SOLDIER, SURGEON, SCHOLAR

SOLDIER, SURGEON, SCHOLAR

The Memoirs of William Henry Corbusier, 1844–1930

Edited by ROBERT WOOSTER

UNIVERSITY OF OKLAHOMA PRESS • NORMAN

ALSO BY ROBERT WOOSTER

*Soldiers, Sutlers, and Settlers: Garrison Life on
the Texas Frontier* (College Station, 1987)

*The Military and United States Indian Policy,
1865–1903* (New Haven, 1988)

History of Fort Davis, Texas (Santa Fe, 1990)

*Nelson A. Miles and the Twilight of the
Frontier Army* (Lincoln, 1993)

*The Civil War 100: A Ranking of the Most
Influential People in the War between the
States* (New York, 1998)

*The Civil War Bookshelf: 50 Must-Read Books
about the War between the States* (New
York, 2001)

This book is published with the generous assistance of The
McCasland Foundation, Duncan, Oklahoma.

Library of Congress Cataloging-in-Publication Data

Corbusier, William Henry, 1844–1930.
    Soldier, surgeon, scholar : the memoirs of William Henry
Corbusier / edited by Robert Wooster.
        p.   cm.
    Includes bibliographical references (p.   ) and index.
    ISBN 0-8061-3549-2 (alk. paper)
    1. Corbusier, William Henry, 1844–1930.   2. United States.
Army—Surgeons—Biography.   3. Surgeons—United States—
Biography.   4. Medicine, Military—United States— History.
I. Wooster, Robert, 1956–   II. Title.

RD27.35.C67A3   2003
617'.092—dc21
[B]

                                                        2002044446

The paper in this book meets the guidelines for permanence and
durability of the Committee on Production Guidelines for Book
Longevity of the Council on Library Resources, Inc. ∞

CONTENTS

ILLUSTRATIONS

MAPS

WILLIAM HENRY CORBUSIER'S CONTINENTAL UNITED STATES

Camp Tacoma

Fort Mackinac

Camp McDermit
Fort Washakie
Pine Ridge
Camp Sheridan
Fort Wayne
Elmira
Nyack
New York City

Sacramento
Winnemucca
Auburn
San Francisco
Gilroy

Jeffersonville
Fort Monroe

Fort Lewis
Fort Hays
Nashville
Fort Macon

Los Angeles
Camp Verde Agency
Camp Date Creek
Fort Grant
Camp Supply
Memphis
Chattanooga
Charleston

Amite

San Antonio

0   200   400 Miles

N

INTRODUCTION

Army surgeon, ethnographer, and writer, William Henry Corbusier (1844–1930) witnessed the emergence of the United States from young republic to world power. When he was born, the nation consisted of twenty-six states and the territories of Florida, Iowa, and Wisconsin. The most recent census had reported a population of seventeen million. Nearly 90 percent of Americans lived in rural areas; New York, his birthplace, was the country's largest city with nearly four hundred thousand residents in its five boroughs. American Indians still dominated much of the trans-Mississippi West, and only adult white males could vote. Doctors were generalists who often had little formal education and observed only rudimentary hygienic procedures.

By the time of his death, Corbusier's nation had expanded to forty-eight states and the territories of Alaska and Hawaii. The United States also controlled the Panama Canal, Cuba, Puerto Rico, the Philippines, Guam, and assorted other Pacific Islands. Its population numbered nearly 123 million, 56 percent of whom lived in urban areas. New York City now had almost seven million residents. American Indians had been confined to reservations, women and blacks (at least according to the Fifteenth Amendment) had achieved the right to vote, and doctors now understood germ theory, the ties between medicine and science, and the importance of good hygiene.

William Henry Corbusier's career as an army surgeon during the Civil War, the wars against the Indians, and the occupation of the Philippines spanned the army's development from frontier constabulary to world power. Fortunately for posterity, Dr. Corbusier, his wife, Fanny Dunbar Corbusier, and their five sons were prolific writers who carefully recorded the developments they witnessed. One son's diary would eventually be published, and the elder Corbusier took careful notes through his many transfers. His retirement in 1908 afforded both him and his wife even more time to write. Mrs. Corbusier tackled her reminiscences; an avid genealogist, Dr. Corbusier completed a 363-page typewritten family history in 1912, explaining that he wished "to leave this information in such a form that his children, their children and children's children and others who may honor their fathers and mothers may know who their ancestors were and what they accomplished in their day." This massive tome, replete with biographical sketches of immediate family members, appendices, bibliography, and index, traced the family's roots back to Bermuda, England, Belgium, and France. He would continue to edit and update this genealogy for the rest of his life.[1]

Fanny died in 1918 following a long illness, leaving Corbusier without his helpmate of half a century. Lacking a permanent residence as a result of his lengthy military service, a lonely Corbusier compiled a moving six page conclusion to Fanny's work, which he called "Recollections of Her Life in the Army" (hereafter referred to as "Recollections"). In 1924, spurred by the surgeon general's call for autobiographical materials from army medical officers and looking for things to do while recovering from the amputation of the toes of his left foot, he began working in earnest on his own autobiography. He completed the task two years later, giving it the straightforward title of "Memoirs of William Henry Corbusier, Colonel, U.S. Army, Retired" (hereafter referred to as "Memoirs"). The work seemed to have been intended for publication; typescript copies were distributed among a few family members, with some eventually winding up in a handful of libraries and archives.[2]

Corbusier's widespread experiences over eight decades give his memoirs an extraordinary breadth. Obviously, his reminiscences of two wars, a major campaign against the Apache Indians, and life at numerous army posts have tremendous value for military historians. Change came slowly to the army of his day; his account speaks to the continued influence of Civil War and Indian wars veterans upon the armed forces of the new century.[3] Yet his memoirs should not be relegated to the shelves of a few specialists, for what a full life he lived! From the streets of New York to the wilds of Arizona to the jungles of the Philippines, his writing reveals one man's honest observations of his varied adventures. Always fascinated by the theater, for example, Corbusier witnessed some of America's most legendary stage performers, including the diminutive Tom Thumb, the exotic Lola Montez, and the powerful Edwin Booth. His frequent comments on these activities remind us of the influence of the stage on nineteenth-century American popular culture. Further, Corbusier's recollections of his years in the California gold fields provide excellent insights into relations between whites, Hispanics, and Chinese immigrants in that booming region. Much the same can be said for his richly detailed accounts of life in the Philippines and among the Yavapai, Sioux, and Shoshoni Indians. His descriptions of medical techniques, though tantalizingly short, serve as a useful record of the momentous changes in his craft. Finally, the doctor's description of his retirement years offers an intriguing glimpse into the history of aging in America.

In 1968, the Corbusiers' only surviving son, William Tremaine, published *Verde to San Carlos: Recollections of a Famous Army Surgeon and His Observant Family on the Western Frontier, 1869–1886*. Privately printed in Tucson by Dale Stuart King, the book featured extensive excerpts from both Dr. and Mrs. Corbusier's manuscripts. Unfortunately, the layout of *Verde to San Carlos* intermixed primary materials with editorial comments and was confusing for readers. As western historian Dan Thrapp concluded, "They are very confused and were ineptly edited. Otherwise they would have comprised historical matter of considerable usefulness."[4]

Thus the extraordinary accounts of Dr. Corbusier and his wife seemed destined for continued obscurity. But an indefatigable granddaughter, Nancy Corbusier Knox, subsequently took up the task of securing a publisher for the works of her grandparents. Realizing that both of the Corbusiers have an important story to tell, the University of Oklahoma Press is now publishing them as companion volumes.

———— ᥴᢙ ————

William Henry Corbusier was born in New York City in 1844. His father left for the gold fields of California five years later; young William joined him on two occasions during the 1850s and early 1860s. The junior Corbusier returned east in 1864. Having just turned twenty, he was hired by Illinois officials as an acting assistant surgeon (sometimes called a "contract surgeon"). "I was fairly equipped for the work before me," Corbusier later explained, "as I had studied medicine in California under a surgeon who had done quite a practice among the Mexicans, as well as among the Americans, but he couldn't speak Spanish, so I interpreted for him and assisted him in all of his practice." Created to help meet the army's desperate need for medical personnel, the position paid one hundred dollars a month but bestowed no military rank. Attached to the Sixth and Ninth Illinois Cavalry and the First Illinois Light Artillery regiments, he served in the Franklin and Nashville campaigns.[5]

Following the war, Corbusier returned to New York City and secured his degree from Bellevue Hospital Medical College, one of the country's best medical schools. He then signed another army contract as acting assistant surgeon. In 1867–68, while on Reconstruction duty at a small post at Amite, Louisiana, he met his future wife, Fanny Dunbar. They would have five children, all boys: Claude Romeyn (1871–1927); Harold Dunbar (1873–1950); Philip Worthington (1875–1945); Francis (Frank) Addison (1877–1958); and William Tremaine (1882–1973).[6]

A brief experiment with civilian life proving unsatisfactory, Corbusier returned to his old government job as contract surgeon in 1869. After two-and-a-half years at Camp McDermit, Nevada, he was transferred to Arizona, where he worked for the army as well as the Bureau of Indian Affairs. His interest in the Yavapai Indians there blossomed into a lifelong avocation. In 1876, Corbusier passed his Army Medical Board examinations, which led to his regular commission as first lieutenant and assistant surgeon. The list of Corbusier's stations over the next two decades— Fort Macon, North Carolina; Charleston, South Carolina; Chattanooga, Tennessee; Jeffersonville, Indiana; Camp Sheridan, Nebraska; Fort Washakie, Wyoming; Forts Wayne and Mackinac, Michigan; Fort Grant, Arizona; Fort Hays, Kansas; Fort Lewis, Colorado; Fort Supply, Oklahoma; various army posts in the New York City vicinity; Fort Monroe, Virginia; and Angel Island, California—not only reads like the index to a United States atlas but demonstrates the army's central role in national development.

With the outbreak of war against Spain, Dr. Corbusier, now a major and surgeon, was dispatched to the Philippines, where he served two tours of duty. Fanny, along with twenty-six boxes of their possessions, accompanied him on his second tour. They left thirty-six other boxes behind in San Francisco. Tragically, these cartons, filled with journals, diaries, and priceless American Indian and Filipino artifacts, were destroyed by the earthquake and fire that ravaged the city in 1906. Corbusier returned to the states as chief surgeon, Department of the Columbia, during which time he conducted an extensive inspection tour of military posts in Alaska. Officially retired in 1908 as a lieutenant colonel, he and his wife traveled extensively.[7] Heartbroken by the loss of his wife in 1918, Corbusier rejoined the army during World War I as a member of the General Court-Martial for the Port of Embarkation at Hoboken, New Jersey. In 1919, he left active duty once again, this time having reached the rank of full colonel. Restless and hobbled by a series of foot ailments, he tinkered with his genealogy and visited family members, friends, and old haunts, usually accompanied by a Filipino servant named José. He also completed his own memoirs and oversaw their typed transcription. Corbusier died in San Francisco on February 9, 1930, and was buried at Arlington National Cemetery.[8]

Colonel Corbusier had compiled an admirable if unspectacular military career. One contemporary officer, George O. Eaton, remembered him as "a real man" on the campaign trail. "The real thing, through and through," Eaton continued, "no kick, no complaining in the daily march with much work of all sorts." A dutiful officer, Corbusier kept abreast of medical advances; in his 1894 efficiency report, for example, he noted his interests and publications in ethnology, his "reading knowledge" of French and Spanish, and his continuing study of "all the sciences bearing upon or relating to medicine." But promotions came slowly in the army of his day, and Colonel Corbusier, like most of his comrades, secured his advances by virtue of seniority rather than merit.[9]

The only minor blot on Corbusier's military record came during his first tour in the Philippines. In 1898, a supercilious colonel of volunteers accused him of engaging in unauthorized money changing with enlisted men of the First South Dakota Infantry "at the rate of two Mexican silver dollars for one of gold, for his own private gain." The official exchange rate was $2.03 to $1.00. Stubbornly insisting that he had done nothing wrong, the proud Corbusier pled ignorance of any regulation forbidding such actions. The investigating officer found that he had charged the prevailing exchange rate and had not cheated anyone. In dismissing the allegation, Assistant Adjutant General Thomas H. Barry explained that although Corbusier had erred in changing money with enlisted men without their commanding officer's consent, "the impropriety committed is void of all evil intent and . . . is not of that gravity which necessitates the action of a court-martial."[10]

Corbusier's interests extended far beyond the army and medicine. Fascinated by his years of interaction with American Indians, he witnessed the Sun and Buffalo Dances, experienced a sweatbath, and treated prominent figures such as Sarah Winnemucca, Red Cloud, American Horse, and Young Man Afraid Of His Horses. Dr. Corbusier was the first to systematically record the culture and language of the Yavapai. His works on that southwestern tribe were published in the *American Antiquarian* and the *Zeitschrift für Ethnologie* (Berlin), and they remain essential sources for Yavapai scholars. Noted ethnologist Garrick Mallery credited the doctor with having been "a valued contributor" to his 1879–80 report on the use of sign languages among Plains tribes for the *Annual Reports of the Bureau of American Ethnology*. Later in his life, Corbusier tried in vain to help Mike Burns, a Yavapai Indian whom the army had captured as a boy, to develop and publish his own autobiography.[11]

Corbusier's memoirs, completed in 1926, record his life's experiences and adventures. Proud but honest, Corbusier left a factual account, largely free of self-promotion, of his long life. More a chronicler than an editorialist, he favored description rather than analysis. The doctor is remarkably accurate, with an especially keen eye for details and names. Even more striking is the lack of exaggeration or hyperbole about his own affairs. In an original manuscript of 156 typed pages, only twice does one have reason to suspect Corbusier's veracity in matters of personal achievement. In one case he refers to himself as having been a "Surgeon" (a position that bestowed military rank and privileges) during the Civil War, when in fact he held the less prestigious job of contract surgeon. The second instance concerns his suggestion that his recommendation during the Philippines insurrection had led directly to the army's decision to issue military identification tags to all soldiers. The army indeed did so in 1906, but Corbusier's specific role in the process has not been documented.[12]

Of course, autobiographical accounts reflect the values of their author, and Corbusier's are no exception. Most obvious is his sense of class and race; not surprisingly, given the society in which he lived, his writing occasionally reflects a Kiplingesque "White Man's Burden" view of the world. Corbusier also inherited a strong belief in the importance of education. Comfortable but not affluent, his family of Dutch ancestry made it possible for him to secure a sound grounding in grammar, history, languages, and the physical sciences. Combined with his natural inquisitiveness, this seems to have stimulated his lifelong passion for learning.

Perhaps more intriguing are the things Corbusier chose not to include in his memoirs. In recording his movements over eighty years, he casts himself as a dependable family man who relished the simple pleasures of everyday life while never losing his desire to experience as much as circumstances would allow. No evidence suggests otherwise. But as one would expect from a document that seems to have been intended for publication, Corbusier's memoirs do not give a complete record of his life. One must look to his genealogy, for example, to find his physical descriptions of himself and his wife. In that latter document, he reported that he stood five feet, nine-and-a-half inches tall and weighed about 150 pounds. He had straight dark brown hair, dark gray eyes, and dark mustache, eyebrows, and eyelashes. He seemed a bit self-conscious in describing his nose: "straight and somewhat large and thin . . . with conspicuous nostrils." Fanny was five feet, two inches tall, weighed 106 pounds, and had brown hair, blue eyes, and a fair complexion.[13]

It is not surprising that he also fails to mention several family matters in his memoirs. Here again other sources help to complete the record. Corbusier's memoirs acknowledge the death of a brother, Stephen, but not that of an older sister, Laura, who had died as an infant in 1843. The latter fact he reserved for his more private genealogy. Likewise, his father, William Morrison Corbusier, who seems to have abandoned his wife and son, simply vanishes from the "Memoirs." Indeed, his father's side of the family receives but short shrift in this public document. But the genealogy allows Corbusier to report that his father—who receives only cryptic treatment even here—died in Shasta County, California, during an 1880 construction accident, and to trace the roots of his forebears back through Bermuda, England, France, and the Low Countries. Of his mother, Mahala, the brief comments found in Corbusier's genealogy reinforce the affection for her that his more public memoirs only suggest. His mother, who possessed "a keen sense of humor," eventually remarried. She lived happily with her new husband, Henry B. Jones, in Elmira, New York, frequently entertaining her son's growing brood. Like her son, Mahala seems to have become estranged from most of her ex-husband's relatives.[14]

Corbusier's superficial treatment of his wife in his memoirs reflects the Victorian values of the day, which frowned upon public expressions of emotion from males. Here Fanny appears as little more than a loyal army wife and the "Little Mother" of his five sons. But his genealogy, surviving diaries, and conclusion to Fanny's "Recollections"—safer places for a man to discuss personal matters than in a patriotic officer's memoirs—reveal more private details, such as her love for flowers and the sewing and shopping she did in excited preparation for her sojourn to the Philippines. Likewise, his touching addendum to Fanny's "Recollections" includes emotions absent from the memoirs. "Always bright and cheerful," she had a "sweet" smile and "looked supremely happy as she nestled her head in my hands and placed her arms about my neck" even as her health slowly deteriorated. Devastated by her death, a grieving Corbusier returned to the rooms they had taken at Plainfield, New Jersey. "I came back to 120 Crescent Avenue and there I was alone with everything in the rooms as they were when my beloved was carried out," he writes. "I had her sweet face before me as I have it now and the loving happy smile as she cuddled against my hands when I stroked her face."[15]

Short passages about her death found in a few surviving letters reveal even more about William's relationship with Fanny. As a friend wrote, "If ever there was a brave, loving spirit, your lovely wife had one. She spoke to me last winter about your dread of her leaving you." Son Frank, who had been unable to attend the funeral, wrote his father a note that also suggests warm family relations. A recent letter had "brought us closer to you and made us feel that we were not so terribly far away," Frank explained. "How I wish I could have been with you."[16]

On several occasions, Dr. Corbusier directs readers to Fanny's "Recollections" for further details. Indeed, he seems to have conceived of his "Memoirs" as complementary to her work, a classic illustration of the "separate spheres" that middle-class men and women of that period often strove to uphold. She dealt with the domestic matters of their family life; he concentrated on his childhood years and the public issues that he considered to be of historical interest and record. It seems especially fitting, then, that their manuscripts be published as companion volumes.

EDITORIAL NOTE

William Henry Corbusier deserves to speak for himself. Thus this edition includes only minor deviations from the typescript. The book has been separated into chapters to improve its readability. A 1919 War Department letter thanking him for his recent services has been moved from the text to the notes. In addition, a few of the lengthier paragraphs have been divided; a paragraph mark (¶) has been inserted to indicate where this has been done. Annotations provide readers with further information or clarification of the text. Obvious typographical or transcription-related errors have been corrected, but mistakes judged to have been Corbusier's have been retained and marked as [*sic*]. Missing words or phrases have been inserted in brackets [ ]. Finally, the doctor used a complex and often inconsistent series of abbreviations. For clarity, abbreviations of states, months, numbers of military units, and ranks have all been spelled out and ship names italicized.

ACKNOWLEDGMENTS

Several people and institutions have helped to make this work possible. My mother and father, Edna and Ralph Wooster, instilled values and habits that have served me well for over two decades in my chosen profession. Lieutenant Colonel Thomas "Ty" Smith brought the Corbusier manuscript to my attention, and through his close reading of my work, saved me from numerous errors. Durwood Ball also made several important editorial contributions and suggestions, for which I am extremely grateful. Noemi Ybarra performed the laborious task of inputting the original typescript to a word-processing program; her meticulous work helped to make this a much better product. The Frantz History Enhancement Fund supported research trips to Santa Fe, Austin, and Washington. Nancy Corbusier Knox offered not only generous hospitality but cogent suggestions on the manuscript. And once again, my wife, Catherine I. Cox, took time from her own professional obligations to read and comment upon this work as it developed. To each I offer my sincerest thanks. Of course, all errors are mine and mine alone.

ROBERT WOOSTER
Corpus Christi, Texas

SOLDIER, SURGEON, SCHOLAR

CHAPTER ONE

Boyhood in New York

I can remember as far back as romping on a bed with my baby brother, Stephen Myers, and after that his sickness and his death on September 30, 1847, the return of some ragged soldiers from Mexico, a parade and a ball of the Lafayette Fusiliers, which had its Armory at 421 Broadway, in which my father was a corporal in 1848, and the uniform of which was a red swallow-tail coat with brass buttons, white trousers, broad white leather belt, which had white supporters crossed in front, a high bearskin cap, and, fastened behind to the belt, a fatigue cap near the cartridge box.[1]

We lived above a jewelry store in a red brick house on Hudson Street, New York City, not far north of Charlton, the back windows of which looked out on a large open space. We had a large black New Foundland dog and a small light colored one of another breed which we took to the Hudson River to swim. A little girl used to call for me to take me with her to school and I carried a green covered primmer [sic]. I had for many years a "Reward of Merit" dated June 1, 1848, signed by Miss B. Buxton. We had one maid, Phoebe Wannamaker. Hickory and Virginia pine were used for cooking and heating wax candles, lard oil and whale oil for illuminating purposes. The lamps had large glass globes from which depended glass prisms which shed many colors and tinkled when moved.

My father collected books, which he rebound, and among them I can recall Aesop's Fables, Ossian's Poems, Boswell's Johnson, and the lives of Red Jacket, Napoleon and Henry Clay. My mother did much hemstiching [*sic*], made wax flowers and fruits, wire baskets which she hung in large stone crocks filled with a solution of alum to allow crystals to form on them, white rabbits of canton flannel, having red beads for eyes and pink lined ears, and she painted a window shade in oil. She also worked on perforated cardboard in colored worsteds and rolled colored paper for alumetts. She had a steel hook made by her father from a shoemaker's knife with [which] she knitted babies socks and mitts.

I was taken to a theatre in the winter of 1847–48 and saw the actor Edwin Forrest and his wife in Hamlet and Macbeth.[2] Once when I was sent for peanuts, I was given a large silver coin and returned with as large a basket as I could carry nearly filled with nuts, but no change. The mingled odor of cherries and roses always brings to my mind's eye a visit to Hoboken, which was then quite a resort. I see a large rock amid rose bushes near a cherry tree, the long veranda of a hotel, to which I was hurried after a fall, probably from the rock, and my head bandaged. For many years I carried a scar on the upper part of my forehead. After this, I often did my fingers up in bandages. One night I saw what to me was a wonderful sight, the whole sky red from the burning of the old Park Theatre.[3]

I can often smell the Madeira wine and hickory-nut cake and other things on the table for two days when there were many calling on January 1, 1848, and women on the second. We visited my grandparents that year and I stood by grandfather Stephen Myers while he planted a cherry tree not far from the front door of the house.[4] A baker passed once a week and I always bought a big square of ginger bread or some round hearts with a big copper penny. Old Dutch, a big shaggy dog, died and was burried [*sic*] under a pear tree at the stone fence in the garden. I was with my father when he shot at a bird in the apple orchard, which flew away and gradually grew smaller, and, when I returned to the house, I said that he had turned a big bird into a little one by shooting at it.

My mother and I went to the foot of Burling Slip to bid my father good bye on January 31, 1849, the day he set sail on the Bark *Mara* for San Francisco, California, in a party of 157 men.[5] He had a cedar keg with a capacity of about three pints, having a strap to suspend it from one shoulder, and a muzzle loading revolving six-shooter, with barrels about five inches in length, later called a "Pepper Box," and, which when a little worn, would all go off at once. Shovels and pickaxes were scattered about, and, as the moorings were cast off, the whole party joined in singing "O Susanna don't you cry for me, I'm going to California with a pickaxe on my knee."[6]

Afterward, my mother and I went to my grandfather Stephen Myers' farm on the hills back of Nyack and about a mile from the Hudson River. During a heavy snow storm he went to the county town to attend to some business for a relative (DeBaun), contracted a severe cold and died of pneumonia on February 25, 1849. I saw his doctor bleed him from an arm and the blood in a basin taken from the room. I never saw him drink any alcoholic as a beverage or smoke tobacco. He had a snuff-box, but I never saw him open it. Snuff taking by the nose was quite common, and I often saw it offered and taken. His dress coat was a dark gray cloak with a broad collar and a cape which reached half way down the arms. It was fastened at the neck by mean of a large metal clasp. Men's tailors went from house to house to sew by the day.

We sometimes drove over to granny Myers', my great grand mother's farm—Elizabeth Stevens Myers—near Rockland Lake, and in the winter foot-warmers filled with live coals and ashes were put in the wagon or sleigh to keep us warm. She lived in an old one story brownstone house built before the Revolutionary War, and I can see her looking over the lower door as we drove up. There were two doors, one above the other, so that the upper could be left open for ventilation and the lower one shut to keep out chickens, etc. The ceilings were low and hewn sills held up the floor above to form a garret. The floor was sanded white, and figures made with the broom were seen. The fire-place was very large and in it were round-bottom iron pegs each with three legs. There was a strong, large iron crane and heavy iron andirons. The dishes were stood on edge or hung on a sideboard which stood against the wall. A very large, round mahogany table had its top turned up and it shone. When needed, it was rolled out, and, after knives and forks were taken out from the space in the top of the huge legs, the top was lowered to its place and pegs run through the holes beneath. On one side of the fireplace was the door of an oven in which baking was done once a week. Great pies were made in large, red, earthen dishes in the bottom of which, in yellow script, were the Dutch names of girls, as Jannetje, Maritje, Margretie, etc.

There were in and around Nyack many kin folks, closely or distantly related, as De Bauns, Remsens, Demarests, Greens, Snedekers, Blauvelts, Lydeckers, Waldrons and others. Great pride was shown by the girls in the many patch-work designs which they made at school and at home. The women had many quilting parties, the patches were sewn together, cotton batting was laid between two layers and sewn in. Then was the time when family traditions were handed down and the news of the neighborhood and country discussed. About sunset, the men came for tea at which several kinds of preserves would be served with hot biscuits, pound cake, etc.

The calico frocks that the women wore week days were not of fast colors and had to be treated with a salt solution before washing to prevent fading. Every woman who could afford it had a black gown to wear on Sunday and special occasions. Old clothes were cut into strips and sewed together by the children and their elders, rolled into balls, and sent to the weaver to be made into carpets, usually a yard wide and the length of an ordinary room. Old clothes that couldn't be made into rag carpets were exchanged for tinware, which was brought around about once a month by a man whose wagon inside and out had a display of all sorts of tin utensils wanted by the housewife. I was a good producer of rags, and the seat of my breeches were rarely without patches due to sliding down the large inclined cellar doors. Under clothes were usually made from bolts of cotton bought unbleached and bleached on the grassy lawn in the bright sunlight until quite white and soft. My grandmother Myers had bed-linen enough to last a lifetime. Her father had raised and prepared the flax which she and her mother spun and it was then sent to the weaver. The bedsteads were high and had testers from which curtains were suspended and there was a valence [*sic*] which hid a trundle bed when it was not in use and pushed underneath. A bedtick was filled with rye-straw laid lengthwise and placed on rope supports. A feather bed was thrown on the tick and a linen sheet over it, patchwork quilts and blue and white spreads over all. I had to climb a bedpost to get into bed and in winter I snuggled between two feather beds.

The farmers usually did their own cobbling and harness repairing. Cowhide boots were worn in the fields, and, in winter by the men, and heavy galoshes of pure rubber over dress shoes. The women wore prunella—a black fabric—which had no heels and which were no protection in rain or snow.

Men and boys wore their hair long, quite to the collar, and there curled under. It was parted on the left side, except when the young fellows went courting, to church or a party, when some of them roached it, i. e., parted it on two sides and curled it over into a sort of topknot. A few years later, they went to a barber to have their hair curled. Girls usually combed their hair straight back and held it with "a round comb," or braided it to hang down the back in two plaits. The mothers wore high combs and their hair over their ears and sometimes fluffed.

I used to wander up to the barn, and one day a hen that had a brood of very young chickens rushed at me with outstretched wings and drove me back; at another time a gander hissed at me and sent me home, but I was more afraid of a sow that had a litter of young pigs and ground her jaws in anger. The odor of corn pollen comes to me, the cawing of crows; the sound of the whetstones when the harvesters in the field sharpened their scythes, the smell of the fresh grass when it fell before the mowers as they swung, their scythes in unison, cutting wide swaths, or the cradling of the rye; the occasional rest to go to the shade of a big tree for a drink of cider vinegar and brown sugar or molasses in water. How delightful it felt to be thrown up on a load of hay and to be driven to the barn, there to be tossed on the hay mow.

¶I liked to sit on a stone fence under a peach tree to watch the many sails on the Tappan Zee, while I helped myself to the fruit from the tree.[7] Along the stone fence, on my way back to the house, I picked blackcaps and strung them on straws of timothy, which with red clover was stored for winter's use. Berry picking was great fun, and blackberries were plentiful. The only set-back was the fear of snakes and especially the black snake. When apple-picking time came, the air was filled with the fragrance from the fruit. The cellar was not large enough to hold all of the fruit and it was cached in trenches dug in the garden, lined with rye straw and covered with the same and soil, to be taken out when needed. Potatoes were cached in the same manner. Wagon loads of wind-falls were hauled to a cider-mill to be brought back as cider to drink or be boiled down and apples peeled and quartered added to make apple-sauce. Red currants, red raspberries, and gooseberries grew along the garden fence, and along the front fence was a great row of hollyhocks, and beyond them beds of larkspur, sweet william, tansy, sage, lavender, etc., and a few love apples bushes—tomatoes—the fruit of which the family had only recently learned were good to eat, from Germans. They were very small, about the size of a cherry, and covered with a thick sack or balloon.

¶When the nuts were ready to gather, it was great sport for the children and their elders to go nutting. When the winds hadn't blown the nuts off, the men would thrash the trees with long poles, while the women and children filled their baskets with chestnuts, hickorynuts, walnuts and butternuts, which, after drying, were piled on the floor in the garret. I liked to go up there to listen to the patter of the rain on the shingled roof and look at the things stored there, as the big spinning-wheel, the mahogany cradle which had a hood and which had held many members of the family. There was a very old hair covered leather trunk, an old muzzle-loading musket which once had been a flint-lock, but then percussion caps were used to fire the load. Near it was a bullet pouch containing globular lead bullets, muslin patches and a bullet-mould. Over it hung an old powder-horn, all dating back to the Revolutionary War and the War of 1812, and had been carried by grandfather in the latter war and on muster days since then.[8]

Hogs were fattened to be killed late in the fall and made into hams, sausage, headcheese, lard, etc., enough to last throughout the winter. The hams and livers were smoked in the so-called "wash-house," the chimney of which was very large. Most of the cooking was done here in the summer time. The hogs were fattened mostly on corn, skimmed milk and buttermilk. Churning was done every day or two, and it fell to the lot of the younger members of the family, and in winter they had to cultivate patience, and the dasher of the old-fashioned churn would go down and up many times before the butter came. Clabbered milk was made into pats of "potcheese" about two and a half inches in diameter, to be sliced and laid on bread and butter, dried and grated or allowed to "rot"—ripen— as we say now—until the ones who ate it wished that the mouth had been placed above the nose. We often had "buttermilk pop" which is made with flour mixed with egg until almost dry and then dropped a little at a time into boiling buttermilk while stirring it. Brown or maple sugar was added to taste at the table.

The threshing of the rye and buckwheat was left for winter, and then for days could be heard the rhythmic sound of the flails on the big barn floor. The grain was sent to be ground at a mill, and after that, the rye, sometimes mixed with corn meal, was made into bread with sour dough and baked in the oven and the buckwheat made into cakes with yeast baked on a griddle were eaten with butter and molasse[s], or soused headcheese or pigs feet fried was the breakfast dish. Steel forks were still in use, and a few of them had only two tines. If you were given one of them, there were times when you would be forced to carry food to your mouth with a knife. The excuse then might be made that knives were made before forks, but fortunately we also had forks with three tines. The silver spoons that dated back to the Revolution, six of which were tea spoons and came into my possession, were light in weight, but those made about 1812 were very heavy, and my aunt Jane Tasman once told a woman, who was bragging of her silver, that the Myers children cried when they had to use these spoons, they were so heavy.[9] There were few pewter dishes still at my great grandmother Myers's, which, it was said, were brought with the family when it came from Holland about 1650 to New Amsterdam.[10] Some of it was used for bullets during the Revolutionary War.

My Aunt Lovenia Myers was still attending school, and she took me to the village in which Mrs. Catherine Remsen had a school in the basement of the Methodist Church.[11] We spent from 9:00 A.M. to 4:00 P.M. in the study and recitations, with a recess of twenty minutes in the morning, the same in the afternoon and an hour at noon. We read a chapter of the New Testament every morning. All work ceased at sunset on Saturday, after the cooking had been done for Sunday. The big family Bible was brought out from the parlor and a chapter read and then there were prayers to prepare for the morrow. The big bell in the steeple of the Reformed Dutch Church called the faithful Sunday morning to hear long sermons, ringing twice and ended by tolling. There were two other churches, the Presbyterian and the Methodist. At the latter revival meetings were held in winter which the other denominations did not attend, as they did not approve of them, nor did they approve of the methods at camp meetings which were held in summer.

The odor of Jamaica rum, spice and lemon pervaded the house New Year's eve, and even the children were allowed a sip of the punch. We hung our stockings at the fireplace and chimney which were large enough for Santa Claus to ride down. In the morning we found big copper pennies, candy, mitts, comforters, etc., in our stockings. In February the sugar maple trees on the back part of the farm were tapped, the sap collected to be boiled down into syrup and sugar. I enjoyed tramping through the snow in the woods with my uncle Peter. On Paas—Easter—there was a great pile of eggs of various colors on the breakfast table and there was the cracking of the shells to see who could win the most. Peach leather is one of the delicacies I remember, but haven't seen since those days. Jujube paste was another sweet I liked. When planting time came, I heard the phases of the moon discussed and the proper time of the moon to plant certain vegetables or crops.

For disorders of digestion, sulphur was given in molasses, and springtime seemed to be the time to take it. Sassafras root tea would be drunk instead [of] coffee at breakfast. Hot boneset tea was insisted upon for anyone who had a cold, and about a quart of it would have to be drunk. Goose grease was rubbed on the neck for sore throat and a woolen sock bound around the neck. Cornmeal gruel was given and panada—soda crackers with hot water poured on, sweetened and flavored with wine. Tamarind water was given to quench thirst in fevers. A sort of tamarind jam, imported I think, was to be found in every grocery store.

My grandfather Myers had offered to each of his children on marriage a piece of land on which to build a house, but my Aunt Jane Tasman was the only one who accepted and received a lot in the southeastern corner of the farm, on a road to Piermont, and on this her husband, Thomas, built a house, which many years afterward they sold to one of the Towt daughters. None of the sons wished to remain on the farm, so my grandmother sold it to John Towt, and went to live in Nyack, where she bought a house on Bird Street, the south side, about fifty yards east of Broadway. Here I lived with her until about the middle of 1852, and continued to attend Mrs. Remsen's school, which she taught in a house she and her husband had built about two blocks southwest of the Methodist church and about a block from a grove of trees in which picnics were held and through which ran a brook in which we boys loved to wade. It is now a ditch with very little water in it and the grove has disappeared. There is a railroad station just south of its site.

¶In summer, school opened at 8:00 A.M., and we were under its rules from the time we left home until we returned there, and for their infraction the rattan was laid on the back of both girls and boys. I soon learned that it was not best to stand and pretend it didn't hurt, as some of the boys did, but better to cry out and wriggle, which didn't increase the anger of the teacher, but lessened the number of blows. My whippings were mostly for looking off of my book at study time, when a girl monitor, Elizabeth White, a distant cousin, told on me. She, however, received more than I did, as she was always getting into trouble. We had long lessons in spelling, and went up and down in the class. I managed to get next to head and very rarely to the head, which a girl held most of the time. It was not a pleasure to spell her down, as when she missed a word, she cried.

We ran and hopped, skipped and jumped, and had long jump matches a great deal, and played "one old cat" and "two old cat" ball. In the latter, a batter, when he struck a ball, exchanged places with the other batter. If caught out, the catcher took his place. In one old cat, the one batter, when he struck a ball, had to run to a base and back before the catcher or pitcher could hit with the ball or touch him with ball in hand. In early summer, most of the boys trapped yellow birds and bob-o-links. I didn't become expert with top or marbles, but after seeing my uncle Peter make me a kite, and showing me how to select straight ash sticks and where to center them, balance the leaders, and hang the tail, I became a great kite maker and flyer, and not infrequently had two balls of white twine out, my kite higher than all of the others. We played hide-and-go-seek at night around the block, and tag was a common game. There was a game in which two sides were chosen and one of them would go through the motions of some trade or calling for the other to name dumb-crambo.

My uncle Samuel Myers and aunt Maria died in June, 1850, of the Asiatic cholera in Cincinnati, Ohio, and left two young children, Elizabeth and John, who were cared for by some distant relatives, named Stephenson, and the family wanted to bring them east. My mother volunteered to go after them and her undertaking was considered a great one, as Cincinnati was a western wicked city, and for a lone woman to venture there was risky, but she came back with my cousins, and my grandmother took charge of them, so there were three children in the house.[12]

By this time there was a dancing master in the village and music teacher. The choir sang by note, a long note-book in one hand and a hymnal in the other. The leader had a tuning fork and would strike the key for the choir and congregation, as every[one] sang. Occasionally there was a concert in the church, but never a circus or a theatre in the village. My grandmother, Rachel Myers, had a fund of stories relating to the Revolutionary War and the War of 1812, some of which she had heard from the participants.[13] The most thrilling one was about the killing of the sentries at a certain outpost. Several mornings the one on this important post was found dead and scalped, and the men dreaded going to it, until one of them volunteered to take it. Towards morning, while it was very dark, he heard the grunting of a pig, and, shortly afterward, saw what seemed to be a pig rooting and gradually coming his way. He watched it and when the animal got within gunshot, and he could see it well, he up with his musket and fired at it. There was an Indian yell, and when his comrades came, they found a dead Indian covered with a pig skin. While I was at Nyack, there was only one left of the many Indians that formerly lived at the sight [*sic*]. She was called Yawney—Jane—and used to wash clothes and do other work for my grandmother.

The reading of fiction was thought a waste of time. The Bible had stories that sufficed, and the psalms and hymn book had all of the poetry that most people cared for or had time to read. My grandmother, however, was very liberal in her ideas, as she had finished her education in a young ladies['] school in New York City, on North More street, but she wouldn't tell us fairy stories, and when asked for one, she would begin with: "There was an old man and an old woman who went to the barn to pick straw. Did you ever hear it before?", and for a long time we answered "No," and then she would repeat what she had said, until one day my Aunt Louise, who was tired of hearing the repetitions, told us to say Yes and when we did so, our grandmother said, "Then I will not tell you again," and one of our great pleasures was spoiled. We heard about the hoop-snake which with its tail in its mouth was rolling very fast down a hill towards a farmer who stood near a riding-rail fence. He jumped to one side, and the snake struck a rail in the fence, and, while fast, the farmer killed it. Another one: A snake was charming a woman when a man happened along the road just in time. He pulled her back and broke the charm. A glass snake, which a man had killed, as he supposed, broke into pieces and he put them into his pocket, but the pieces joined together and the snake got away. A woman woke up one morning feeling something fast to one of her breasts and saw that it was a milk snake. She cried for help, but no one knew what to do, so they sent for an old Indian woman who asked for a saucer of milk. This she placed on the bed near the woman and the snake let go and went to the saucer to drink. A man who had killed many snakes carried them home tied to a stick which he swung over one shoulder. He died as soon as he reached home from inhaling the poison from the snakes. Formerly there were so many snakes on rocky and heavily wooded Snake-hill that the neighboring farmers had regular hunts to try to kill them off. The copper-heads were venomous and were numerous.

There is an old stone church at Upper Nyack about which my mother told a story which indicates the faith of its congregation. The pulpit was old and unsafe and badly needed repairing, but there was no money to pay for a new one, and, after waiting in vain for some time, one of them said, "Let's pull it down. The Lord will provide money for a new one." When they tore up the old floor, there beneath was a great store of honey. This they sold and raised enough money to build a new pulpit.

My first dream that I remember was, I think, on the farm. I saw my father home from California, and in the morning asked for him as soon as I got out of bed and couldn't believe that he was not in the house. We called a tin cup or dipper a "blickey," a swing in the back yard a "scup," a porch a "stoop" and an auction a "Vendue." A frock worn by a bride the Sunday after her wedding was called, "A walk bride dress" and her bonnet "a walk bride hat." When we had enough to eat we were "fiest." Sickness and misfortunes were usually attributed to sin, and the people had an inkling of what was much later learned, that they are caused by breaking the laws of nature, which we were so long in discovering. When they prayed, they expected an answer, and believed that God took an interest in all of their doings. My Sunday school teacher was Mrs. Eliza Snediker Remsen, and when I was older Mr. Prall was at the head of the Bible class of which I was a member.

Mrs. Catherine Remsen had a May-Day celebration for her scholars, and we went over to the grove and there crowned Elsie Depew, "The queen of May." The smaller girls wore pantalettes and the large ones skirts that swept the ground. Later the skirts had string fastened around the bottom which ran through small rings inside up to the waist so that they could be raised out of the mud or dust. Later still, women wore hoops. I boarded with Mrs. Remsen for a time and she treated me as if I were her own child. She had a class in astronomy at night. Mr. Remsen— a gentleman of the old school—looked after our writing, wrote many a trite saying for us to copy in our copybooks, and sharpened our quill pens. On entering and leaving the schoolroom, the boys bowed and the girls curtsied in the old school way.

When I left Nyack in 1852, I was well advanced in my studies for a boy of my age, as Mrs. Remsen was very thorough in her teaching. I could spell and define most words in the speller, had learned all of the tables, weights and measures, and could work all of the examples given to me as well as those in U.S. and English money, knew the "Rule of Three" and vulgar and decimal fractions as well. In geography, the states and their products, capitals where located, population and all of the rivers and mountains as well. Parsing had become easy and was a sort of mental gymnastic we rather enjoyed.

Back in the city, the streets were still poorly lighted with oil lamps, and some wells were still in use, but most of the water was taken from hydrants in the streets or yards, sperm oil and lard oil lamps were used more for illuminating purposes than candles and wood was mostly burned as fuel. Two horse omnibusses were driven over the cobble-stone pavements from the Battery to 23rd Street and Eighth Avenue. Passengers entered by steps at the rear and the drivers, who sat high up in front, pulled the door shut by means of a strap which he held under one foot. This a passenger would pull when he wished to get out. There was a hole, about six inches in diameter, back of the driver through which he received the fare. The City Reservoir was out in the suburbs at Fifth Avenue and 42nd Street, and the water was conducted there through the Croton Aqueduct.[14]

After [Lajos] Kossuth came to the U.S., early in the fifties, a hat named after him became the vogue.[15] It was of black soft felt, with a crown about four inches high and brim about that wide, but for full dress a high crown, white or light gray beaver was worn, the fingers sometimes run against the fur to form spirals. It was at length adopted by the "Know Nothings"[16] a political party opposed to the admittance to citizenship of more foreigners, and especially the Irish, who controlled the elections in the city.[17]

My next school was Theodore June's 1852–53 at Stanwich, a few miles north of Greenwich, Connecticut. We took a car of the Hartford and New Haven Rail Road at Canal Street, which was drawn by horses to the suburbs, probably 23rd Street, where the train was made up to be drawn by a steam-engine. We left the train at Greenwich and from there drove to the school in a two-horse surry [sic] or stage. There were no other buildings near by, and the boys had quite a stretch of country to roam over. The small boys had "short bounds"—a radius of about a quarter of a mile and could not go farther without a teacher. The large boys had "long bounds" about three miles every way. For breaking a rule, a boy would be limited to certain bounds for three days. Three days for small boys meant that long on the lawn around the school. It wasn't very long before I was sentenced to three days. The large boys had a stage at a stone fence in a field near by, where they sometimes had acts, mostly minstrels, led by William Christy, brother of George Christy, the popular negro minstrel.[18] The leader ordered the small boys around and, when he tried to boss, I told him that he was only a negro minstrel, and that was a low down name to me, as actors were not held in any esteem among the people whom I had been brought up among. For this I was given the three days, but I could hold my own among the boys after that.

¶We took long walks out in the open with one of the teachers, or in the woods after huckleberries and blackberries, and once went fishing on the Sound. Mr. June made us sinkers by pouring molting lead into holds that he drove into the sand. There were corn fields and apple orchards all around us. One road led over a bridge at a swampy place and we liked to wade in the water to let the leaches [sic] cling to our legs and then come out to rub them off and see the blood run. Fighting hornets was a major sport, and to go right up to a hornet[']s nest and punch it to stir up the hornets, was a daring act. We always threw stones, when out for fun, sometimes at a mark, but oftener to see who could throw the farthest and skipped stones on the water to see who could make the most skips. Fried scallops and doughnuts were frequently among the dishes we enjoyed, and they were served in great stacks which would disappear among the thirty hungry boys.

Mesmerism was introduced and had become the vogue. Mr. June read about it and then looked about for a boy on whom to try his hypnotic power. As I was the youngest, and he thought me the least sophisticated one in the school, his choice fell upon me, and I was ready to play my part, as I had seen the performances among the people in the city. I knew what was expected and acted to his suggestions and satisfaction, and the wonder of the larger boys who were permitted to see the performance. I think it was the second seance that his wife, who didn't approve of his experiments, came into the schoolroom and broke the spell that I was supposed [to] be under, by pushing me back against a desk upon which I suddenly sat down. I looked upon the affair as an entertainment and didn't know they were taking mesmerism seriously. I felt sorry afterward, when older, for what I had done, as Mr. June really believed that he had hypnotized me. Later Spiritualism became a hobby and table-rappings

were practiced, but the tricks were never suc[c]essful in my presence. I had
faked once and was wise to the way in which a table could be moved.[19]

In 1853 I was sent to Paulding's Institute, which was a higher class
school than June's. We wore grey clothes on week days and dark green
on Sunday, the roundabouts of which had black velvet collars and cuffs
and brass buttons. We marched to the Episcopal church two by two. The
Rev. Mr. Spencer was the pastor, and his son was an Episcopal missionary
at Zamboanga, Mindanao, Philippine Islands, when I was the Chief Surgeon of the Department of Mindanao under General Leonard Wood in
1904.[20] We had Wednesday as a holiday instead of Saturday and we usually
spent it in the woods on the hills east of Tarrytown, where there were
stone enclosures which had formerly been used as blinds from which wild
pigeons were shot when they came in immense flocks, but came no
more, having been annihilated. Among the games we played was "Duck
on a rock," in which a stone was placed on a rock of some size and stones
were thrown at it until one of the players knocked it off. Great attention
was paid to our habits, and especially to the care of our bodies and clothes.
Regular inspections were very thorough to see that we bathed, teeth
cleaned, hair parted just right, clothes brushed, and shoes polished. We
had lessons in the Bible every Sunday afternoon and prayers every day of
the week, all of the boys on their knees. I read nearly all of the books in
the library, mostly ancient and modern history and biography, and of
course, all of Washington Irving's works. We were taken to Sleepy Hollow where he received us, and we came away well pleased.[21] I had the
measles while here and had a good time while isolated in the family part
of the house under a nurse, although I did miss the winter sports of
1853–54. By the time I left Mr. William G. Weston's school, I had been
attending school steadily for six years and was far advanced as very few
children of my age were.

CHAPTER TWO

❧❧❧❧

The California Gold Fields

I left New York for San Francisco, California, on July 5, 1854, with my father, on the steamer *Prometheus*, which carried 381 passengers.[1] Chickens, ducks, pigs, steers, and sheep were taken on the steamer alive, to be killed as needed. The boat was rather crowded, as this was an opposition line and the route lay through Nicaragua, where William Walker, the filabuster [sic], was at that time.[2] After I had recovered from the sea-sickness, which lasted two or three days, I spent much of my time climbing masts and ropes. We stopped at Kingston, Jamaica for coal, which was carried on the heads of negro women, mostly in tubs made of casks sawed in two, and which required two men to lift to their heads. We were long enough ashore to have dinner on the veranda of a hotel. Drove around for a time and then strolled around the plaza, and I for the first time ate bananas, mangoes, avocados and other tropical fruits, the only varieties of which we had in New York were oranges, lemons, coconuts, and preserved tamarinds.

We should have disembarked at Greytown, Nicaragua, but there had been some trouble between the natives and passengers of another steamer, and the U.S. ship *Cyanne* [*Cyane*] was there to prevent further trouble, so we transferred to flat boats which took us to a stern-wheel steamer which lay at the mouth of the San Juan River.[3] We ascended the river very slowly on account of the many sandbars and were the rest of the day and all night reaching the Castillo Rapids, sitting around or reclining on chairs and benches, as there were no staterooms or beds usually needed as the trip should be a short one. We made many stops and sometimes passengers went ashore so as to lighten the boat, although it drew very little water. After the boat cleared a sand bar, we would board her again. There were many native shacks along the river, at some of which we bought limeade, fruits and occasionally cakes or other food. Meals were not furnished on board, so my father produced his champagne-basket in which he had brought crackers, a large pineapple cheese, sardines and prepared coffee in cans, went to the engine-room and brought back hot water with which to mix the coffee extract and we had quite a lay-out. We had breakfast at the Rapids, July 16, 1854, and I ate fried plantains or bananas for the first time. Afterwards, we leisurely walked past the Rapids to the side-wheel steamer *Ometepe*—named after the volcano—which had staterooms for all of the cabin passengers, and on which we were to cross Lake Nicaragua.[4] Every one was rejoicing at the change and enjoying the comfort; the women went to their rooms to make their toilets, which they had not been able to do for nearly twenty-four hours, and some of them were asleep when along in the afternoon there was a shock and the boat shook and then began to sink. It had struck a rock and the passengers were shaken rather roughly. All rushed to get to the upper deck, and the doors were soon blocked. A very fat woman in dishabille, with hair flying, ran out of her stateroom and tried to climb out of a cabin window, but got no further than her waist. She tried to back in again, but didn't succeed, and could do nothing but kick and throw her arms about. My father and some other men, seeing her predicament, went to her rescue and pulled her back in to the cabin. All except the back part of the hurricane deck sank into the water.

Our party, consisting of my father, my uncle James A. Corbusier and the ladies, Mrs. L. Forrest, Mrs. Butler, and Mrs. Forrest's daughter Ida, were among the last to get up there and we stood there awaiting our turn to be taken ashore. The small boats were already carrying passengers to the rocks and fallen trees in the swamp, only a short distance away, and others were coming from up and on the river to assist in the rescue. My father looked after the ladies to see them taken from the steamer, and returned to me with a rope in his hand. It was to help me in case the deck all went under, but we reached the big rock where the ladies were seated. By this time it was getting dark and then the rain began to come down rather heavily. My father placed us back to back, with wraps over our feet and gave me a big umbrella, having whalebone ribs, which were then used, to hold over us. There we sat, listening to the men firing their revolvers at alligators to drive them away, for hours.

¶Towards morning we heard the whistle of a steam-lighter and we were soon crowded into it, to be taken over to Fort San Carlos at the outlet of the lake, a few miles distant, and here we remained about twenty-four hours. A party of about a dozen of us found an empty native hut of upright poles and thatched roof with a dirt floor and took possession, and then the men went out to forage for food. Other men were out in the same quest and all of the chickens were soon bought up. Some paid in advance of the cooking, and didn't wait for the delivery, so the natives accepted pay a second time, and the last comer was the one who took the chicken. My father stayed by his chicken and brought it away, and also brought several yards of jerked beef, so with the provisions he brought along, we fared very well, although some one had stolen what remained of his pineapple cheese. Later in the day, a few hams were issued, but we didn't succeed in getting any. We had a good swim in the lake, and visited the old overgrown fort on the hill. A few Nicaraguan soldiers, bare-footed and in high straw hats, shirts and trousers, strolled about, not clean or well-fitted, but very picturesque.

¶We slept on the ground, with our wraps under and over us until shortly after midnight, when the whistle of the *Central America*, which had returned after taking the steerage passengers and baggage across the lake, awakened us and we had only to jump up and walk down to the water's edge to climb on the back of an almost naked native and he carried [us] to a small boat which took us to the steamer.[5] We had made no toilet, as there was not water except at the lake. We passed the volcano Ometepe as we crossed the lake to Virgin Bay where there was no wharf, so a hawser was carried ashore and fastened. By pulling on this rope, natives brought a flat boat to us and on this we were pulled nearly to shore to mount the backs of black fellows and be carried to the strand. A wagon drawn by four very small mules was procured and the six of our party drove over the mountains to San Juan del Sur on the Pacific Ocean, which we did not reach until some time after dark. I walked a good part of the way, as there was much of interest along the road. Armadillos in their shell armour were plentiful and there were some sloths up in trees. Well up the mountain, I saw upright green leaves about half an inch in diameter moving across the road in a column about four feet wide, and, on investigating, I saw that each leaf was carried by a large ant. I followed along, and not far up hill was an anthill higher than my head which was the destination of the ant army.

The hour was so late when we reached the hotel that every bed had been taken, so I had to sleep in a grass hammock or on the floor. I took a hammock and slept in one for the first time. People had to move their pallets in the morning before I could get out of the hallway and go breakfast. The ocean steamer, the *Pacific*, lay some distance out from shore and we had to go native-back to rowboats to take us to a small steamer which carried us the rest of the way out.[6] We were very happy to get back to comfortable quarters again.

We entered the harbor of Acapulco and, when inside it was not easy to tell where we entered. Very few of the passengers had ever seen a Mexican town, so nearly all of them went ashore. Of course we went and the boats had cushioned seats and awnings of striped canvas. Limes, pineapples and bananas were very cheap. Sea shells of many kinds and pearls were for sale. The very old church was of great interest to me and I climbed up into the tower to see the ancient chimes, one of the bells of which had the date 15. . . [date not completed in typescript]. I was here afterwards—I think in 1864—on Palm Sunday and saw the Mexicans, all in white, bearing palm branches, going to mass.

When we disembarked at San Francisco, July 31, 1854, the married ladies joined their husbands, and my father, Uncle James and I went to a hotel—the St. Charles, I think—which was built on piles over the water of the bay, on a street which is now some blocks from the water-front. As I entered our room, I saw the ceiling coming down and dodged back and stood to see what would happen, when it went up again. The rooms were all lined with white canvas which moved whenever a door or window was opened or closed. I didn't see Mrs. Butler again until the latter part of November, 1873, when she was the wife of Lieutenant [Edward R.] Theller of the Army, who was on General Ord's staff in San Francisco. She had been in an ocean wreck and two Indian fights. Lieutenant Theller was killed in the Modoc Indian War.[7] Alexander Sloat, a grand uncle of mine, was in San Francisco and took us to a Chinese restaurant and there I ate my first olives. He also showed us through the El Dorado, a great gambling house on the lower side of the Plaza, in which all sorts of gambling games were openly conducted and every one could play a game. Many a miner, who had earned his pile in hard labor and was on his way to the States, didn't get any farther than San Francisco, losing all in this place.

The dime was the smallest coin in circulation and was called "a bit," but it wouldn't buy much. Twenty-five cents was "two bits." Give a silver quarter and buy something for a bit and you received a dime in change, so there was a long bit and a short bit. A Chinaman would always get change so as to give a short bit, and not a long one, when making a purchase and so saved 20%. Slugs, i.e. $50.00 gold pieces were in circulation and gold dust was often tendered, so we saw gold scales in every store.

After a few days, my father, Uncle James and I, went to Sacramento by boat. My ticket read "For Popsie's Boy." The days there were very hot, and I remember the delicious watermelons we had at the hotel. We visited Sutter's Fort, which was yet in a good state of preservation and in which my father had spent some time with Sutter as well as at Sutter's Mill, now Coloma, in 1849.[8] We went to Auburn, Placer County, about forty miles, in a Concord coach, passengers inside and on top, the U.S. mail in a boot in front and baggage behind.[9] Off we drove at a fast gate [sic], but the four horses soon had to lessen their gait and come down to a stead[y] gait. After leaving the valley of the Sacramento, which was very soon, we began to ascend the Sierras, and then came some pretty steep grades up which we walked. We saw Auburn from the top of a hill near a tavern called the "Traveler's Rest," and descended into Auburn Ravine, in the bottom of which rested the small town. As we dashed in, a great gong sounded the dinner call and, after eating, we climbed into my father's spring wagon and drove out to his ranch about three and a half miles north east, called "Spring Ranch" on account of the two fine large cool springs, the only water within two miles or more, which gave control of fine grazing for a long distance. Only about a hundred acres were fenced in on which to raise oats and barley for the horses, and cut what hay— worth $40.00 a ton—was needed when the grass began to give out. On a beautiful knoll stood the house of four rooms, with a garret, built of upright boards and battened. Two large pine trees and many live-oaks shaded the grounds in front and one large oak at the back. On one of the front trees hung the skin of a huge grizzly bear that had been killed not far away, near which we swung, two grass hammocks, which we had brought from Mexico, and here I lay many a time listening to the soughing of the pines and whispering of the oaks in which doves often took refuge and uttered their mournful calls of oo-oo-ooo. My uncle James didn't remain long on the ranch, but went down to San Francisco and later returned to the States by sailing vessel around Cape Horn.

We at first had to do our own cooking, and bacon and eggs were a stand by. Bacon wasn't a common meat in the north at that time and I had to learn to eat it. We had shanghai chickens and plenty of eggs, but the miners around us rarely had any except gull's eggs which were gathered on the Farallon Island and boiled before they were shipped. We soon hired a Chinaman cook and paid him $25.00 a month as Chinese labor was very cheap.[10] Later my father had an Alsatian man and wife, who had two boys and a girl, who, all but the little girl, did the work inside and out. I learned to milk a cow and much about caring for chickens and pigs, and had a hand in all kinds of jobs. I was soon able to ride the worst broncos on the ranch, which I had to blindfold to saddle, bridle and mount, and I had to learn horse sense to succeed. Horse-shoeing, wagon repairing, harness and saddle overhauling, were carried on at the ranch, and I was always around receiving lessons from my father who wished me to be able to do what anyone else could do. I learned to plough, harrow, cut grass with a scythe and every other kind of work that had to be done around a ranch of that kind, branding and marking the different animals as well.

My father soon gave me a shotgun and taught me "Safety first," so that I wouldn't shoot myself or be a menace to any one else. I at first winged many birds, as crows, doves, quail, etc., which I often kept as pets. I also had large grey squirrels, rabbits, etc., and made pets of some of the domestic animals, one of the most interesting of which was a young pig. I rode young bulls and trained one of them to obey my touch of foot and hand. During the rainy season the cattle that were thin would often mire and we had to haul them out with a team of horses by a rope around their horns.

I usually wore a blue or grey flannel shirt, trousers stuck in top boots which had a colored top in front, a colored sash and soft grey hat. In winter I had a black horsehair serape, with a colored border of red and white roses, to shed the rain. I always turned my boots over and shook them before putting them on, as I had heard or read about rattlesnakes having crawled into them over night. I was on my pony Julie many hours a day, often out after stray cattle. She was black with a white face and two hind white stockings. Her tail almost reached the ground, but her mane was kept roached. No fence could keep her from roaming about at will, and I jumped her over fences, ditches, logs and bushes, rode her up and down flights of stairs—a dozen or more steps. No matter how far away she was and she heard my whistle, she would come running. Sometimes she would knock at my bedroom door at night and, knowing she wanted sugar or salt, I would get and give her some. She would then jump the fence and go off to graze again. I could guide her by my feet and hands, riding bareback, without bridle or hackamore. Once only did I slip off, and that was when I was loping up a steep hill without holding on except with my knees, and slid down over her tail. I could mount over her head or tail, or from either side, crawl under her and between her fore or hind feet. She would at command get down on her knees, lie down, roll over or lie still until told to get up. Her running gaits were pacing and loping and I drove her single in a buggy.

¶My father had bought her from a Missourian, who had bought her out on the plains. He was one of several families that had been several months crossing overland from Missouri, bringing along all of their earthly possessions. My father bought nearly the whole outfit, wagons, buggies, American horses, Durham cows and a bull, etc. He had no use for six yoke of fine large oxen that he bought, so rented them to Bob Hilliard, who had a sawmill over on Bear River, to be used for logging purposes, and had to take pay in lumber. Most of the cows, some of which had worked under the yoke, were let to a Mr. Stevens who was running a dairy and sold milk for a dollar and a half a gallon in Auburn. For a time my father kept the cows, and I remember selling milk to some miners a few miles away and returning with a good many silver dollars.

One of our two springs was about six feet deep and had a trout in it. It was inside a hewn-log house about eighteen feet square, around the sides of which were shelves for milkpans and crocks for butter. For a time I carried the water used at the house and soon learned to use a pole similar to the one used by the Chinese and had to make fewer trips. I learned to handle an axe and then for a time cut most of the wood.

I missed the companionship of boys, and whenever I could, would select our fastest horse and ride over to the Auburn and Grass Valley road where there was a wayside inn to race with a boy about my own age. I have always been fond of horse-racing, not, however, as a looker-on or to bet, but when riding one of the horses. It was so with other games, as baseball, football, etc. I wanted to take an active part in them. I had a horse, pointer dog, a bull dog and a shotgun and all sorts of pets, but was lonesome, and was very happy when I was left in Auburn to attend school.

Once when my father was away for the night, a stranger happened along and stayed with me, and in the morning gave me some silver money which I showed to my father on his return. He told me that I shouldn't have taken it and never again to take money from anyone whom we entertained at the ranch. All must be welcomed to whatever the ranch afforded, man and beast.

A Prussian, Englebert Bauer, occupied a cabin on the knoll and worked when he felt so inclined. I spent many an hour listening to his stories about "mina contree" and the wonderful deeds of his family, while he cut tobacco from a plug, rolled it between his palms, pressed it into his clay pipe, and skillfully picked up a live coal to light it and then lazily puffed away. When there was water above the ranch in the rainy season, he did some ground-sluicing and washed the earth[,] deposited it in a cradle, making about seven dollars a day, not enough to pay him for the time he put in, so he went prospecting, carrying his pick, shovel and pan, to do some pocket hunting. One night he came back with fifty dollars in gold dust and almost as much on several other nights. I then caught the gold fever, as the most I had panned out was when we cleaned out the spring which extended down to bedrock and I took out about .25¢ to a pan, so I went with him and returned with about seven dollars. I was satisfied, probably as pocket mining with a pan is no easy job or it might have been that I had very little use for money, for there was nothing in the town for me to buy.

There were some Digger Indians camped not far away and near some oak trees on which there were acorns at least two inches long which they dried, shelled and ground in holes in the granite rocks in a creek, using a long round rock as a pestle.[11] They boiled this meal in baskets, as they had no pottery. Cobble stones four or five inches in diameter were heated in an open fire, picked up with two sticks and dropped into a basket of water and meal. These were replaced as fast as they cooled off until the water boiled and the meal was cooked to their taste. The mush was dipped out and carried to the mouth with two or more fingers and it constituted their principal food for a good portion of the year. When the clover came up in the beginning of the rainy season, they would lie prone in a patch of it and eat it right as it grew, just as the lower animals ate it. They were skillful basketmakers, and often ornamented the outside of the water-tight ones with the top-knots of the quail and other feathers closely woven in. They burned their dead and mixed the ashes with pitch from the pine trees to cover their heads which was a long time wearing off.

Rattlesnakes were very numerous, and I killed many of them, one a few feet from the house, where we had a hen with a brood of young chickens in a small coop. I heard her utter a cry of fear, and on going to the coop, found a rattler with body bulging. I cut it open, and out fell two dead chickens. It had killed two or three more, intending, probably, to swallow them also.

We had a large Durham muley cow—one without horns—that some-times failed to give any milk, or gave very little, and one day we caught her in the very act of milking herself. She was one of the cows that had worked in a yoke on the plains, and, when grazing was scarce, would suck herself. We put a rack on her neck, so that she couldn't turn her head around to reach her udders.

The Missourians and others told me of many of their experiences on the plains. When miles from any wood, they cooked over dry buffalo chips—the dry dung of the buffalo—which would be in a big heap, and, as soon as the young men could unyoke the cattle and unharness the horses, there would be a race to see who would reach the nearest heaps and secure them. I also have eaten a meal cooked over buffalo chips. A popular song was "When I got alkalied," and I have been alkalied.[12] There was a story current among them of a wagon-train of families that had been chased by Indians and some of the party killed or wounded. The Indians came in sight again, and the father of some children who had the measles, took one of their blankets and threw it out for the Indians to pick up, saying, "Damn them, let them have it." It started an epidemic among the Indians and many of them died of the disease. In the Corbusier "Win-ter Counts" there is a winter named because of the disease.[13]

Auburn caught fire [in 1855] and nearly every house in it was burned, and my father, having so much lumber due him at the mill, had much of it hauled there.[14] He bought a lot and built a house large enough for two stores. In one of these, Englebert started a restaurant and fruit stand, and I went to town to live with him, to return to the ranch at week-ends and look up stray horses and cattle, as I now knew their habits and ranges.

There were a few children in town by this time and a school had been opened in which a well-educated Irishman was the teacher. My father had him give me special attention so as to make up for the time I had lost on the ranch, where, however, I had read all of the books that I could find, some histories, but mostly about pirates and highwaymen.

Chinatown was up hill, a short distance from the stores and some times there would be trouble. Hearing the yelling and beating of shovels and the banging of miner's pans, one would think that some one was getting killed, but, although the whole of the Chinese community seemed to take part, very rarely was any one more than a little bruised. There was a Chinese theatre, and I went frequently for a while, until the play got too long for me and seemingly never would come to an end. Englebert thought I was wasting my time by going, so [he] gave me some apples and peaches to sell and was satisfied when I brought back the money for them, but I wasn't cut out for a vender and soon went out of business. I once followed a Chinese funeral procession out to the grave-yard where the dead were to be fed, and when the food was distributed, I was given some spiced barbecued pork and a cake that looked like an apple dumpling which had some Chinese characters printed on it in red ink. These I tore off and then took a bite finding some finely hashed meat inside. After swallowing a mouthful, I asked a Chinaman what the meat was, as I had never tasted any thing like it before and when he informed me that it was "all some lat"—rat—I felt like I did once after I had swallowed a fly. The meat staid [sic] down, but my appetite left me for any more chow at that time. Some weeks afterward, our Chinese cook told me that the rats they ate were caught in the rice paddies and had hair on their tails.

Gambling was carried on openly, and on Sunday—the miner's wash-day—many miners came to town to make their purchases, and, after securing their supplies, would enter a game and play until all that was left of their gold dust or money was gone.[15] Those that came from Rock Creek, just south of our ranch, averaged about ten dollars a day sluicing, as long as they had water during the rainy season. Others bought water by the inch from the Bear-River Ditch Company and could work their claims throughout the dry season. A miner's inch was the water running through an opening a foot wide and one inch high. Three or four sluice boxes were usually used, each one made of three one-inch boards twelve feet long. One was fitted into the end of another and a cleat about an inch high was laid across the lower end of each to retain the gold which when very fine was held by quicksilver placed at them to catch it. They were given a slight incline, so that the water led into them, would wash the earth that was shoveled into them, from the stones, which were taken out with a fork, having about six strong prongs, by a man who stood with a foot on each side of the trough. When water was less plentiful, or a man worked alone, a Long Tom was used, which was a kind of sluice two feet or more broad at its lower end and a foot or so at its upper end, the bottom of which was of sheet iron half way up full of half-inch holes at its lower end. Water carried the earth that was thrown in at its upper end down through these holes to an inclined tray beneath, which had a cleat near its lower edge to hold the gold. When there was no running water, or not enough, recourse was had to the rocker or cradle which was about three feet long and fourteen inches wide on two rockers end with an upright piece at the left upper corner for a handle. The bottom had a slight incline and a cleat across its lower end. The upper half held a tray, or box, above it, which had a perforated sheet-iron bottom, into which the earth was thrown and water poured on with a large dipper, while the cradle was rocked until all of the earth was washed off of the stones onto the piece of canvas below which let it fall gently to the floor, where the gold was caught by the cleat.

My father never gambled, nor did he drink alcoholic beverages, except occasionally a glass of claret. He smoked a cigar after supper and sometimes between meals, but I never saw him with a pipe. After a smoke at night, he would pick up his violin, banjo or accordeon [sic] and play for a time, always by ear. He now collected firearms, and had old pistols and rifles besides his shotguns. Among them was an old long Yager with which he was a good shot at a hundred yards. It was too heavy for me to carry, but I would sometimes shoot at a mark. Nearly all of the men gambled and the boys imitaded [sic] the men, but played the Mexican game of Monte with Mexican cards, using marbles for stakes. I tried my luck, but lost. Finding that the cards usually ran in favor of the dealer, I procured a monte deck and became dealer and banker. Very soon I had nearly all of the "alleys," as we called them, which were not numerous, and I lost interest in the game, as there was no sport in getting them so easily, and I cared more for games in which there was more action.

The accordeon was the principal musical instrument, and one could hear it nightly in all of the saloons and elsewhere. The jewsharp [sic] was sometimes heard and it was the favorite of the Indians. I saw Edwin Booth play Richard III in Auburn, in 1856, I think.[16] Once a one-ring circus came and it was well patronized, $2.50 admittance. I saw a bull fight and a bear and bull fight. The bear was a grizzly which had belonged to the notorious Lola Montez—Maria Dolores Eliza Rosan[n]a Gilbert—whom I had seen petting it on the lawn in front of her cottage in Grass Valley, California, where she lived for some time after she came to the U.S. after she had caused a revolution and the dethronement of Ludwig, the King of Bavaria, whose favorite she had been.[17] The bear's play at length became too rough for her and she sold him. For the fight, he was chained by a hind leg to a post set deeply in the middle of the arena with its top only above ground, and he could not quite reach the high strong fence that surrounded it. The bull was goaded and driven within his reach until it made a few lunges with its horns and, when its head was down, the bear grabbed it by the nose and the skin of the neck, when the bull could do nothing but bellow until it was released. The bull stood no more with a bear than with a man. The toredo [toreador] is in very little danger and the so-called sport is a very cruel one. The men have mantas to throw over the head of the animal, which, after it has been maddened with pain from darts covered with fancy colored papers hanging to it, closes his eyes to rush at his tormentors, is very easily dodged as his head is covered. If a horse is to be sacrificed to please an audience, a poor plug is selected and ridden close to be gored to death. The man's part couldn't be a more shameful one. A woman was once advertised to take part in a bull-fight on stilts, but she almost fainted when she saw the bull and her part had to be called off.

Women were rarely seen far away from Sacramento and the few who went to the mines, were well treated.[18] Two German girls made a trip into the car diggings with a hand-organ and a tambourine. When they returned through Auburn, they had, it was said, thirty dollars that they had made with their instruments and voices.

When water was scarce, and often when it was plentiful, the miners didn't always do their washing on Sunday, as was usually the custom, but would hang their clothes in the hot sun for a "dry wash." The lazy ones would become louzy [sic] and the busy ant would help them out. Their clothes and blankets were thrown on an ant hill for a day and [would] be taken off at night quite clean and free from couties [*sic*].

My father contemplated a trip to the States and thence to Europe to take the West with him, so we fitted ourselves out for a camping trip with a tent, beds, cooking utensils, guns, fishing tackle, etc., loaded them into a large covered spring wagon and selecting two of our largest and best mules, drove to Teheme by easy stages. We visited an Indian reservation in sight of Mount Shasta and there my father tried to induce some Indians to go with him, but they didn't know him and none would consent to go, so he couldn't carry out his idea of a wild west show.[19]

I began my first diary on my way to California, and have with some breaks, kept one ever since. I lost that I wrote up to 1896 [1906] in the great fire after the earthquake in San Francisco, April 16 [18], of that year, but writing so much, fixed events in my memory which I might not have otherwise been able to recall.

CHAPTER THREE

On Both Coasts

I was very tired of the simple life and glad to leave the ranch and go to the States[.] I felt that I never wanted to see California again. We were in San Francisco at the time of the disbandment of the Vigilance Committee and its great parade on August 18, 1857. I visited Fort Gunny-bags and went through the building and into the room in which Yankey [sic] Sullivan, a prize fighter and gangster, had committed suicide. The Committee had done good work in driving out the lawless element and cleaning up politics so that the ward heelers had to watch their steps.[1] The express company—Adams—I think—had failed, and my father was afraid to entrust his money to any express company, so he filled a chamois vest with twenty dollar gold pieces and gave it to me to wear.[2] I rambled about the city, went mussel hunting, fishing, and crabbing, etc. with at least $1000.00 on me for some days. We returned to New York via the Isthmus of Panama in September, 1857, stopping some hours at Acapulco, where we went ashore and roamed about.

We took many curios with us and among them a very fine collection of beautiful arrow heads made by the Digger Indians of different colored stone and a bow, the back of which was covered with sinew and the string of twisted sinew. We had a black monkey with a white face, purchased in Aspinwall—now Colon—but [he] had a bad disposition and drew too many children around the house, so he was sent to Barnum's Museum, corner of Broadway and Ann Street, which on holidays was crowded with children and grown-ups to see the many freaks of nature, and here I saw the dwarf Tom Thumb.[3]

My father went on to Europe, but I remained at my Aunt Eliza Polsome's in 83rd street, in Yorkville, where I attended Grammar School No. 37 in east 87th street of which Mr. Boice was the Principal, entering the highest grade and in which I was prepared to enter the Free Academy, now the College of the City of New York, but which I never entered.[4] The boys nick-named me "California" and I was supposed to be a fighter, so the Irish boys, who went in gangs, wanted to try me out, I wasn't accustomed to fist fighting and tried to avoid them. At length one day, half a dozen of the toughest ones set upon me and I ran into an alley in which I found a shinney stick, and grabbing it, I went for them and drove them before me. That was enough for them and they didn't like my way of fighting, so after that they left me alone. I at length had a little band of my own, of a better class, who liked my stories about the wild west. After a time, to tell them some new ones, I had to call upon my imagination. My trained whales took well, until one of them asked if it was all true, and I had to admit it was just a yarn. They were disappointed, and my stories had to be changed. We had minstrels and other shows in a large barn belonging to the father of one of the gang. An Irish boy, who was full of stories and superstitions, told us many of them, and once, just after sunset he began to tell some of them, and, at length said he knew the words to use with which to call up the devil, so we told him to go on. There would be no danger if we stood within a ring which he would make and we said go ahead and call up the fallen angel. The ring was made, and we all stepped inside, and the boy began to repeat the magic words, first telling us not to be afraid, even if old Nick came very close, as all we had to do was to make the sign of the cross and that would frighten him so that he would instantly disappear. It was now quite dark, and we must have heard some unusual noise, as with one accord we dashed for the open air to get out of the barn as quickly as possible.

Target excursions were very popular and the men would wear the same kind of cap, red stripes were sewn on their black trousers and some of them had guns. A target, two feet or so in diameter would be painted and a negro hired to carry it, just back of a brass band. Then came half a dozen or more men on long tail black coats and high silk hats, the invited guests, carrying the prizes donated by them, usually plated ware, at least one piece a basket with a handle. They marched to the selected place in the woods or on the shore of the river. We boys imitated the men, and I, at the head of a gang, in my father's red coat and carrying the only gun, the boys not in our ranks hooting at us and hoping to start a fight. We went over to where Central Park is now, but didn't have the fine dinner after our target practice, as the men had.[5] I was the only boy in that part of New York who had a gun, and I often shot birds in the present park. I lived with my Uncle Edward and Aunt Esther Corbusier for nearly a year and then with my Uncle James.[6]

Street horse-cars were now running to Yorkville and there were other lines replacing omnibusses; sewing-machines were coming into use.[7] There [was] gas in place of oil lamps in the streets, and kerosene oil, having a very strong odor, was driving out whale oil, lard oil, and burning fluids. The latter had caused many deaths by explosion and camphene was one of them. Coal was used for heating and cooking. Water had been lead [laid] into most houses, and bathtubs and toilets introduced, although there were some wells and pumps left.

During the Christmas holidays, the Bowery Theatre was a popular resort, as every one wanted to see [George Washington] Fox in pantomime.[8] Admittance to the pit was sixpence and it was always crowded with newsboys, boot blacks and others whose criticisms and applause were a good part of the show. A man with a rattan in each aisle preserved order. That part of the theatre is now called the "orchester" [orchestra] and the seats are no longer sixpence. I usually paid a shilling for a seat in the first balcony. I think it was an old English sixpence, but the figures on it were worn very smooth and indistinct. It was recalled from circulation after this and a silver three-cent piece was coined and circulated for some years. There were not so many bootblack[s] as there are now and all of them were boys who went about with only a box of black paste and a brush. I think that the paste was made of burnt sugar, as dogs liked to lick it from boots and shoes. The boys spit on the paste to thin it, and one day a boy, whose mouth must have been very dry from the large demands of his customers, was heard to call to another one, "Say Johnnie, lend me some spit." Pareppa Rosa [sic] was the popular prima donna and we often went to the Academy of Music to hear her.[9] Airs from the operas she sang were heard on the streets and in nearly every house, and my cousins, Alice and Henrietta and I improved English words for many of them. I was in New York City August 17, 1858, the day the first message was received over the first Atlantic cable after its successful laying between Valentia [Valencia], Ireland, and Heart[']s Content, Trinity Bay, New Foundland, and it took 67 minutes to send a message. It had been completed on August 3, under the direction of Cyrus W. Field, by the British ship *Agamemnon* and American frigate *Niagra* [*Niagara*]. The celebration was a great one, and sections of the cable were worn as watch charms and placed among the bric a brac.[10]

My uncle James went over to Williamsburg, Long Island, to live for awhile, and I went with him to continue my studies in Grammar School No. 18 a short time and then took a course in double entree bookkeeping, etc., at Paine's Business College on the Bowery, New York, as my uncle was getting ready to go to Toledo, Ohio, to open a hat, cap, straw goods and artificial flower house. We went there in December 1859, I think, via Albany and Dunkirk, crossing the Hudson River at Albany on the ice in sleighs. I became a clerk, and my principal work was to set the samples out for inspection, but I also helped with the books, making out monthly balance sheets, etc. The chief clerk—Mr. Butler—and I fitted up a large room in the third story of the brick building, which we reached by the freight elevator, which we raised by pulling on a large rope which ran over a huge wooden wheel. We took our meals at a hotel and paid $3.50 per week, often having venison and other game. During the dull season I read much of the time, caring more for books than for money. I remained here about a year, and then, having written to my mother that I wished to go on with my education, she sent me money to go to Nyack.

There I entered the Rockland County Classical and Commercial Academy, of which Christopher Rutherford was the Principal.[11] It was one of a number of such schools along the Hudson River at that time in which boys were educated, pursuing the higher studies which prepared them for a college course or the study of a profession. Greek, Latin and the modern languages were taught, Algebra, Geometry, etc. Much attention was paid to reading and elocution and each boy had to recite a new selection on Friday. Here are some of mine: Landing of the Pilgram [*sic*] Fathers, Psalm of life, Bingen on the Rhine, Speech of John Adams, The Seminoles reply and many parts of Shakespeare. We started a debating society and had some warm discussions on slavery, the right of the South to seceed [*sic*], and other political questions. We rowed on the Hudson and swam. In winter, we skated, often going over to Rockland Lake to do so. There was fine coasting on sleds in winter and on wagons in summer. Some of us often camped in the woods on my grandfather's old farm, which was now owned by Mr. John Towt and which I knew so well. I taught the other boys how to camp and to cook. I could climb any tree, as I had learned to climb on the steamers going to and returning from California.

Mr. Towt liked boys and had some of his own. He let us go into his fine orchard, which had been planted by grandfather Myers, and take all of the fruit we wanted, but requested us not to break any of the branches, so we treated the trees as if they belonged to us, I in particular, as they had been planted by my grandfather. On the other side of the road, between it and the turnpike, was a much younger orchard, the fruit in which was not so good, and we really didn't want it, but after the owner had warned us to keep out, we watched for his coming and when we saw him coming along the pike we would jump his stone fence to pretend that we were after the fruit. He would shake his whip and yell at us until we ran away as if we were afraid. I think that often he was playing a game, just as the boys were. The falls of ten or twelve feet were a favorite for pic nics. We hunted snakes on Snake Hill where formerly there were so many that the neighboring farmers had gone on regular hunts to try to kill them off. The copperhead was the venomous one and there were a few of them left.

Base-ball, played on four bases, had taken the place of the other ball games.[12] I became the captain of one side and Mr. Rutherford of the other, and nothing gave him greater pleasure than to beat my side. Many Cuban boys were educated in the schools on the Hudson, and one of them, Arturo Betancourt de Guiterrez [*sic*] Castillo, Mirando de Bethancourt, was assigned to a room with me, so that he might learn English and I might learn Spanish. The first night was warm, and he was going to get into bed naked. I told him that wouldn't do, so he put on his trousers to sleep in, but I said "No." We then looked into his trunk and there found nightshirts that his American guardian had provided him, the use of which he didn't know. I was probably the poorest writer in school, so I was surprised one day to have my copybook was [*sic*] held up as an example of neatness and cleanliness. Only once had I worked for a prize, and that was when I was in Yorkville when a colporter [*sic*] visited a Sunday-school

which I was attending and offered to give a book to the one who committed to memory the most verses in the New Testament. I learned the
twelfth chapter of St. Matthew, but he never returned.

Several of us boys liked to listen to the village post, a writer of fiction for
the county paper and shoemaker, who spoke Spanish and was a socialist.
The story writer would tell us what he was going to do with some of his
characters. A fourth character was a fisherman who quoted Shakespeare.

When the Civil War began my mother was in Memphis, Tennessee
and my father in California, so I had to leave school owing to the lack of
funds to pay my expences [sic], and I went to the farm of a relative and
hoed corn for a time, but soon went to New York and staid [sic] with the
Bakewells, who were relatives. The father had an army contract to make
tents, and I learned to use a palm and sew canvas while looking around
for something to do. Boys were not wanted, except for training in a business house or permanent jobs, but I at length went into a cloak and man-
tilla store on Broadway, a couple of blocks above Canal Street and about
four blocks from where I was born, at $8.00 a week, where I remained
until I received money from my father with which to pay my way to California. There were many friends or relatives who would welcome me to
visit them, but I didn't think of depending on any one except my parent[s]
to help me and I wanted to help myself.

The political campaign of 1860 was a very exciting one. There were
nightly parades of men in water proof capes carrying torches, and I
attended many meetings to hear speeches of both parties, and when
[Abraham] Lincoln was on his way to Washington to be inaugurated as
President, I was at Nyack and watched the railroad train on the east side
of the Hudson, hoping that he would safely reach the Capital.[13] I was in
New York at the beginning of the Civil War when the first troops left for
the South, first the Sixth Massachusetts on April 16, 1861, the Seventh New
York on April 19 and the Ellsworth Zouaves later, Durye[e], etc.[14]

Shortly afterward, I left by steamer for California, crossed the Isthmus
of Panama by rail and was in Panama long enough to visit the old cathe-
dral, up the steps of which the natives entered on their knees. On the
Pacific, fifty or more men would assemble around a large man who had
a stentorian voice and led in singing, "A Life on the Ocean Wave" and
other songs of the day, and at night a crowd gathered around a young
lady, who played a guitar, and sang "Ben Bolt," "Lilly Dale," "Old Black Joe,"

"Tranquadillo," etc. When about midway between Panama and Acapulco, just after sunset, while most of the passengers were on deck, and we were wondering where the Confederate ship *Alabama* was, which had unexpectedly appeared at many places and done much damage to our shipping, might be [*sic*], and we hoped not on the Pacific, when stars appeared in the east and great stripes of alternate red and white came up from the western horizon, spreading to the zenith, I exclaimed, "Our Banner in the Sky!" and every one looked upon it with reverence and as a good omen.[15] We were in Acapulco for some hours and I went ashore to visit the very old church and an old bridge again.

I joined my father at Gilroy in the Santa Clara Valley, about thirty miles south of San Jose, and, after a few days we went drove [*sic*] to a ranch he had located in the mountains, about three miles northwest of the Henriquete and Guadaloupe quicksilver mines.[16] Here we built an upright board house of one large room and began to plough with a yoke of oxen which I tried to guide but without success. Our stay was very short and we abandoned the house and went to San Jose. Two of our best horses had been stolen and we had only one left, so we had to "ride and tie" the twelve miles to town. The rainy season had set in and we had to wade a swollen stream which almost swept us from our feet. My father knew a Frenchman named Prevost, who had a tree and flower nursery, and I thought that I might like the business, so I went to the nursery and learned much about the cultivation of fruits and flowers, planting, transplanting, grafting, budding, setting out hedges, and especially about roses. I improved my Spanish by going to a Romish church every Sunday morning to hear a sermon in good Spanish. Mr. Prevost read aloud every night, usually a French novel, and on Sunday had friends to dinner, when not only French, but also Italian and Portuguese were spoken and often sung, and there were two ex-Garibaldian followers who told of their services under their great leader, so I could enlarge my French vocabulary and pick up a little of the other languages.[17]

I at length realized that I was not in my element and that I wanted to study medicine and surgery. Dr. J. J. Braman of Gilroy, wanted a helper who could speak Spanish, as he had quite a practice among the Mexican population, but couldn't speak their language, so I accepted his invitation to join him.[18] The first books that I happened to pick up were on homoeopathy and water cure, and, after reading a while, I thought that if such very small doses of medicine could do good, none at all would do the same, and I thought of quitting. Anatomy and physiology, however, interested me and I soon became interested in the cases I saw, and they were all sorts of medical and surgical ones, enough to keep me thinking. Questioning them in Spanish, I had to bring out their symptoms, and that was good practice for me. I had to study anatomy on my own body and sit before a looking-glass to watch the movements of my muscles. At length a Mexican was lynched and I was able to procure his body to study, and this was the time that I secured the skeleton that my son Harold has in his possession.

An American from western New York was hauling lumber from Bod-fish's Mill up the canyon west of Gilroy over to the San Joaquin Valley with two wagons and six yoke of oxen and had with him $400.00 in gold which he wished to send this family. He was informed in Gilroy that he would have to wait for a check from the main office in San Francisco, so he carried the money with him. After delivering the lumber and returning to the Santa Clara valley, he went into a wayside house in Pachoco Pass to get some tobacco. He took some gold from a pocket, looking for a silver piece with [which] to pay for it. Two Mexicans saw the gold and left the room before he did. A few hours afterward, some Americans as they came up the road saw yoked oxen grazing at its side, and, looking about to find the driver, they found his dead body in [an] open space among some bushes in which there were signs of a struggle. A blood stained knife lay near the body and around the neck was the noose of a lariat which had been out. The two Mexicans were suspected and word was sent to arrest them. One was found over in the Pajaro—"Bird"—Valley, where he was spending gold very freely. He was brought over to Gilroy, where a Justice of the Peace held a court in a hotel, which was still stand-ing in 1922. An American, for whom the Mexican had herded sheep, iden-tified the knife that had been found near the body as one he had sold to the Mexican, and a piece of a lariat, that the latter had in his possession when arrested, was found to be the rest of the noose which was around the murdered man's neck, whose body showed several knife wounds. The prisoner was ordered to be taken by the deputy sheriff to San Jose to await trial for murder. While the examination was in progress, a man went into one of the two stores and selected a piece of rope of an unusual length. When he took out money to pay for it, he was asked if it was to be put to good use and answering "Yes," was told there was no charge.

On the veranda of the hotel there were 35 or 40 of Bodfish's mill-hands, some of whom quietly slipped between the deputy and his prisoner[. A]s they stepped out of the door of the hotel, the rope procured at the store was thrown over the latter's head and surrounded by mill-hands, he was taken to a line-oak tree a hundred yards or so southwest of the hotel, a few feet from the one road leading south through the town and on the road that ran up into the canyon where there were two saw-mills— Hindman's and Bodfish's—sawing redwood into lumber. Before reaching the tree, the Mexican slipped the noose from his neck and it caught at his feet by which he was dragged on. At the tree he slipped one of his hand-cuffs off and struck out with his manacled hand, when a young man was thrown against him, fell on top, caught him by the neck and held him down until he stopped breathing, when the rope was replaced about his neck and he was strung up to a branch of the tree. An elderly lady, Mrs. Eigleberry, who came out to her gate, a few feet away, was heard to call out, "Hugh, you ought to be ashamed of yourself."

I had been making a call on the canyon road, and was walking quite rapidly after dark, along a path that led beneath the tree, when I struck against the body, which bounded back and made me jump. Hearing voices approaching, I stepped back against a fence, and saw two men come up, light a match, hold it up to the face of the body, and one of them said, "He is dead all right." The body hung there until noon the next day, when the justice of the peace, who was also the coroner, came from Old Gilroy to hold an inquest. It was found that the hanging had been done by persons unknown. I requested the coroner to turn the body over to me and I would save the county the expense of burying it, and he told me that according to law the body must be buried. I promised to comply with the law, so had a coffin made, placed the body in it, hired a wagon and a driver, went out into the country about five miles, dug a grave and made the internment [sic], having Stanford Moody and the driver assist me. Moody was a typical westerner who sometimes worked in his father's blacksmith shop, but spent most of his time looking after their cattle or breaking bronchos. We had taken a liking for each other and spent much of our spare time in each others['] society. He was always ready to join me in a hunt, prospecting trip or anything else in which there was action. The night after the burial, I met the other two outside of town and went after the body, going and coming as quietly as possible, not knowing [if] the murderer had friends in the neighborhood, but we afterward learned that he was a stranger to the Mexicans around Gilroy. We put the body in a room next to the office in which I could work at my leisure. I afterward cleaned the skeleton and took it east with me. Years afterward my son Harold had it articulated and he now has it hung in a case in his office.

I studied Pharmacy and made all of the tinctures, syrups, mixtures, powders, Pills, etc. An English surgeon, who had lost his wife and taken to drink, came over from the Pajaro valley quite frequently to visit us, as his practice was nearly gone. He was well educated and had had much experience, some of which he imparted to me. He had a wonderful memory and one day, after reading aloud several pages from a history, handed me the book and repeated verbatim the whole chapter. He was sometimes seen walking along a road striking with a crop, which he always carried, at his coattails, and I learned one day why he did so. We were talking in the office, when he suddenly turned to an open door behind him and in a very angry tone called, "I know you are there." He then said to me that the devil, who was always following him to drag him down to hell, was behind the door, but his wife was at his side to guide him above. He was then in a repentant mood, after a hard drinking spell.

The willows at Old Gilroy had been one of the rendezvous of the murderous road-agent, Joaquin Murietta [Murieta] who often hid his stolen horses there and the Mexican, some of whom had probably been associated with him, told of his exploits.[19] There was an old Mexican woman Senora De Castro, who had had twenty-two children and was sometimes dubbed "Old twenty-two."

I hunted a great deal, as game was plentiful, quail, doves, blackbirds, ducks, geese, rabbits, and some deer, and I always came back with my big gamebag full. As soon as the grass began to spring up, after the first rains, flock after flock of wild geese would appear and drop down to feed, and I have seen them so thick that they looked like large patches of snow. When there was low fog, they would fly low, from patch to patch and within easy gunshot. A young fellow killed seventy in one day from behind a trained ox and salted them for future use. My liver-colored pointer bitch was a good retriever and would even swim out in a salt lake to retrieve ducks, but not willingly when the water was quite cold. Once she ran across a bear and came back very fast, and, as I had only a shot-gun along, I climbed the side of the steep hill to get as far away as possible. I often prospected as I hunted, taking a few reagents with me, and I found copper and antimony southeast of Gilroy. We sunk a shaft on the antimony and there was quite a ledge of it, but there was no market for it so we quit work.

Only twice did I go out with a party to hunt, once after grizzly bear about forty miles south of San Juan Bautista, when the young fellows made so much noise that all large game was driven away and I had to kill quail to secure meat for supper one night. Deer bounded away in the distance and only the fresh tracks of Grizzlies were to be seen. Another time I went with a party of six or seven south of Pochece Peaks. I had to borrow a horse from a neighbor who told me to rope any one in his pasture. I selected a black one which I saddled and rode about for a while, to try him out and I found him very tractable. I rode with the party the next morning, a roll of blankets strapped to the castle of my saddle and my rifle in a leather holder in front. We stopped at a well about ten miles to get a drink of water, and going to remount, while throwing my right foot over the blankets it happened to touch the horse's rump. Before I could get the foot into the stirrup, he gave a great buck and threw me over to his off side while jumping up a low hill towards some oak trees against which he would have dashed me, and I let go of his mane and the pommel of the saddle dropped. As I did so, he kicked my left shin and broke a sliver of bone about two inches long from it but without breaking the skin. My companions were a long time roping him and brought him back free of saddle and bridle of which he had managed to rid himself. All laughed and joked me about my horsemanship and I invited any one who wished to do so to ride the horse. My friend Moody, who was riding a horse that had to be blindfolded before he could be mounted, said he liked to ride just such a horse and I told him to go ahead and get on. He asked if I could sit his horse and I said, I might if I blindfolded him to get on, he gave the bridle of my horse a jerk and said "I will ride you all right." He then, in a very nonchalant manner placed his left foot into the stirrup and

was carelessly throwing his right over, when the black dropped his head, humped his back, bounded up and came down on all fours, easily bucking Moody off. He then quickly turned and jumped, trying to strike Moody with all of his feet, but just missed him, his feet astride him. We all yelled and charged the horse which ran off again and gave us a long chase before he was caught. He had to be blindfolded before he could be resaddled. Moody mounted him carefully and had both feet in the stirrups before taking the handkerchief from over his eyes. Once in the saddle, the black couldn't unseat Moody and he rode to the mountains, by which time the horse was in lather and I mounted him again.

Hugh Martin—a half Mexican—with whom neither Moody [n]or [I] was on good terms, talked a good deal about how he could ride bad horses, so the next morning I said to him, "Hugh, you are such a good rider that I wish you would try my horse before I get on him," and he replied "Ride your own horse." But when some of the others accused him of being afraid, he had two of the party help him bridle, blindfold and saddle the horse and then turned its head up hill while he mounted. He then jerked off the blind, put spurs to the horse, dashed quickly up hill a short distance and then quickly turned and came down just as fast. I then mounted, left the party and rode down into the valley, the horse trying to buck me off whenever we came to a level spot. One time he bucked my hat off and after picking it up I had some difficulty in remounting. At night, I lighted a big fire, gave him plenty of rope under an oak tree, where the grass was a foot or more high, rolled up in my saddle blanket, having left my others behind, and went [to] sleep. The next morning the horse nosed me and held perfectly still while I saddled bridled and mounted him. He must have been poisoned by the loco weed, as he had bad spells every now and then. During one of them he struck his owner with his forefeet and the man, who had broken him to harness, in anger beat him over the head with a fence picket until he killed him. When I left the party in the mountains, I had intended to go to Gilroy that day, but I rode so hard that the horse was trembling from fatigue, and for that reason I stopped and spent the night under the stars. I had been advised by my father long before that to always carry matches and food with me, but this was a time that I didn't have some jerked venison, bisquit [sic] and coffee with me. I however, reached town in time for breakfast.

A horse at the Twelve-Mile-house, a stage station south of San Jose, was a wise one and knew a trick or two. One day when the stage out from San Jose stopped to change horses and the passengers to eat dinner, no horses were to be found in the barn, the door of which stood wide open, so the driver had to go on to the Eighteen-Mile-House to get a relay. There he found his lost team. One of them had untied himself, gone around and untied all of the others, raised the bar that held the doors closed, opened them and led the others to the next station. A different knot had to be used in tying this horse and a different fastening for the doors. At that time it was not safe to go on foot along this road, as wild long horned cattle grazed all through the Santa Clara valley. In the mountains I often ran across manadas, a stallion at the head of each one, which, when I approached, circled and rounded up his mares, faced me and snorted defiance.[20] Horse racing was a Saturday sport, when the hitching-rails were crowded with saddle horses and buggies and wagons lined up along the two roads. Herds of long-horns were frequently driven through the town and would usually mill when they came to the road that led west and the vaqueros would have to sing to get them started again. I became a good vaulter of fences from having so many times to get out of their way.

He was a very poor man who didn't own at least one horse and to be without one, a man was down and out. To steal a man's horse, was a great crime and the thief, if caught, was lynched. People traveled mostly in their own vehicles, or on horseback or by Concord coach. To get from San Francisco to San Jose, many travelers took a boat to Alviso, at the south end of the Bay of San Francisco, and from there by coach. In the rainy season, the men often had to get out and pry the wheels out of the mud with fence pickets. There was a front boat for the Mail sacks and small articles, and a rack behind for trunks, etc. A seat by the driver was always sought and when there were Mexican women inside, American men took to the outside and sat with legs hanging over the iron rail that ran around the top of the coach, not liking the smoke from the women's cigarrettes [sic]. Very few Americans had yet taken to the cigarrette and a young fellow who could roll one was looked down upon and was thought to be fit for nothing else.

I made a specialty of raising geraniums and soon had many different varieties, as they were so easy to propagate. For a time I took up the solving of puzzils [sic], which were sent to me from near and far, until there were none left to solve. I took up the guitar for a time, learned part of a Spanish fandango and then quit, as I was too active to spend my time learning to play well and go about mooning.

There were many southern families, mostly from Missouri, the men of which met at the post office, when the daily stage came in with the mail, to read the newspapers and discuss the war news. One time, when a southern army had started from Texas for California, there was much rejoicing, but its defeat in the fight at Pigeon's ranch—La Gloriatta [*sic*]— in New Mexico, dampened their ardor.[21] Very few of them, if any, had been slave owners and their talk was simply to unburden their minds. All, however, joined in to celebrate the fourth of July, 1863, with a barbecue in the willows at Old Gilroy. Trenches were dug and the roasting of the various kinds of meat was begun the night before. Quarters of beef, whole veals, sheep, pigs and chickens, donated by people from the North and South, were cooked for the feast[.] Tables of long boards were made and the food placed on them and even a barrel of wine was put on tap near by. The Speaker of the day who began his speech with, "When Freedom from her mountain heights unfurled her standard to the air" was a little late on account of a hot axle of his carriage and the report was spread that he was tight. The Missourians were delighted and enjoyed the day the more as he was what they called a "Black Republican," "Abolitionist," etc.

Five or six of us boys borrowed two anvils, bought powder and began very early in the morning to fire a salute and kept us the firing all day, except when we were at the barbecue or stopped every four hours to rest and eat great hunks of barbecued beef and slices of bread. When our powder was giving out, we set off our anvils in front of one of the stores until the merchant came out and offered us powder to burn if we would go to the other store, so our supply didn't give out until we had celebrated to our heart's content. One of the anvils was placed on the ground, a playing card and a small cone of powder laid on, with a trail of powder leading from it. The other anvil was then set on top and the powder touched with a heated iron bar about six foot long. The report could be heard a long way off.

On a trip by horseback over the mountains into the Pajaro valley to collect some money, I saw great tracks of a grizzly crossing the road. I stayed in a hotel in Watsonville over night. There was no key for the door of my room and I put the money I had well down under me when I went to bed and laid my revolver so that I could grab it quickly. A brass band was playing patriotic airs as I fell off to sleep listening to it. After a time, I heard my door open and foot steps approached my bed. I slowly moved my right hand toward the revolver and, as a hand went under my pillow, I grabbed the revolver, sprung over onto my left side ready to pull the trigger, but there was no one there to shoot.

I once acted as a clerk at an election, and at least once helped to dig a grave. There was no undertaker and no grave digger, so we young fellows volunteered to assist at funerals. I rode all of one night with a ranchman, who was taking the body of his wife to Santa Clara, 35 miles, for burial.

There were three churches, a northern Methodist, a southern Methodist and a Christian or Campbellite.[22] I often went, in which old Mr. Rule, who raised vegetables and fruit and peddled them, expounded the Bible, as it rarely had a regular minister to lead the services. One of the members was a blacksmith, who was the sole support of his wife, a child and his old father and mother, and lived about a mile from the town. His mother had a badly burned back which was slow in healing and my preceptor and I made her frequent visits. The man met with an accident, and for some time couldn't work at his trade. His scanty savings were soon exhausted, so he suggested to his wife, who had a cultivated voice, that she teach singing. I secured pupils for her and the class met in the church, the first singing school in the part of the valley. The young people had their first lessons in singing and she was able to support her family until her husband could go to work again. We had no organ or other musical instrument, so I sent for a tuning-fork to give us the key. After the class had learned to read by note, we formed a choir to lead the singing in the church. Our teacher was quite timid, so I had to be the leader. I would strike the key and sound Do, Re, Me [sic], Sol, Do, breaking the stillness, and she would then take the lead, beating time with one hand. We drew the young people and the Methodists had to start a singing class of their own to prevent any more of them from joining ours.

¶One of the pupils lived with her sister, Mrs. Hindman, at the sawmill, six miles up the canyon and I drove her into town for every lesson, asking a total distance of twenty four miles with a horse and buggy, but she was an interesting girl just from New York and I didn't begrudge the time spent with her. Before she came out, her sister, before her marriage, stayed with us, and on Christmas day, 1863, I drove her to San Juan Bautista, twelve miles south, where we attended mass at the old mission church, which at that time was in a good state of preservation.[23] Thousands of Indians had been buried in the small enclosure at the east end of the church whom the Spaniards had baptized, set at work to build the church and at length buried them. There were at least a dozen couples in buggies, with the fastest horses in Gilroy and mine, a roan mare, probably the fastest, in the lead. There was a bull-fight, but we cut it out and after a good dinner in the old adobe hotel—still standing in 1922—we drove home in the late afternoon.

We had many dances until a revival in the Methodist churches caused many of the girls to join the church on probation and they were not allowed to dance, but before the order was announced, we had a candy-pulling, which didn't last long, as we had the fiddlers near by[. W]e just had a dance to enjoy our selves, but we couldn't get the probationers together again. We, however, had one more dance. The two Methodist churches made peace and held a festival and donation party in an unoccupied hotel. After a supper and an auction of articles which were for sale, some of the young men asked the most liberal of the two ministers if there would be any harm done if we had just a little dance all among ourselves, and he said "No." Before any objections could be made, the fiddlers started and the young people were dancing. Some of the two congregations left in high dudgeon and went across the road to a hall in which they had kissing games. The next day and for several days after that there were many disagreements and much back talk, but the dancers usually came out ahead, as they ridiculed the others and asked which was worse, dancing or promiscuous kissing. Both at last seemed at last to have been banned.

CHAPTER FOUR

The Civil War

I went to a camp of instruction as a substitute in a California militia company from San Jose for about two weeks.[1] I was growing restless at not being in the army and wrote to my mother that I must get into it in some capacity. She replied that she could secure me a position in the volunteers, so I set out for the "States," leaving San Francisco about March 1, 1864, up to which time there had been no rain. I saw fifty cows, some of them with calves, sold at $2.50 each—just what their hides would bring. We paid three cents a pound for the beef we ate.

I went ashore at Acapulco again, although the French had blockaded the port.[2] I hadn't heard the order forbidding passengers to land, rowed ashore with two tough looking men, who didn't return to the steamer. Another man and I had some difficulty in getting natives to row us back until we brought our revolvers around where they could be seen, stepped into a canoe and ordered the men to row us out. I crossed the Isthmus of Panama the third time, and on the Atlantic ran into a big storm, during which we saw many water spouts for which a cannon was kept loaded ready to fire at one to break it if it came too close.

I remained in New York long enough to run up to Nyack to see my grandmother, and then went to Memphis, Tennessee, to join my mother, part of the way by rail, but from Cairo, Illinois, down the Mississippi River on the *Belle Memphis* which was probably the best stern-wheel steamer on the river.[3] The Ninth Illinois Cavalry were on board, returning south after re-enlisting and enjoying a veteran furlough at home. Major George B.

Christy was the surgeon of the regiment, but I didn't know that he was the friend of my mother who was going to recommend me for the position of Acting Assistant Surgeon, U.S. Army, and I didn't become acquainted with him until introduced by my mother in Memphis, where she was living in the corner house opposite the southeast corner of the Navy Yard.[4] She used to send coffee and sandwiches to the guard at the corner about midnight and Colonel Thomas, in command of the regiment, had her watched for some time, thinking she was a rebel, but when introduced to her and learned she was a northern woman, he was reassured and laughingly told her how he had suspected her, and he had more than coffee and sandwiches at her table.

Photographs and ambrotypes had long ago taken the place of daguerreotypes. Chloroform and others were used as anesthetics. Later nitrous oxide and other anesthetics came into use and local ones replaced freezing with ice and salt. We had a wooden tube about four inches long with a trumpet shaped piece at one end and a flat disk at the other, as a stethoscope to listen to the sounds of the heart and lungs.

The Army needed surgeons and I had no difficulty in getting a position. The surgeon of the Sixth Illinois Cavalry was the Medical Director of the brigade and the one assistant had been sent to a Kansas regiment, so I was assigned May 30, 1864, to that regiment and Battery K, First Illinois Light Artillery as their Surgeon. They formed a part of the brigade commanded by Brigadier General Benjamin H. Grierson, in which brigade were also the Seventh and Ninth Illinois Cavalry and the Twelfth Tennessee Cavalry.[5] Chaplain [Augustus] DeFoe, who was a graduate in medicine, assisted me until I familiarized myself with the work.[6] There were two men dying, when I took charge of the regimental hospital and Major Christy, who was near by, came to my assistance when I asked him for advice. All of the older men were ready to help me and tell me their experience in camp disease from the beginning of the war. I had nothing to unlearn and was ready to profit by their advice. I had seen more medical and surgical cases than most men of my age, and I wanted to learn how to treat all such cases. My hospital was composed of half a dozen tents about fourteen feet square, and I had men detailed from the regiment as cooks and nurses, and drivers. My two hospital stewards were enlisted as such. I had one two-horse ambulance and one four-horse with beautiful cream-colored [horses] which didn't last long in the field.

After we left Memphis for active service I had much less work to do. Men who had chronic bowel trouble and could hardly sit their horses were cured as soon as they could get fresh pork, chickens, eggs, green corn, watermelons, persimmons, pawpaws, muscadines, scuppernongs or other fruit, green or ripe. Change from wormy hard bread and rusty bacon, and the muddy water of the Mississippi doing in most cases more good than medication. As soon as I learned to give large doses of quinine, malarial fevers were controlled. Following cavalry with ambulances through all kinds of country was hard on wagon-tongues and I broke many. Even the new ones that I made of green saplings, which would stand much bending, after a time became dry and broke. When a horse gave out I had to send men out to press in a new one, leaving the wornout one in exchange, or giving a receipt, which was of little use to the recipient, unless he could prove that he was a Union man.

Part of the regiment was in bivouac at Colliersville [Collierville], Tennessee, on the Memphis and Charleston Railroad while General A. J. Smith was returning from his unsuccessful Guntown trip.[7] Patrols were sent out every morning on the different roads, and I, having very little to do received permission to accompany one of them. I spent the night with Captain Edward Ball of Company E, Sixth Illinois Cavalry, and early the next morning, about 5 A.M., July 23, 1864, we started, having a detail of ten men from his company and Quartermaster Sergeant Pollock with us.[8] We could just see the road as we wended our way south. A dog ran out about a quarter of a mile down, indicating that men were near by watching us. The Captain was very much depressed and said that he had a bad night and thought much about his past life. We crossed a small stream on a bridge at the first break of day and entered a more densely wooded stretch of road which led to the Coldwater. As we reached the latter, the Captain said to me, "When I was here the other day, I thought what a good place for guerrillas to surprise us," and then turning to the men, he ordered "Unsling carbines." The words were scarcely spoken when we heard in the clear morning air the order, "Fire," which came from the other side of the creek. Then there were the reports of guns and the whizzing of bullets and slugs causing our horses to plunge forward. Captain Ball's horse made only one jump, the Captain swayed and both he and the horse went down. He and his men were on white or light gray horses. My horse was a bay and not easily seen in the darkness, but theirs were good marks. I was on his right and protected by his body, as he was nearest to the creek. My horse, which had been under fire once before and had reared and went over backward, when I slipped off on one side and remounted, when he got up. But this time he simply bolted and dashed down the road until I managed to guide him into the woods away from the road that led along the creek, and stop to look around. The weather was very warm and I had worn a straw hat, which had fallen off as my horse bolted and I didn't stop to pick [it] up as I was no longer a good mark. All except two of the men had followed me and as we turned back, they came limping along, having received loads of slugs, chunks of lead, about a quarter of an inch thick, in their legs and arms. Their horses had been shot under them and killed outright, so I mounted them behind two of their comrades to return to the main road, which we reached near the bridge over the small stream which ran into the Coldwater.

¶I estimated that the party that had fired at us must number about twenty-five. Hidden as they were among the trees, logs and bushes on the opposite side of a deep stream with steep banks, which we couldn't cross except over a bridge half a mile away, we couldn't get at them, and we didn't know but there was another part[y] at the bridge, so we rode fast, crossed the bridge, pressed in a wagon at the first house to carry our wounded, and returned to the camp. Most of the other men started at once for the scene of the bushwacking [sic] and the surrounding country was searched, but no armed force was found, only people attending to their affairs as if nothing had happened, but some of them were probably the very ones who, after the shooting, had disbanded and hidden their guns. Captain Ball's body was brought in and I found that he had received a bullet and a large number of slugs in his left side, and his horse, which was also killed, had received many bullets and slugs.

The Sixth Illinois Cavalry numbered at least a thousand men armed with sabres and Spencer carbines, having one shot in the chamber and six in the breech, which were carried on the right side depending from a broad black leather sling over the left shoulder. I saw one regiment, Iowa, I think, with six-shot revolving rifles. The cartridges were metallic, and there were no more paper cartridges which required good teeth to tear, so men with very poor teeth, or no teeth at all, could be enlisted as soldiers. Some of the men were troublesome while we were on the Hernando Road, in the suburbs of Memphis, as they could procure all of the whiskey they wished. For punishment, they would be made to carry a stick of cord-wood in front of the guard tent. Occasionally one would have to be "bucked and gagged" to keep him quiet, i. e., tied in a sitting posture, under his knees and over his elbows with a piece of wood tied in his mouth. One so tied, had threatened to shoot the Colonel after he was released, but in the first fight in which the regiment used the carbine, the cartridges soon gave out on the advanced line and this man was the first to come back over the brow of a hill in a hail of bullets to carry back his hat full of cartridges. At this time, the Colonel was in front riding along the line. When the man was asked after the fight why he hadn't shot the Colonel when he had so good a chance[,] "He's too brave a man" was his reply. At the end of the war and I was leaving, he said "I know that you will remember me, I gave so much trouble."

The first time I went out with the whole regiment, I took several barrels of whiskey along to issue with quinine for malarial fevers, but unless I had it [in] sight all of the time, it would be taken and men got drunk, so I never took any more. There was plenty of it in the mountains of Tennessee, if any was needed and the quinine acted as well without it.

We went on the brow of a ridge overlooking the Tal[l]ahatchie River, August 9, 1864, the first time I was under fire. The screaming of the bullets, etc., caused me to dodge, when the officers near by laughed good naturedly, and then a missle [*sic*] of some sort came with a louder scream over us and caused the laughers to dodge, but I was ashamed to do so. I laughed then, although not very heartily. It was time for me to go back and establish a dressing station, but back of the brow of the hill, where the horses had been left with every fourth man, more men were wounded than on top of the hill and I had to go back still further. After the fight, and we had taken the river-bottom, we had to build bridges on which to cross the river before we could get at the enemy, so [we] had to camp in the river-bottom. At night a heavy rain flooded it and there wasn't standing room for all on the slight elevations, so many men climbed into the trees. Colonel Mathew H. Starr and I rested as well as we could on some hard-tack boxes, but the exposure caused him heavy chills the next day and I sent him back to Memphis in [the] charge of Hospital [Steward] Robert Tyler.[9] His departure left Major Charles W. Whitset in command.[10]

General Nathan B. Forrest escaped us and made a dash for Memphis, which he entered August 21.[11] Colonel Starr had command of the convallescent [*sic*] camp and other troops on the outskirts of the city and was wounded. Steward Tyler took him to Jacksonville, Illinois, where he died, October 1, 1864. He was a Kentuckian by birth and his relatives would have nothing to do with him after he enlisted in the Northern Army. Just before his death, he asked to be propped up in bed to have Tyler sing, "Just before the Battle Mother, I am Thinking Dear of You," a song that he Tyler and I often sang together when we drove into Memphis behind our striking four-horse team of cream-colored horses and accompanied by Tyler on a piano whenever we came across one. He joined Tyler, as well as he could in his last song.

Colonel Starr and I picked up boys on the same day. His was a mulatto who had been a house boy and was quick and very bright. All laughed at my boy, a very black field hand, slow and deliberate, whose name was Ned Cherry, but sometimes it was McGowen, the names of two different owners. The Colonel's boy left him in about a week, taking a horse and a revolver with him, but Ned stayed on and served more faithfully as groom and valet. I mounted him on a horse and he always carried a small Dutch oven and coffee pot, the only cooking utensils I had for some time. He knew a good deal about horses, and, when the mess wasn't running well, he baked a very tempting corn pone, [which], with the boiled backbone of a hog, made a very substantial meal. He at first demurred at taking roasting ears for us to eat and feed for our horses from the fields, and to do so was the same to him as stealing. I taught him the alphabet and to spell simple words, and one day, to test his proficiency, I asked him, "What does a-n-t spell?" "I don't know Sir" was his reply. One night, the officers' boys were bragging about their masters and their rank, and after the Colonel's boy had his say, Ned was heard to say, "Go away niggers, I'm the doctor's boy." Doctor to him was a higher title than that of colonel. It was the only time he was heard to brag. At the end of the war, a captain asked me to leave Ned with him, and I did so, knowing he would have a good home up in Illinois.

Stacy Heminway [Hemenway], the assistant surgeon of the Ninth Illinois Cavalry seemed to be fearless.[12] While preparing for an examination for promotion, he carried a book in his saddle pockets to study whenever he had a chance and one morning sitting against a tree the open book before him the enemies' [*sic*] artillery opened upon us. He closed his book and arose to attend to any wounded there might be. He had taken only a few steps, when he saw a solid shot ricocheting along the ground. He calmly raised his right foot and the ball passed over the very spot where the foot had been. Finding that no one was hurt, he returned to the tree and his studies. I have seen men turn pale and sweat break out on their faces when fighting began and they dismounted to advance to the firing lines. The desire to go to stool was irresistable [*sic*] and they would empty their bowels and bladders and then run to catch up and take their proper places. The older soldiers always eased themselves in this manner, so that in case of a wound of the abdomen the bowels would be less likely to be injured.

In October, 1864, on arriving at Clifton, Tennessee, on the Tennessee River, under Brigadier General Edward Hatch, we had to wait for supplies of all kinds.[13] We often had to stop and make horseshoes and nails, and grind corn while on route, as there was very little food in the country through which we had come. One noon, while here, I had nothing whatever to eat, so went over to see what Heminway had. I found him in a room of a house which had been vacated by its owner, sitting on a horse such as is used to hold shingles when shaping them. I seated myself at the other end and he called his orderly to bring in some refreshments. The man appeared with two army hard tack biscuits and two tin cups of water. The next day the expected fleet of stern-wheel steamers arrived, and we were allowed to go on board of one of them and get one meal and drink of beer or whiskey.

¶We left the day after that to join Major General C. C. Washburn, and were soon in a country in which we could find something to eat when our rations gave out.[14] This often happened, and we had to take corn from the plantations and grind it ourselves at the water-mill to make unbolted "branch meal." In the proper season, we had plenty of roasting ears, which went well with the boiled backbone of a hog. Possession would be taken of the smoke-houses, and hams, shoulders and bacon issued. We fared very well when we had for dessert pawpaws along the rivers, muscadines, scuppernongs, apples, peaches and in the fall of the year after a frost, persimmons. But when we went into winter quarters at Gravelly Springs, Alabama, I remember that for a few days we had parched corn and a few sour Chickasaw plums, without even a little sorghum to sweeten them. Parched corn, cracked with a stone and boiled, was a very poor substitute for coffee. The men craved sugar, and, when they found sorghum molasses, they would leave only "a few," and where there was only "a few," they would leave none. When soldiers were not fed on candy in three days and when we were where the sutlers could follow us, they did a big trade in molasses cake and dried apple pies. While we were in Memphis and our mess drove to the city, we would, on the hot days get a cherry cobbler and a big piece of jelly cake for dessert after our camp fare. Tobacco was grown nearly everywhere and one of my men would dampen the twisted leaves at night and roll them into cigars in the morning. When I was a boy on the ranch, Chinamen gave me some of their cigarettes to smoke, but I didn't care for them and never formed the habit, but I now began to smoke cigars, finding that they satisfied a craving for food when it was non appetizing [*sic*], and I have smoked in moderation on and off ever since, never in the morning, but usually once after luncheon and once after dinner. There were distilleries all through the mountains, which had been in operation long before the imposition tax which the mountaineers did not feel called upon to pay.

On our march through the country, Brigade Headquarters would take possession of a large plantation house, and no white woman would be seen until Brigadier General Benjamin H. Grierson would sit down at the piano, begin to play, and the officers would gather around and begin to sing the popular war and other songs, when the women would quietly enter the room and sit near the door to listen, but ready to slip out. Soon their reserve would be broken, and they would enter into conversation. As I was a New Yorker and a surgeon, not fighting against their beloved south, they usually became friendly with me before they did with the others. Then too often they wanted my professionable [*sic*] services. They had only household remedies with which to treat diseases for which there very few doctors to consult about them. Fodder tea made from the leaves of corn—maize—, dogwood and cottonwood bark, prickly ash and hickory ashes were used for chills and fever, as quinine was contraband and very rarely procureable [*sic*], and they couldn't get opium in any form. While on the road, some of the men would break out into the song "We'll Rally Round the Flag Boys," "When This Cruel War is Over," "John Brown's Body Lies Mouldering in the Grave," "Just before the Battle Mother," and other songs about Mother. Very soon the whole company would join in and the refrain would be carried back to the whole regiment and others back of it until the whole brigade would make the whole country ring with voices.[15]

In the mountains of Tennessee, the married women smoked corncob pipes and all through the states, even in the cities, the women, young and old, dipped snuff, and a bottle of Rapp's was a very acceptable gift. At a reception given by one of our generals in Memphis, I noticed that every now and then there would be a thinning out of the women, and I was told that they went into another room to dip snuff. I questioned a young lady, whom I suspected had just come from dipping, about the habit and wether [sic] really nice girls dipped, and she naively replied, "Oh, they clean their teeth with the snuff." The end of a stick, a little smaller than a lead pencil, is chewed to form a brush which is dipped into the snuff and then rubbed on the teeth and gums. A young Tennesseean said that if he caught his wife dipping he would leave her, but he hadn't caught her up to the time I left Memphis, although she was a devotee.

I always carried two shelter-tent halves to button together and set up on two sticks, just high enough to crawl under, and two rubber ponchos, one to place under me and the other over me at night, when it rained, and one over my neck and the other over my legs when riding. If the ground was wet, I slept dry, if not comfortably, on four split fence-rails. Several of the officers were good chess players and we had many a game. We were resting one morning after having ridden many days and some nights and lost the count of days, when an officer passed the chaplain and me and informed us that it was Sunday. We had just finished a game of chess and the laugh was on the chaplain, but he had enjoyed the game as much as if it had been a week day.

I had an orderly who foraged for me when rations gave out. He was a Tennessean [sic], William Duer, who had a rather asceting [sic] looking face, and when he tied a white handkerchief around his neck and assumed a serious expression to approach a house, needed no introduction as a parson.[16] If there was anything good to eat in the house, he always brought some of it away with him, a pone of cornbread, a chicken, etc. It was a long time before I learned how he managed to get into the good graces of the women folks. It happened one day when I approached a house and saw him on the veranda talking to the women, while some of his cronies were upsetting several beehives to rob them of their honey. Just then the bees swarmed out and attacked the men who retreated in great disorder, on the jump, with heads down, arms flying about, followed by the enraged bees and the laughter of the women, who saw the Yanks defeated and on the run.

I was placed in charge of the ambulances of the brigade, and my experience on the ranch in California served me well. To see that the horses were properly cared for, the ambulances repaired, the sick and wounded carefully transported, besides looking after the sick and wounded of the regiment, kept me alert. At Holly Springs, Tennessee, I was assigned a rather disagreeable duty. A platoon of cavalry under a lieutenant was placed at my disposal and I was sent to procure mattresses for a temporary hospital. I went to the large houses on the outskirts of the town first. Whenever I went, I showed my order, asked how many persons were in the family and then commanded as many mattresses as I thought could be spared, be brought to the entrance of the house from which my men loaded them into the wagons. At one house in town, two sharp featured women looked out of a second-story window and called me bad names, after I had knocked at their door and told them what I wanted, until I pointed at the double line of cavalry drawn up on the opposite side of the street and told them that the men would enter the house and take what we wanted. Then the poor creatures, who had probably been told what terrible things the "Yanks" had done, promptly sent down a mattress. On the opposite side of the town, a very attractive young lady answered my knock at the door, weeping bitterly, and said she was alone, her mother having gone out. She begged me to wait for her mother's return. I thought that her mother had wisely left on purpose, but the girl's tears seemed so genuine that they prevailed, and then too I still felt the berating I had received from the mouths of the two angry women, and I had nearly the number of mattresses we needed. At the next house, there were enough mattresses on the gallery waiting for me to supply our wants. There also were blankets and cots and offers of more, as here were Union people anxious to do something for the cause. We left all of the bedding behind when we resumed our march, and the people could recover what had been "borrowed" from them, although some of it was soiled.

After General John B. Hood's forces crossed the Tennessee River and the fight at Shoal Creek, Alabama, on November 9, we fell back and fought at Lawrenceburg, Tennessee, November 22; Camp[bells]ville, and Lyn[n]ville, November 24, we entered Columbia, Tennessee, on the night of November 25, while the Fourth Army Corps, which had been stationed then for some time, was leaving, we had some difficulty in securing a house in which to place our wounded.[17] There were still some of the officers left, who had been treated well by the people, and asked us to go elsewhere, so on we went, but all had been kind and we felt grateful. It was midnight when we reached the middle of the town, our wounded needed attention and we couldn't go any farther, so we parked our ambulances on a beautiful spacious lawn under great oak trees and notified the occupants of the large colonial house that we must have a room, and they cleared one over their large dining-room and we took possession. By the time we had dressed our wounded, we were pretty tired and not having had anything to eat since morning, were quite hungry, when, much to our surprise, the mistress of the house, herself, came to the door and invited us to come to breakfast. We then broke a fast of about twenty-four hours on fried chicken, cornbread and coffee, such a meal as we hadn't eaten in many a day, cooked by an old colored woman, born a slave. Afterward, on our return south, while chasing Hood's army, I stopped at the house to leave a present of some coffee, which was a luxury to people who had been using parched wheat, dried, parched and ground sweet potatoes, when I was made to feel mean and petty at having abused the hospitality with which we had been received and treated, on being told by a lame daughter of the house that one of my men, to whom she had entrusted her pony, which she had been hiding in the house for safe keeping, had stolen it. When I questioned the fellow about it, he said that he had tied the pony to one of the ambulances and it was stolen one night.

From Columbia, we had a rapid march to Shelbyville, Tennessee, on November 28, and thence to Pike Ford, twenty miles below, where we learned that General Forrest had crossed Duck River the day before, six miles farther down. We swam the river and skirmished with the enemies' [sic] flankers for eighteen miles, and then camped within sight of the fires of Hood's army, and so near that the chopping of wood could be heard. The regiment resumed its march very early the next morning and rejoined the main army about noon at Franklin, Tennessee, with a loss of eight men missing. It took an active part in the battle of Franklin, which began about noon the same day.[18]

There were times when the opposing forces would be on opposite sides of a stream and the men would fraternize for a time. One would call out "Hello Yank, got a match" or "Come over and have a smoke." The reply would be, "All right Johnny," and they would meet, one probably with matches, coffee or hard bread and the other with tobacco or whiskey.

What wouldn't some of our men do for a smoke or a drink. They would hob nob until an order was given or bugle blown to begin firing or advance, when they returned to their own side to resume the fight.

During the battle of Nashville, Tennessee, on December 15, 1864, while we were resting on the Granny White Pike and eight or ten men were resting on a side hill under an oak tree, one of them called "Look out," and all except one jumped to one side.[19] A solid twelve pound shot passed through his abdomen and buried itself into the ground behind him, about eight feet from me. The men usually made light of artillery fire, and during this battle when the enemy unlimbered their cannon and began firing, they would yell, "Go for them" and charge on foot. They took several batteries with very few casualties. On the night of December 16, our Twelfth Tennessee Cavalry, came in contact with the Twelfth Tennessee Confederate and mingled with them. One would call out in the dark, "What regiment," and receiving in reply, "Twelfth Tennessee," joined our men who out numbered the others, and on returning to our lines were surprised to see the prisoners they had unknowingly brought in, and the Confederates were no less surprised to find themselves prisoners.

While driving General Hood's army from Nashville to the Tennessee River, after leaving Duck River December 20, the pike was littered with all sorts of impedaments [sic] which the Confederates had to abandon in order to retreat faster, even to firearms. They were in a desperate condition, as shown by the many prisoners we took. They were mostly in rags and their feet were tied up in rags. All were very hungry and glad to get a square meal once more. White bread was a luxury, but their cornbread was just as good if not better, to fight on. Back in the country, they usually had hog and hominy, better food than our men had, except when they were among the plantations. The southern women deprived themselves of the best of everything, so that they might send their fighters the best food and clothing that they could secure. By this time the blankets, ingrain carpets etc., had been sent to their army, often in the form of coats, etc.

I was once sent from Huntsville, Alabama—about November 5—to Nashville, Tennessee, in charge of a railroad train of sick and wounded in freight cars. The men lay on the bare floor, having only one or two blankets as bedding. I telegraphed ahead and had a meal prepared for them at Stephenson [Stevenson]. After transferring them to the hospital at Nashville, I returned by rail to Pulasky [Pulaski], Tennessee, where I spent a couple of nights in a brick Presbyterian church, which had been converted into a hospital. Surgeons were needed here, but I had Jaundice and was feeling badly. The only communication with our brigade was by courier at night, and it was long ride. This I didn't mind, as I felt better in the open air, so I accompanied the courier, riding fast, and reached the regiment at Shoal Creek early in the morning of November 9, just as it was going into action. We crossed the creek and advanced to the Tennessee River which Hood was crossing. Dispatches that we captured, told when he would advance, and we fell back, skirmishing with his cavalry until the infantry caught up, drove us back and his artillery opened upon us. At Lawrenceburg, November 22, they were so close behind a stone fence that I had very little time in which to hitch up my ambulances and go galloping away. Luckily the harness was still on the horses. On the road to Lynnville, I was just ahead of Captain George Anderson of Company C when he was killed.[20]

After the defeat of Hood, and he had recrossed the Tennessee, we encamped for some time at Gravelly Springs, Alabama, and afterward crossed the river to Eastport, Mississippi. I was Surgeon of the Ninth Illinois Cavalry from January 24, to March 15, 1865 and accompanied it on a scout to Russelsville [Russellville] and Tuscumbia, Alabama under Colonel Joseph W. Harper.[21] At Eastport an expedition was fitted out to go south, and I was ordered to take charge of the Small Pox Hospital, March 16. It was on a gentle slope of a spur from a ridge about a mile long which ran down to a large creek which emptied into the river. This ridge ran parallel with the creek and on it, a little farther west, was a picket post. The buildings were of pine logs, cut and laid up by soldiers, and the roofs of shakes rived out by them from the grove of trees in which they were situated. The largest held twelve beds, having a great air-space, and the small ones two and three beds. The largest had one door, a huge fireplace, and a window without sashes at each end. The spaces between the logs were only partly chinked and those under the eaves were open. I was quartered in an enclosure of boards about four feet high and covered with a tarpauling [sic], on the main ridge, which the Grand Rounds passed every night. Just below me was a clear spring of cold water. I not only had soldiers, but also white and black refugees as patients. The death rate was small among the whites, as they had been vaccinated and were partly protected. There was less pitting among those who recovered than is usually the case. I attribute this to the darkness, the ozone in the pine forest, more than the local treatment of painting each pock on the face [with a] tincture of iodine several times a day.

A negro was found hiding under some casks on the steamer *Crescent City*, which had come up from Paducah with commissary supplies, and he had a suspicious eruption on his face which I found to be small pox. While I was at the boat getting some supplies, the officer in command of the guard asked me to look at his sergeant and when I told him that the sergeant had smallpox, the latter said, then we all have it, and sure enough they had, and I took all ten of them and the chief civilian clerk to the hospital. Great sympathy was shown for my patients, and I was given a permit to trade at a picket post down in the valley on the road leading to Iuka Springs [Iuka]. In exchange for salt, I received milk, eggs, chickens and a few vegetables. The troops cared very little for rice and gave me all that I could use, and rice pudding was seldom missing from the hospital menu. I was given a credit of $500.00 in the Subsistence Department and bought canned goods from the boats that came up the river with supplies. The Sanitary Commission sent me dried fruits and clothing, and once a barrel of raw potatoes in vinegar, which my cook never could boil or roast soft enough for my patients or nurses to eat, and they couldn't eat the hard raw pickled potatoes.[22] One day some men in gray uniforms called from an adjoining ridge and asked what the log houses were, and when one of my nurses yelled back, "SmallPox Hospital" they disappeared in haste.

While I was on duty here, I heard of the assassination of President Lincoln, April 15, 1865. The news cast a gloom over the whole camp. We had been afraid that an attempt would be made upon his life, as some southern sympathisers [*sic*] were heard to discuss the probability of it and seemed to approve, but the Confederates were horrified when they heard of his death. I afterward met at a boarding house in New York the volunteer captain who captured Wilkes Booth, the murderer, and later still, at Camp McDermit, Nevada, Lieutenant Alexander Grant of the Cavalry, who [w]as a sergeant and member of the squad of soldiers who buried Booth at the Arsenal near Washington.[23]

The small pox was very fatal to the negroes, but the whites, and particularly the soldiers were pretty well protected by vaccination from scabs, which were not always well selected when there was so great a demand for them at the beginning of war, and very sore arms were the

result and the persons not always rendered immune. I had been vaccinated several times unsuccessfully when away at school and was surprised
when my mother wrote to me, after I had gone to the hospital, that I had
been vaccinated when a babe and afterward had varioloid [*sic*] in a mild
form, so I was well protected. After I had discharged my last case, I burned
the hospital, went down the Tennessee and up the Cumberland River to
Nashville, where I requested the Medical Director to annul my contract
on June 14, 1865.

CHAPTER FIVE

Reconstruction

From Nashville, I went to Memphis and thence to Mound City, Arkansas, on the Mississippi River a few miles up from Memphis, where my mother was on a cotton plantation a little back from the west bank of the river. Here I practiced my profession until September, when I went to New York to attend lectures at the Bellevue Hospital Medical College and here completed my course of study for my degree in medicine. In the country around the plantation, malarial fevers [were] very prevalent and nearly every one had a chill every other day or once a week at noon and dosed himself regularly with blue mass and quinine. One elderly planter said that if people would go to the second story of their houses as soon as the sun set and make a fire and sleep up there, they would be free from fever, as he was. We didn't then know that the mosquito spread the malarial parasite which caused the fever and chills.

There was a "slash" across the road from the house, the outlet of a lake, which was full of minnow, feeding probably on the larvae of mosquitoes, and after a rise in the Mississippi River trout fed along the shore on the minnow. Fishermen from Memphis tried to take the trout with all sorts of bait, but caught none. I wanted some of those trout, so loaded my shotgun with large shot and fired at those near the shore. I stunned them and my little negro Pete would jump into the slash and pull them out by the gills and I shot all that we could eat the largest weighing seven pounds. The slash was full of cypress trees and their knees and water moccasins were thick. A negro shot a rabbit which ran into a hollow in one of them near the water, and, putting his hand in to grab the rabbit, was struck by one of these snakes. He came to me a few minutes afterward and I gave him aromatic spirits of ammonia and whiskey until the bad effects of the venom wore off, after applying bandages to his arm to retard the circulation of the blood. He recovered, probably not having received much of the poison.

¶Chigoes, or redbugs, were thick and we had to sponge off with a strong solution of salt before venturing into the bushes, otherwise they would bore into the skin and produce small ulcers. We had to go into the underbrush to gather blackberries which were thick and could be gathered by the bucketful, and there were the wild turkeys to hunt, which we could hear among the pines not far from the house. One of our old negroes made a turkey-call of a small block of wood scooped out and a nail driven through the middle which he would rub, and he shot wild turkeys for us frequently. I one time caught a turtle over a foot across in the swamp back of the plantation and found near by over fifty turtle eggs. Our black cook said that there were all sorts of meat in a turtle and she cooked all of them for us. I placed its heart on a plate and saw it pulsate every now and then, and when I wet it with water at the end of twenty-four hours it began to pulsate again. Asiatic cholera appeared in the country as an epidemic and I had three cases which an old country doctor pronounced pernicious malarial fever, but years afterward I raised some of the cholera germs on gelatine plates and they had the same peculiar sickening odor as the cases I treated.

I received the degree of Medicinae Doctor from the Bellevue Hospital Medical College, March 1, 1867, at the Academy of Music, New York City, after having attended lectures and clinics. I had also received instruction in a special class under Dr. Stephen Smith who was still living in New York in 1923, aged over 90 years and had a course in auscultation and percussion and diseases of the heart and lungs, under Dr. Austin Flint, Senior.[1] The bi[n]aural stethoscope had been invented by Cammeman [Cammann], but the clinical thermometer was not yet known.[2] Our sense of touch "tactus eruditus" had to be educated as well as our senses of hearing, sight and smell under tutors at the bedside. My sense of smell is very keen and I learned the odor of many diseases, and the many kinds of pulse which are unknown to the later doctors, who have so many instruments of precision, but few of them have the "tactus uruditub" [eruditus] of the

early doctors. Bellevue was the first medical college to make clinical lectures the great feature in its course of study. Flint, Sr., taught us the natural history of diseases and the course one would take without medication,
under good and bad conditions, as he had seen many such. I had witnessed
many autopsies to see the appearance of the organs as affected by disease.

After I had received my diploma at the Academy of Music on 14th
Street, which was filled with friends of the graduates to hear the speeches
and listen to the grand orchestra of fifty instruments and witness the presentation of diplomas, I was connected with a dispensary on 59th Street
east of the Central Park, along the southern boundary of which, on the
rocks were the shanties of squatters, mostly Irish laborers who received a
dollar a day. These shanties were usually of one room, built of castoff
materials picked up here and there. Goats roamed at will among them,
and, where there was any soil, there was a cabbage patch. The occupants
of these hovels sweltered in the summer and the children had to be looked
after by the authorities, and it was these children I had to treat, while
wrestling with the ignorance and superstitions of their parents. If a child
recovered, the parents were greatful [*sic*], but if one died, the mother
would probably blame the doctor and yell her denunciations.

There were several families crowded together in a tenement on the
south side of the street, and one morning I entered a room in which a
woman was frying batter-cakes for breakfast on a long griddle, while her
three children were carrying on a great rate. She tried to quiet them, but
not succeeding, she raised the clothes of one who was about four years
old and spanked it with a shovel-shaped pancake-turner and then went on
turning the cakes on the griddle with it. I wasn't invited to stay to breakfast. I soon learned that it would take a long time to build up a paying
practice and my funds were running low. My life in California and service
in the army had unfitted me for life in a city, so I made a contract as an Acting Assistant Surgeon U.S. Army, for a year, on August 19, 1867, with the
Chief Medical Officer of New York City and ordered to Amite, Louisiana,
where there was stationed a company of the First U.S. Infantry, under
Brevet Major Robert J. [H.] Offley.[3]

Before leaving for the south, I went to Patterson [*sic*], New Jersey to
visit Dr. G. W. Terriberry, who, after returning from the war and attending a course of lectures at Bellevue, settled there to practice his profession, and, while I was there, several doctors and their wives gathered at the

house of Dr. [Henry C.] Van Giesen to spend the evening and have a little sport in taking Nitrous Oxide gas—Laughing Gas—Dr. Terriberry made and administered the gas, and Dr. Van Giesen was the first to take it, inhaling from a large rubber bag.[4] He stood in the middle of a large room from which all of the furniture had been removed, and we all stood around him, making faces and laughing until he lost control of himself and began to laugh in a most upro[a]rious manner. He then made a rush for his wife, threw his arms around her neck and madly kissed her. Mrs. Van Giesen was to have been the next one to take the gas, but she now declined, nor would any of the ladies consent. One of the other Vans, of which there were a Van Houtan, a Van Blarkom, and a Van Winkle, inhaled and stood perfectly still, with a most pitiful expression on his face as if he were about to cry. We then went into the Doctor's office, and I wondered if I could control my risables [sic] after inhaling the gas, so I grabbed hold of an office chair and inhaled, while the others laughed, and shouted and danced, trying to make me laugh. They tried to break my hold on the chair, but I held on and thought what big fools they were making of themselves, and I didn't smile.

At Amite, the company of infantry was camped just south of the town in tents and the officers in a row of tents on the town side.[5] Besides Major Offley, there were First Lieutenant Charles D. Viele and Second Lieutenant Hubble [Shadrach Hubbell], who shortly went to New Orleans and died there of yellow fever.[6] The first sergeant's wife ran our mess and we had large grey squirrels which had been shot in the pine trees by a Cherokee Indian as our meat diet mostly. After a time Mrs. Offley joined her husband, and we all moved into a new frame house just across the street from the camp and Mrs. Offley took charge of the mess. The Sergeant's wife had become a mother some time before and had given up the mess. The child was a boy and was the first child I ever had named after me and the first U.S. soldier's child born in Amite.

Second Lieutenant John Joseph O'Connell joined a little later, Viele was promoted to captain and left for New Orleans.[7] Lieutenant Allen Smith took his place, and we then messed for a time with a French woman, Madame Clements, who was a perfect cook.[8] Most of her cooking was done in copper over charcoal fires in a large range, in each hole of which was a separate fire. We had chickens, peahens, wild turkeys, wood cock, quail, [and] venison roasted on a spit before an open fire. She learned our birthdays and then had special dinners, when she treated us to champagne and for dessert would cook very attractive doughnuts or fritters and then watch for one of us to bite into the cotton in the former or mosquito bar in the latter. That was sure to happen and then she and her little French girl assistant would laugh until tears rolled down their cheeks. I had boarded with her a short time just after I arrived in Amite, and very early every morning she would send up a cup of delicious black coffee, until I said I would rather sleep. She had many cats that sat around in the kitchen windows, and asked why she had so many, said she served them as squirrels to the officers. This was one of her pleasantries, as she thought too much of them to have harmed them in the least. Years afterward I called upon her, when her vision was so feeble that she could scarcely see me and when I told her who I was, she hugged me and kissed me on both cheeks.

The two young officers and I drove, swam in the Tangipahoa River and tried all sorts of feats on our improvised gymnasium, on parallel bars, ladders, rings, trapeeze [sic], etc., and kept adding to our repertoir [sic] until Smith let me fall twice as I hung by feet to his feet, and after that I wouldn't trust him again. We had a croquet ground laid out on an old well-beaten road on which we learned to play so well and carom on the wickets that we had to change their direction and the rules so as not to be able to become a rover the first play. But the croquet court at Dunbarton was on a grassy lawn and we played our best games out there. Darkness would often overtake us and we would light fat pine on a platform at each end of the grounds raised and covered with earth.

Before Mrs. Offley came, we had become acquainted with a few of the people when the Episcopalians had a festival and fair for the purpose of raising money with which to build a church. Mrs. George T. Dunbar and her two daughters, Fanny and May, were the prime movers and had made most of the articles that were for sale, among them white shetland wool jackets for babies made by Fanny, and mouchoir boxes by May, and for which they took orders. The food was mostly donated by others. It was at this festival that I first met her who was to become my beloved companion for nearly half a century. After the supper, the eatables that were left, were raffled off and all of the chances I took I bought from her. I had won a chicken, a ham, a roast pig and a pyramid of cakes, when I heard one of the young townsmen say to her, "Sell your chances to that Yank, he wins everything," so our party took all of the chances, knowing that the young fellows had very little money to spend. We took our winnings over to our mess and the next day had a picnic, having to buy ice cream only. The Dunbars and the Davises were our guests and we took them on a long drive through the magnolias hollys and other trees up the Tangipahoa River. We had many drives after this, and when Mrs. Offley came she often invited the young ladies to dine with us and play croquet, and we as often went to their houses.

The people were left impoverished by the war and had to let much of their land go in payment of taxes. Mrs. Dunbar lost 1200 acres of piney woods for this reason and had only a few acres with some buildings, and some eight or ten squares of land in Amite left which brought in nothing. George T.—"Buck"—her son, had been badly wounded in both thighs at the fight at New Hope Church, 17 miles from Atlanta, while in Captain Charles Fenner's Battery of Louisiana Light Artillery.[9] Hospital gangrene set in and he nearly lost his life. His mother went to nurse him and when he was strong enough, he was placed on duty in a medical depot of a cousin, Dr. Benjamin Miller, a medical director in the Confederate [Army], but he was never strong afterward and was unable to cultivate the ten or twelve acres that were left. After the death of his mother, March 21, 1869, he went to St. Louis, where he married and had several children and where he died, December 21, 1903.

A prominent lawyer, who owned [a] large tract of land, found it difficult to raise money enough to buy a calico dress pattern for a daughter. He couldn't pay a dressmaker and she didn't know how to cut and make the dress, so [she] went with tears in her eyes to Madame Clements to teach her how. She had been brought up in town and didn't have the training that women on plantations received, who had to look after their slaves, train their cooks, house maids and boys, look after the dairy, the carding of the cotton, its spinning and weaving to homespun and afterward cutting and fashioning into clothes. There were the aged and sick to care for, and the children to educate. The teachers were usually governesses from the north. The poor whites were mostly illiterate, as their forebears had gone into the country when land was cheap and schools were few and far between. The Civil War closed most of the schools and stopped the education of the young. But now the woods are settling up and many of the educated class have been driven to teach, after having lost their all during the war, and it is surprising to see how many bright minds there are among the piney woods people. They have been lying fallow for three or four gen-

erations and are the product of unmixed blood—not of the melting pot, but thoroughbred Americans from away back and the hope of our country.

Yellow Fever was epidemic in New Orleans, and Lieutenant Smith had the disease while on duty there. He came to the company to replace Captain Viele who was a wonderful racounteur [*sic*] and his stories were very entertaining. One day he told us of a wonderful jump his sister had made on a horse over a high gate, and afterward, Major Offley brought me a novel—*Charles O'Malley*, I think—and there was the story he spun almost as he told it.[10] One day I expressed a doubt as to the veracity of one of his stories and he said, "Well, it amused you, didn't it." So we accepted his stories with a grain of salt.

We had an outpost at Madisonville and some of the men were reported sick, so I went over to look after them. An Internal Revenue Officer, a former Volunteer officer, accompanied me and as we drove through a heavy shower, we got slightly wet. The horse flies were so thick in the savannahs that we had to fight them to keep them off of ourselves, and they bled our mules so badly that we had to cover them with gunnysacks. We stopped at Judge Hennin's place about halfway, or eighteen miles or so. He was home and received us very cordially. As we undressed to go to bed that night, the assessor had a chill and I was chilly. He died at Covington three days afterward of yellow fever or pernicious malaria. I found that the men at the outpost had intermittent malaria fever, but as there were some cases of yellow fever in the neighborhood, I thought [it] best to bring them back to Amite.

There were some families of clay-eaters in the piney-woods, and clay might be seen drying against the chimneys which were built of cages of split sticks filled with earth, such as we built in our winter camps during the war.[11] These people were quite yellow and their faces and bodies apparently fat, but they were very anemic.

The southern girls teased me about my pronunciation of log, frog, dog, etc., which they pronounced, laug, fraug, daug, and I would retort by calling them you-uns and myself we-uns and by repeating:

"Tis hard for you-uns to live in camp.
Tis hard for you-uns to fight the Yanks,
Tis hard for you-uns and we-uns to part,
Cause you-uns have got we-uns heart."

On leaving, I would say that I would stop by again very shortly, but these little differences acted as attractions and there were many inter-marriages between the people of the different sections. Slavery had kept them apart only to a slight extent, and most of the people of the south felt that slavery was a handicap to their progress. Mrs. Dunbar freed her two slaves after her husband's death and then paid them wages, one, Mary as cook, and Mingo as butler. The latter was her husband's body servant at the time of his death December 29, 1850, on the Steamer *Alabama* at the mouth of the Coatzoecalcos [Coatzacoalcos] River. Mr. Dunbar had set free the slaves that his father left him by his will.[12]

The infantry company was sent to New Orleans and both black[s] and whites requested its return, as they feared trouble between the races, so the troops were sent back. While I was in New Orleans, I saw Edwin Booth and Miss McVickers [Mary R. McVicker] in several Shakesperian [*sic*] plays.[13] They were engaged to be married at that time and the balcony scene of Romeo and Juliet was the best love making that I ever saw on the stage.

On returning to Amite, I spent all of my evenings at Dunbarton and in October Fanny and I became engaged to marry. May was an accomplished pianist and she played for us every night, sometimes a whole opera. I decided to remain in the army, so went to New York City intending to go before the medical board as a candidate for an appointment as assistant surgeon, but when I arrived there, December 16, 1868, the board had been dissolved and I decided to go to San Francisco and enter into private practice.[14] I returned to Amite a few days before the date fixed for our wedding and found Mrs. Dunbar dangerously ill with pneumonia. She died, March 21, 1869. Mr. Charles Miltenburger, an uncle of the children, came from New Orleans for the funeral, and he advised that our wedding should not be postponed, but that we, as well as May and Henry Addison, who had been engaged for some time, be married before the funeral, and after some hesitation on the part of the daughters, his advice was taken and the two weddings on March 22, 1869, were sad ones, Rev. Jno. Frs. Girault of St. Peter's Church, New Orleans, officiating. There was no wedding feast, as the New York Herald published heartlessly, "A Death at a Wedding and Marriage Feast" on noticing the marriages and death.[15]

Fanny and I remained at the old home until an agreement was made as to the settlement of the estate that the Addisons would take the home,

and Fanny and their brother, George T., would take real estate in the town.
We then started on our long wedding journey to California. We stopped in
Baltimore to visit her Aunt Mary Robinson and her Aunt Amanda Harding
and cousin Louisa R. Harding. After that we went on to New York to visit
my mother and while waiting for the sailing on April 21, 1869, of the
steamer *Henry Chauncey* for Aspinwall—now Colon—we went to Nyack
to visit my grandmother Myers, who was living with my Aunt Jane Tasman, and also to Haverstraw, Tarrytown, Brooklyn and other places.[16]

Little Mother, in her "Recollections," has told about our trip to San Francisco, but I may add, that she seemed to be the authority on plants and fish,
as all questions that came up about them among the passengers were
brought to her to answer. There was a boy on the steamer who had the
Sloat features and I thought he must be one of that family, so on passing the
stateroom occupied by him and his mother, I looked in and saw the name
on a trunk, and when we stepped upon the wharf at San Francisco, May 14,
the first person to whom I was introduced was Reverend Archibald Sloat, a
Presbyterian Clergyman, a distance [*sic*] relative of mine whom I had never
met before, who had come to meet his wife and son. Dr. Braman, my former preceptor, who had introduced us was a member of his church.
Archibald was a cousin of Alexander, who had bid us good-bye in New York
and who had received my father and me in 1854. Every steamer from
Panama was welcomed by a crowd of people, and, as it neared the wharf,
one would hear the call, "Anyone on board from Ohio?," or "Anyone from
Kentucky," etc. If the reply "Yes" was heard, there would be cheers, and the
waving of hats, handkerchiefs etc. and the new comer, when he landed,
would be received with joy and taken in charge to be shown the city and
treated to the best of every thing in drink, eat and smoke.

We went out to Hayes Valley, beyond Van Ness Avenue, where we kept
house and I practiced my profession, more than making my expenses. On
July 4, 1869, there was a grand celebration of the completion of the railroad across the continent, and we sat on the sand hills, near where the
present City Hall now stands, to witness the greatest display of fire works
we had ever seen. The meeting of two locomotives on rails depicted the
place where the last spike was driven. There were many bushes on these
and other sandhills, the roots of which were dug out for firewood as the
hills were leveled. They were very hard thick and knotted and we used
them as firewood, even on the coals of which we broiled our steaks.

¶I was not satisfied with our surroundings and the fogs were bad. My little wife was coughing some, so I secured an appointment as an acting assistant surgeon, July 17, 1869, and was ordered to Camp McDermit, Nevada, to wait for a medical board.[17] There we were taken thrown upon our resources, which were many, and there we spent four very happy years in each other[']s congenial society, with very few other associates. Claude born here August 5, 1871, was a great source of happiness and we watched with great interest his growth and development. I started a record of his doings and sayings which I made for years, but at length lost in the great San Francisco fire, April 18, 1906. We usually had two Piute Indians to work for us to carry water from the creek, bring in wood, keep fires going and do odd jobs. Two Piute girls looked after Claude, and Sarah Winnemucca did our laundering.[18] Old Chief Winnemucca used to come and sit around to talk.[19] I looked after the sick Indians, but received no extra pay for doing so, as they were looked upon as prisoners of War. Mother and I hunted, fished, rode horseback and drove. One winter, another officer and I killed over a dozen coyotes, one on the parade ground near the flagstaff to which it had been driven by our two dogs, one a greyhound and the other a setter. See Mother[']s Recollections.[20]

Lieutenant Henry A. Reed of the artillery was on duty at the post for a time, and he and I had many discussions and we would read up so as to be able to start something that the other one wasn't posted on.[21] I kept ahead of him on chemistry until one day he went over to the hospital and borrowed the books I was reading so as to keep up with me. There was an incentive for both of us to study.

Although we were sad to leave McDermit November 16, 1872, yet we were glad to get to a city once more and our stay in San Francisco was an enjoyable one. We felt like hugging the first large trees we saw in the mountains on our way there. We accompanied recruits in Arizona, leaving November 27 on the steamer *Newbern* and rounding Cape Saint Lewcas [Cabo San Lucas] into the Gulf of California and up to Port Isabel at the mouth of the Colorado River where we transferred to a stern-wheel steamer of low draught, putting over 120 recruits on a barge which we towed up the river, stopping at night to let them camp on the river bank.[22] For sea sickness I oftener used sea-water than any other remedy.[23]

¶The river had many sand bars and when approaching one, an Indian would stand in the home with a marked pole in his hands and measure and call out the depth of the water. Only when he called "mark twain" would the boat slow up and probably stop, Indian deck hands would wade ashore with a hawser, tie it to a tree, and then the signal would be rung for the wheel to be turned backward so as to throw the water under the boat and to wash sand from under it while the hawser was wound up on the capstain [sic] until we were over the bar.[24] Or when the bar was narrower, a stout staff would be placed upright near the bar which would be raised by tackle and the capstain while the reversed wheel washed the water underneath to remove the sand. There were many whirlpools in the river and if a man fell overboard he was almost sure to be carried to the bottom and he drowned, and nearly every batch of recruits that went up lost a man. Captain [Jack] Mellon of the steamer knew his business well, and it was said that he and the other steamboat captains could run a boat if there was dew on the grass.[25] We were landed at Fort Yuma, where we remained about two weeks and was [sic] there on Christmas day 1872, when we had watermelon for dinner which was grown by the Yuma Indians.[26] The stern-wheel steamer *Cocopah*, Captain Polhemus [Issac Pol-hamus], took us up to Ehrenburg [Ehrenberg] and had no sand bars to negotiate.[27] The morning after we left, we had for breakfast beavers' tails and buckwheat cakes. We expected an ambulance to meet us, but as it had not arrived, Lieutenant Orlando Wieting of the Twenty-third Infantry who had been recently married and had his bride with him, and I bought a covered spring wagon two broncos and harness from a man who had just come across the desert with a load of fruit.[28] Freighters hauled our bedding, tents, baggage, etc., and the recruits on foot. We left Ehrenburg January 1, 1873, and had our dinner after a short march under a palo verde which didn't give much shade. Here at the dry diggings, gold was taken out by shaking the earth from the bottom of a shaft in a shallow wooden bowl until it sank to the bottom, so only nuggets were found. The third day out, we had quite a fall of rain, but we had to pay for the water we used, which was hauled up from a very deep well by a mule which went round and round until the large keg came up full of water emptied itself and then he turned the other way to let the keg down. The water was strongly impregnated with soulphur [sic] and we had to add claret to it before we could drink it.

CHAPTER SIX

⊱⊹⊰

Life among the Yavapai

I was Post Surgeon at Camp Date-Creek, Arizona, where we arrived on January 5, 1873 and remained to August 30, 1873, when the post was abandoned.¹ I was also surgeon of the 2050 Tulkopya [*sic*]—Middle or Midway People—Indians, called Apache-Yuma by the whites, under their chiefs Jemaspie—Chaw-ma-se-cha or Looking Over—and Ochicama [*sic*]—A-wha-che-ka-ma, or Striking the Enemy with the Fist, who had been gathered there by the troops in 1872, until many of them were taken to the Colorado River and 748 of them started May 1, 1873, for the Rio Verde Indian Agency, where they arrived on May 12.² Dr. Josephus Williams who had been their Agent at Date Creek since July 6, 1872, had arrived there on April 27, and 1000 Yavapai—Apache-Mojave—had been brought in from the Black Mesa and the Valley of the Verde, and 500 Apache-Tonto under their chief Echatlepan[*sic*]—White Hat—from the Tonto Basin and the mountains surrounding it.³ A reservation extending forty miles along the Verde River and ten miles on each side of it was set apart from them by Executive order, November 9, 1871 as their permanent home. I was proffered the position of Surgeon over there and accepting was ordered to the Agency by the Department Commander, Brigadier General George Crook, on the abandonment of Date Creek.⁴

¶I took my family—mother, Claude and Harold, who had been born at Date Creek, January 14, 1873, only a few days after we arrived there—with me to Prescott and then learning that there was an epidemic resembling the epizootic and much other sickness among the Indians, I took them by

ambulance to Ehrenburg on the Colorado River where I left them to pro-
ceed by themselves on the rest of their journey "Inside," i.e. to San Francisco and East. I returned by buckboard, driving night and day.[5]

I left Prescott, September 12, 1873, and arrived at the [Camp Rio Verde]
Agency, via Grief Hill [that] afternoon, the day that Del-cha [Delshay]—or
Wa-po-wa-ta, Big Rump—a Tonto chief, half Apache Mojave, who had
been there since August 4, and half a dozen or more other renegades, after
threatening demonstrations, left for the mountains.[6] I met them in an
open space, not far below the Agency, where there were no trees or rocks
for them to hide behind, and they came dancing, yelling and capering
along, flourishing their bows and arrows, but they did not attempt to
approach or intercept me. My elevated position along side the driver of
the ambulance, my long range breech-loading rifle and four snorting
mules kept them a good distance away, for their old smooth-bore muzzle-
loading guns wouldn't carry the round bullets impelled by a small charge
of powder very far, or they may have known that I was on my way to give
relief to the sick of their people.[7]

The Agency was located in the river-bottom, the site of Cottonwood
in 1923, about sixteen miles north of Camp Verde and about three miles
southwest of Peck's Lake.[8] It was composed of a few tents and an unfin-
ished adobe house. The site of which in 1923 was on Chas. D. Willard's
place, and the Indians were in their oowas, or brush and grass shelters.
Fifteen soldiers of Troop K, Fifth Cavalry, in command of Second Lieutenant Walter S. Schuyler, guarded the Agency and were on higher
ground.[9] Some of them had chills and fever, but the Agent and all of his
employees were prostrated and scarcely able to attend to any of their
duties. Mosquitoes were thick at night and there were no mosquito bars
over their beds. The Indians were along the river lower down and were in
a miserable physical condition. Before they came in, they were for a long
time in almost incessant flight from our troops who had so harassed them
that they had but little time to search for food and were compelled to
mainly subsist on tunas—prickly pears—and Mescal or American Aloe,
which they couldn't cook, and had to eat the bases of the leaves, young
stalks and crowns partially roasted in an open fire or baked for a short
time in pits on heated stones, so that many of them were half starved and
became subject to dysentery and Malaria. Deaths were so frequent that
the bodies were left in their oowas to mummyfy [sic] in the dry air or the

oowas burned over them, as there were not enough well Indians to cut and carry the wood with which to burn the dead, as was their custom. The kith-e-eys, who give medicines and also sing, were all trying to aid the sick. Several women, who had been accused of bewitching the men, had been found by the soldiers tied up by their wrists to trees, to be stoned to death unless the men recovered, and had to be kept under the protection of the guard.

The day after my arrival, I visited their che-wa-kes—camps—and took with me the limited supply of medicines that the Agency afforded. The interpreters that I had to use at Date Creek, spoke a little Spanish, of which a few of the Indians could understand a very little, but here I had to use signs while examining the sick. I soon caught on to a few sentences, as— Where is the sun when you have a chill? Where have you pain? Open your mouth. Take a drink of water. Have you bloody stools? I administered medicine to over seventy of the worst cases and until my supply gave out. Most of them had a heavy chill and high fever at noon every day. The Agent purchased one hundred ounces of quinine at a cost of ten dollars an ounce, and after its receipt, inside of ten days most of the sick were able to get to the Agency, where they came to beg for the bitter medicine which they had found so effective. The agency employees were soon on their jobs again and eating good big beef steaks instead of dieting themselves.

I gained the good will of their medicine Men by waiting patiently until they ceased a chant, and would then hand them the medicine to give to the patients. Very soon they came to me for some, and I could trust them to give at least two doses. I did not try to stop their incantations, but rather encouraged them, as they soothed the sick, who often slept while they were in progress, and when my Apache Mojave Indian boy, Cobre, one day asked me to let him go to a medicine man to be sung over, I told him to go. The men always wanted to do something for me and brought me mocking birds, which they would come and feed, canaries, kangaroo rats, young coyotes, and even snakes. After the people were able to move about, I recommended that they be moved to higher ground away from the river and where there were good springs of water, and at length they were located near the foot of Hoo-wal-ka ya-na-ya-na (Pine Top) now called Mount Mingus.

Joe, an Indian interpreter, told me that some of their medicine men could bring a man back to life, so one day I gave a rat a little chloroform and threw it out on the ground where the men were standing around some of whom said, "Pih" (dead). I then, after waiting a short time, picked the rat up by its tail and swung it around until it revived when I placed it on the ground. As it started to run, I told Cobre to pick it up, but he said "Kalepi" (Bad) and the men jumped back.

After I had acquired a better knowledge of their language, I learned something of their religious beliefs and was invited by the pasemache to become one of their circle and sit with them during their ceremonials, the most importance [sic] of which took place the next year, when they represented the spirit or sleep land in a sand picture.[10] The spirit who lives at sunrise, Se-ma-che, is their all powerful Spirit, and the woman who taught them the use of the rattle is a lesser one. Her house is this side of sunrise and its roof is a rainbow. (The rainbow referred to is probably the great natural bridge or arch in southern Utah.) There are other Spirits, capable of good or evil, and every pasemache has a twin or guardian spirit or control, and it might do good or evil. Some of the women were supposed to be in league with the evil ones, and they were the ones to be tied up when the medicine men accused them, when they were told to use their influence to cure the sick and if they did not they would be killed. The Medicine men soon began to lose control of the people and I was consulted on all matters medical or otherwise.

An Indian girl, who had been brought up in a family of whites, became the wife of an Apache-Mojave chief, Boo-wa-we-yoo-ma or Ten Yumas, also called Che-ma-wa-ma-sal-la or Piute's Hand. She had adopted the habits and beliefs of the whites and through her superior qualities gained great influence in the tribe and the people were devoted to her, but the medicine men were jealous of her growing influence, and when her husband's horse kicked him in the abdomen and caused his death, they accused her of bewitching the horse. She was stoned to death, and her husband's brother, although he thought much of her, was one of the Indians accused of the deed, and with the other accused who were arrested by the troops and taken to Camp Verde, where they were placed in irons and confined many months. The woman's friends were very angry and lost all confidence in the medicine men, and they named the brother Kalepi or Bad.

We rarely had visitors and when we had, they were officers from the post or headquarters, or contractors who furnished supplies for the Indians, so that late one afternoon while Schuyler and I sat in our tents at the end of the road, we were amazed to see a tall soft white hat with a narrow brim, appear on the road where it dipped down into the river bottom. Then a blond moon-like face came up smiling, followed by the body of a man in a linen duster on a cayuse. "A missionary" said Schuyler, as the man and horse approached us and exclaimed, "Here ve are right among the vild Indians." He was invited to dismount and we led the way into a tent and he was asked to have a drink. He replied "Yaas" as he poured one from the bottle. That left us in doubt until I asked him if he wasn't afraid to come alone, when he said in a very confident tone, "The Lord takes care of me." At dinner we requested him to ask a blessing, when he repeated the Doxology. When he left the next morning to go down to Camp Verde in search of his fellow countrymen to attend to their spiritual welfare, we cautioned him about traveling about all alone, telling him that the Lord took care of those who took care of themselves. The next we heard of him, he was in the hospital at the post and had lost the tips of his toes from freezing. He had started to cross the Mogollon mountains to go to Fort Wingate, many days ride on a road very rarely traveled, taking with him only a small piece of bacon and a few crackers.[11] Three or four nights after he left, after a heavy snowfall in the mountains, a teamster came to the post on a mule and reported that a family was snow-bound, when Brevet Colonel John J. Coppinger, Twenty-third Infantry, sent a troop of the Fifth Cavalry to break a road.[12] The Swede was found on the road, half starved and his feet frozen. His horse had eaten his bacon and crackers, so he was fed and brought in with Mr. Hitchcock and his wife and three daughters. The father was interested in the Big Bug Mine and had been furnished transportation by the commanding officer at Wingate. Not long afterward I was at Camp Verde and the Colonel said to me, "Let's go and see the padre." What do you think of your Lord now?" he asked of the Swede. "Did he not care for me" was his reply.

The officers of the Fifth Cavalry at Camp Verde had a large pack of foxhounds and greyhounds with which they and the officers of the Twenty-third Infantry hunted jackrabbits, and, whenever I visited the post, I rode with them, but they had never caught a coyote, and there were many of them near the Agency. So, I invited them to pay me a visit and bring the hounds along. St. Stephen's Day, the day before Christmas, 1873, the hunters' day, I met them halfway, where we let loose the foxhounds which soon came upon a herd of antelope a long distance away, and by the time we caught up with them, they had sent all of the coyotes to cover by their bayings and we had to hunt jackrabbits, which were plentiful. I was on a very fast horse, and when the greyhounds took up a chase, I was close behind. When a rabbit dodged, the hounds behind would usually get the lead. After one had dodged several times, two hounds gained the lead and were only a few feet ahead of me when I saw one of them—Walapai— strike the rabbit with his nose, and as it went up about two feet, Verde, the second hound grabbed it.

I had a turkey for dinner that weighed about twenty pounds. It was one of two that I had brought from Date Creek with me, coyotes having stolen one of them. They were from a clutch of eggs laid by a wild turkey which a packer had placed under a barn-yard hen to hatch and mother. After din- ner we gathered around a box wood stove in my tent and I brewed a drink out of claret, which I boiled and to which I added some spice and sherry wine, which was only slightly stimulating, but enough so to cause us to recall all of the old, old songs and keep us merry until midnight. The next morning all were still merry, and they smiled for at least a week afterwards, when I was the guest of Colonel Coppinger, who was in command of Camp Verde. We were returning to his quarters after dinner at the mess and had stepped upon the veranda when we heard a rattlesnake. It was a side-winder and lay in the door-way and had to be dispatched before we could enter. So the claret cup had nothing to do with it.

The editor of the *Arizona Miner*, [John Huguenot] Marion, published at Prescott, was reputed to be the ugliest man in the country and had carried the jack-knife for many years. He at last met a man whom he thought had an uglier face and thrust the knife into his hands saying, "I have car- ried this long enough, take it, I know you must be uglier than I am.["]]¹³ A woman in Prescott made herself notorious by associating with the pack- ers and miners. She wore a man's hat and a man's sack coat. She didn't swagger, but frequented saloons and drank and gambled with the men, but showed her womanly qualities by nursing her associates when they were sick and was ready with her money to feed them when they were down and out.

I was in the field against hostile Apache, who, under their chief Eskim- inzin, had left the San Carlos Agency, Arizona, after killing a young officer, First Lieutenant Jacob Almy, May 27, 1873, and committing other murders.¹⁴ I witnessed the issue and inspected the first annuities allowed the Indians of the Rio-Verde Agency, the day before we started, and that night they had a great gathering. All of the 500 A-Yuma, 1000 A-Mojave and 500 A-Tonto joined in dancing and feasting. When the squaw dance began, a daughter of one of the chiefs ran to Schuyler and gave his blouse a tug and one came to me. We didn't know that we were invited to open the festivities, so, didn't follow when the two ran to two other squaws who were waiting for us. Several chiefs then came forward and explained that they wished us to take part, and the girls came again and pulled a sleeve, so we followed and placed ourselves between our two partners, facing in the opposite direction with elbows out, against which the girls leaned. They were washed, dressed in their best and deloused for the occasion. As soon as we were in place, a space was opened for us and we took four steps forward and then back bending our knees a little as the girls did, keeping time with the chorus of nearly 2000 voices of men and women, singing, "See-an-na see-an-na see-an-na hay-hay-hay, See-en-na hah-hah-hah," followed by hearty Indian yells, when we stopped and gave each one of our partners fifty cents silver. The bucks gave their dancing companions a piece of red flannel, a piece of calico or some beads. The dance took place near the Agency among some mesquite bushes about twelve feet high and large fires were lighted to be kept up all night.

We left on February 18, to be gone until May 22, 1874, having 30 men of Troop K, Fifth U.S. Cavalry and 122 Indian scouts, 59 of which were Apache-Yuma, 41 Apache-Mojave, and 22 Apache-Tonto, commanded by Second Lieutenant Walter S. Schuyler, Fifth U.S. Cavalry, and Al Sieber, chief of scouts.[15] We had a pack-train of eighty mules led by a white bell-mare, to carry our rations and ammunition. My medical supplies were very few and took up a space not over a foot square. It was a sight worth seeing when the mules lined up to have the aparrejos [sic] taken off at night and put on again in the morning, each one knowing his place on the square. Schuyler and I had a negro cook who was a trifler, so we soon went to mess with the packers and sat on the ground around the dirty manta which was used to cover a cargo, on which tin cups, plates, etc., were thrown and boiled frijoles—Mexican brown beans—fried bacon, yeast powder biscuits and coffee were served from the vessels that they were cooked in. Sometimes we had a little raspberry or other jam, called dope. The packers' language was of their own choice, but the American was outdone by the Mexican when it came to the abusive names he called the mules, but the latter clothed them in his own tongue.

The scouts were on foot and armed with Spencer carbines, headed by Kelho (Canoe or Boat), who knew the manual of arms and could blow all of the cavalry calls.[16] He took great pride in calling out orders, and only once made a mistake, when he gave the order, "Charge bayonets" to scouts armed with the carbine. At first, the scouts were poor shots, and I saw about twenty of them fire at a deer not even one hundred yards away, and all miss. The deer was at the foot of a high rock and leisurely disappeared behind it. An Indian who accompanied the scouts was unarmed, and we called him the "Senator" as he harangued them at night frequently after we struck the trail of the hostiles. The scouts almost always had fresh meat, as they killed wood-rats, hauling them out of their holes under the bushes with a stick having a crook at one end. After cutting a slit in their abdomens they boiled them, skin and entrails all.

The second or third day out, we met a command, from Fort Whipple at Prescott, which took about twenty of our scouts. We went hunting one day, the Indians forming a long line and then while advancing, closing in the ends so as to surround a small valley in which many deer were shot down. After that, as we entered Tonto Basin, no hunting was allowed, except for hostile Indians, and one day, shortly afterward, we heard a shot on the far side of a range of hills. The scouts charged over them and came back with the carcass of a deer which the hostiles had killed and left behind when they saw the scouts. From there on, we followed their tracks and those of a horse were very plain for several days and then were no longer seen, the animal probably having been killed and eaten. Moccasin tracks were not so easily followed and would sometimes be lost for a time. At length the scouts began to locate chi-wa-kis or rancherias, when night marches were made to surprise the occupants about the break of day, when the killings were usually made. Women couldn't be distinguished from men at the long range and especially when they had bow and arrow to take part in the fight, but usually they ran to shelter, yet some of them were found among the dead. The hostiles led us over high mountains and through the roughest country, but we followed until we had to go into Fort McDowell at the end of thirty days for rations.[17]

The black stiff brimmed hats that had been issued and ordered worn, were not suited for service in the field, and in a few days the brims were completely or nearly gone and the tops full of holes or absent, so that the hair of the wearer stood out. Soft gray hats replaced them at McDowell which were the forerunners of the present campaign hat.[18] We were on the trail again the next day, heading toward the Sierra Anchas and Tonto Basin. We were soon south of Salt River and in the Pinal Mountains. Often the water at our camps had been alkaline and we had to go unwashed or suffer with sore lips and chapped hands. We struck more rancherias and gave the hostiles no rest. The Pima Indians, ancient enemies of the Apache, were out, and one day our scouts reported that there were some dead Indians on a spur high above us, so, I took twenty of them and climbed up to investigate. I had on government shoes and leggings, but the scouts took off their shoes and wore moccasins, and they had to assist me in places where the soil was loose and the climbing hard. By the time we reached the top I was dripping with perspiration. I found half a dozen coowahs and the dead bodies of sixteen Indians, with heads smashed and bodies filled with arrows, most of them at the opening of their brush shelters, as if they had been killed as they attempted to come out. Many war clubs were lying around, some of them broken and covered with hair and dried blood. The che-wa-ki was in the open on the summit at the end of the spur from which there was a long and steep descent and their fires could have been seen for miles away. The Pimas could have had no difficulty in locating them and probably jumped them early in the morning. All Indians are not good trailers, and, when a party is out, the man in the lead is followed by the others, who do so heedlessly. I have picked up a loaded cartridge after a long string of men had passed over a trail in which it was lying.

Some of our packers carried very large horn spoons which had a capacity of about a quart, with which they washed some of the soil here and there, prospecting for gold. The expression "By the great horn spoon" possibly originated from this use. On the way up the west side of the mountains to the old abandoned Camp Pinal, we came upon an old oven on a flat which had been built and used by the troops when digging the trail to the post.[19] In it were entombed the bodies of two prospectors who had probably been jumped by Indians while they were asleep. The end of a box that had held canned tomatoes closed the opening and was inscribed with their names.

After we had been out for some weeks, we met a scouting party of the Fifth Cavalry from Camp Grant and learned that there were two other commands in the field.[20] It had camped the night before at the foot of a mountain in which our scouts had just located some of the hostiles, who were baking mescal in a pit, which they quickly abandoned and the scouts brought us some of the mescal which was very sugary and tasted very good after our monotonous diet. As they were now surrounded, the hostiles made for the San Carlos Agency and we could simply follow them in. Here they were disarmed by Captain George Randall, Twenty-third Infantry, who was in command of the scouts there, and Lieutenant John B. Babcock, and with them was Captain Joseph B. Girard, Assistant Surgeon.[21] Many of their guns had been taken to pieces and hidden beneath the skirts and clothing of the women and children, who squatted on the ground, but their feelings were not hurt when clothes were lifted and the pieces found, only a laugh followed.

After the disarmament, we went south to Camp Grant and left there some of our scouts who had disobeyed orders by hunting, or else had informed the hostiles of our approach and some others who had sided with them and thrown down their arms. The officers there were living in a large stone house and messing together. It had a cupola that could be seen miles away and the house was called "Brown's Folly," as it had been designed and built by Brevet Major W. H. Brown of the Fifth Cavalry.[22]

Our first camp on returning from Camp Grant was in Hog Canyon, and Schuyler and I made our beds after dark under a live oak tree, and, in the morning, happening to look up, saw a piece of frayed rope dangling from a dead branch, which reminded us of the saying that if a man were hung to a branch of a tree, it would die. I said "let[']s look," and when we turned over our beds, there beneath the canvas were the bones of a human being. I learned afterward that a Chiricahua Indian had threatened to kill an officer and was hung in Hog Canyon. Once, while we were unsaddling our horses to make camp, just as the sun was setting, rain fell for about three minutes from a cloudless sky. Late in the summer of the same year, while I was on my way horseback from the Rio-Verde Agency to Camp Verde, Arizona, a shower suddenly came up and as I held my right hand out rain fell upon and wet it, while the rest of my body, my horse and the road remained perfectly dry. I have seen at least four solar rainbows at one time, the colors of some of them reversed as they were reflections from others. At one camp the ground was covered with colites [geodes] and on breaking one of them, I found it filled with beautiful amethyst crystals and if I had the means of carrying them I could have made a large collection.

When we reached Salt River, the water was so high and so turbulent that we couldn't cross and we had to seek a fording place lower down, but there was a great canyon which we couldn't descend, so we made camp about a mile above the site of the present Roosevelt Dam in a grove of cottonwoods, now many feet under the water of the artificial lake. The next morning we followed what is now called the "Apache Trail" over the steep mountains from Tonto Basin, which in some places wound around escarpments several hundred feet high which we had to hug closely. One contrary mule rubbed his load of flour against the rock and went rolling down, leaving us shy one mule and two hundred pounds of flour. We made camp on Fish Creek, where on November 3rd, 1921, I had dinner while on my way to Phoenix over the graded road by automobile from which I could frequently see the old trail that we had followed in 1874. We crossed Salt River a few miles above Phoenix and went to Fort McDowell again and then back to Tonto Basin.

One of our camps was about five miles east of the mountains, on an arroyo, near which at the foot of the mountains, Captain Charles Morton, Third Cavalry, once had a fight with the Indians and killed many of them, and I took ten scouts to visit the battle ground.[23] We followed the arroyo and for a long way it was filled with boulders two or three feet thick, and we jumped from one to another and sometimes down into the sand. I never jumped from a rock and fallen tree until I had looked to the far side to see that there was nothing there, and it was well that I did so this time, as there on the far side of a large rock, lay coiled, ready to strike, a black rattler, which sprung his rattler when he heard my step. I jumped back, caught up a stone and threw it at him, striking him about eight inches back of his head which he threw back and opened his mouth to its full extent, causing his fangs to fly erect as he fiercely struck them into his body back of the wound inflicted by the stone. I never before realized how widely a snake could open its mouth. I couldn't wait to learn what effect the virus he inject[ed] into himself would have, so, I crushed his head with another stone and proceeded up the arroyo. None of the scouts [would] attempt to kill the rattler, and I thought they would rather have left it alone.

I have seen an Apache pasemache handle a rattler with thumb and forefinger encircling it close to its head. Slight pressure caused it to open its mouth, when he dropped some corn pollen into it and rubbed some along its body. The snake was afterward laid along an arm, a leg, or around the head of a patient or wherever the latter said there was pain, while the pasemache chanted for a time after which he swung the snake off with a "Whistch." I am quite certain that the fangs were removed before the snakes were handled in this manner, as I saw none when its mouth was opened. I didn't see an Indian who had been struck by a rattler or hear of one, during the time I was in Arizona, although I was told by them that it did sometime happen, and they cut the part with a sharp flake of quartz, sucked the venom out with the mouth and applied baked red clay, just as they did arrow and gunshot wounds. The fangs are covertly placed in the base of the pole with which they play the pole and ring game—Tu-re-bi—to give good luck. The Indians had a way of testing the nerves of a newcomer and creating a laugh at his expense, by twirling the rattles on a string behind him.

We returned to the Agency May 22, 1874. The scouts had captured many women and these were drawn up in line and each one was asked where she wanted to go. About fifty of them went over to the scouts who were also in line. Each one was asked if he wanted the woman at his side to live with him as his wife and the women were asked if they wished to live with the scouts. All replied, "Yes." Al Sieber then explained that he was going to marry them in the white man's way, and they must always remain faithful. He then told the couples to join hands and he announced them man and wife. All left apparently happy.[24]

Dr. Josephus Williams had been relieved on account of failing health and Lieutenant Schuyler finding that the Indians were complaining of lack of food, discharged the chief clerk, who was in charge and assumed charge himself. After this the Indians were well fed and cared for in every way. All of the men were required to report every day, and each one was furnished with a brass tag on which was his number, the presentation of which entitled him to a certain number of rations, a component of which he received each day and if one died, his check was turned in. When any were missing, Lieutenant Schuyler lost no time in following their trail. I was then left in charge. The Navajos, Moquis [Mokis] and Zunis visited our Indians to trade with them and I learned that a party had brought muzzle-loading guns, powder, bullets and percussion caps to exchange for deer skins, otter, mountain lion, etc. I ordered them away and they asked for a letter to their Agent in New Mexico, as they thought they were doing a legitimate business. I gave them one, telling him about the traffic which was helping to keep up the trouble we were having with the Apache, and he brought it to an end at his end of the line.

While we were in the field, Brevet Lieutenant Colonel Julius W. Mason, Captain Fifth Cavalry came up from Camp Verde and built a dam across the river and dug irrigating ditches, making use of Indian labor.[25] The Indians planted a variety of vegetable seed, [such] as pumpkin, potatoes, turnip, parsnip, corn, watermelon, etc., which they cultivated successfully, and asked for more farming implements in order to plant a larger area the next season, but the Indian Department didn't see fit to furnish them.

Del-cha [Delshay] was still in the mountains with a small following and some of his men, one of whom he had wounded, sent word that they wished to join their friends at the Agency and Del-cha he wouldn't be taken alive. They were informed that they might come in providing they brought him dead. This they agreed to do and said they would be at the Agency in a certain number of days. Lieutenant Schuyler told them that he would wait that long and if they didn't come, he would go after them. He counted the days and not the nights, and then started for the mountains. The night of the day that he started three Tontos of Del-cha's band came to my tent just after dark, handed me a folded dirty rag, saying "Del-cha" and quickly disappeared. On opening the parcel, I found a whole scalp with one ear hanging to it, in the lobe of which was tied a pearl shirt button. I sent the rag and its contents by courier to the Commanding Officer of Camp Verde, fourteen miles down the river, who forwarded it to Schuyler by courier who reached him at his first camp as he was about to leave the next morning. His scouts identified the scalp as that of Del-cha, and now the full purport of the signal fires they had seen the night before, which indicated that someone was lost. The scouting party returned and the Apache troubles had come to an end. I heard later, that Del-cha's head was taken to Fort McDowell.[26]

The former chief clerk of the Agency was back as Agent by the Interior Department and in a few days after he took charge, the wails of the women for food were often heard on the hills near by. He issued rations to the chiefs instead of the heads of families, as had been done during his absence, and many of them must have been misappropriated.[27]

On or about August 10, 1874, I started from Camp Verde to cross the country, about 800 miles, to Las Animas, Colorado, then the terminus of the railroad on the Arkansas River near Fort Lyon, in charge of Captain James Burns, Fifth U.S. Cavalry, and his wife and two children, to send them to their home in Washington, D.C.[28] I had two ambulances, one with thorough-brace and the other with platform springs, and an escort wagon each drawn by four mules, which were driven by civilian teamsters, with an escort of nine soldiers, some of which were to be discharged on reaching the railroad. My Apache-Mojave Indian Boy Cobre, aged about fifteen years, accompanied me and I had two saddle horses. We crossed the Verde River about seven miles above the post and found the road up the Mogollon mountains very rough, but the view was grand and we could see the country for miles as we drove along the southern limits of the red-rock country which is worn into all sorts of fantastic shapes, as forts, temples, sharp peaks, etc. between which were deep canyons. Our first camp was among a clump of aspens which surrounded a spring of very cold water, not far from Stoneman's Lake, which is deep down what appears to be the crater of an extinct volcano. We always camped where there were grass, water and, if possible wood. In the pines on a hillside was a wild turkey roost and we could hear their calls.

Captain Burns died, August 15, 1874, of hemorrhage of the lungs, on what I reported as Carriso Creek, but which I learned afterward was Dead Man's Creek, about 75 miles west of Fort Wingate, New Mexico, to which post I sent his remains ahead for interment. We had just stopped near the wash and I was dickering with three or four Zuni Indians to slaughter a young steer and sell us a hind quarter, when I heard the Captain cough and his wife cry out. I ran to the ambulance, which was only about one hundred feet away, but the bursting of an aneurism in his lungs caused instant death. The cough was caused by a light whirlwind which carried the dust right up the wash. There wasn't a tree or a bush in sight and not a house for miles and miles. A star mail route between Wingate and Prescott was run for a short time, but Apache Indians killed the drivers of the mail buckboards and the route had been discontinued. At Wingate we learned that the Captain's remains had arrived at the post early one morning and the news spread rapidly. The greater part of the command was out after Indians and the women were expecting to hear of an engagement, and each one feared that the officer might be her husband, so they started to run to the hospital, when they were informed that the officer was from Arizona.

I met Lieutenant Philip Reed [Reade] for the first time, but many times later at Zamboanga, Mindanao, Philippine Islands, 1903–1905. He was afterward retired as Brigadier General and died at his home in Massachusetts.[29] While at Wingate I drank grape-cider—now a popular beverage, called Grape Juice—brought to the suttler [sic] freshly pressed by the Navajo Indians, through whose village we had passed a day or two before where we saw them making their blankets, garters and head bands on their primitive looms. We had our first fresh meat there after several days without any, young lamb and kid. We also had thin crisp wafers which they made from milk of young sweet Indian corn, which they ground on their metates and then baked on heated stone. They grew pumpkins, watermelons and muskmelons, but the latter tasted like squash.

At Bacon's Ranch, our first camp after leaving Wingate, a soldier who had helped to nurse Captain Burns, refused to obey my orders and started to run away. I ordered a shot to be fired over his head and he came running back. I was about to send him back to Wingate under guard, when Mrs. Burns, to whom he had gone, came to me and begged me to let him off as she had been so faithful in caring for her husband, so I reprimanded him and asked him if he would now obey orders. He was very humble and I knew that he had been drinking hard the day before. I returned him to duty and during the rest of the drive no man could have done better. When we arrived at Fort Union, I found that four of my mules that were shave-tails were affected by the high altitude and I left them to rest and become acclimated, taking four mules from the post to replace them.[30] The hair on the tails of mules when shipped by steamer or rail was cut very short to prevent the animals from chewing the hair. Hence the name, Shave-tail.[31]

On reaching Las Animas, I drove directly to the railroad station and put Mrs. Burns on the cars to continue their trip home. I learned that the train had come in about half an hour before, and I was about to go to the telegraph office, when across the track came, mother, grandmother, Claude and Harold, who had arrived on that very train. I was covered with dust, my clothes were greasy, my hair long, and I hadn't shaved, as I had intended to go right over [to] the hotel and clean up. Mother and grandmother cried over me, but their tears were mingled with smiles and it was a happy meeting. A good wash, a shave and clean clothes and I presented a different appearance and was my old self again. Little Mother had seen me come in from a scout or a long hunt but grandmother hadn't seen me before in such a disreputable condition.[32]

Just before I left Camp Verde, the telegraph line which connected us with the rest of the world had just been completed by the troops, and I sent a message to mother at grandmother's in Elmira, New York, to meet me at Las Animas. This was the longest telegraph message ever received at Elmira up to that time. I then wrote and told her the probable date of my arrival there and she made her arrangements so that she arrived as she did. Grandmother hadn't seen me for a long time and she came along. She would have liked to drive overland with us, but the trip was a long one, and to get out of Arizona and go "inside," was not always easy, so she went to Salt Lake City to visit a Mormon Bishop, A. Stephenson, whom she had met in a hotel in New York and who claimed relationship.

¶After a rest of two days and laying in a good supply of commissaries at Fort Lyon, including an extra quantity of sugar to trade after we left the Rio Grande, Mother, the boys and I started about September 10, with an escort of only one enlisted man, a corporal, but eight civilians, who asked to join the party and were permitted to do so. One of them was a cook who had been recommended to me by one of the Kitchen brothers, who ran several hotels, and he turned out to be a first-rate camp cook. He had been out in the country trying to sell rosaries and chromos to the Mexicans and came back broke, as the people had no money, they traded with one another for the few necessities they required. We followed the Picketwire (Purgatory) River to Trinidad, crossed the Rocky Mountains by the way of the Raton Pass, passed Dick Wooten's, crossed the Vermejo and the Cimmaron [sic], along which wild plum bushes were thick and we gathered a bushel of the ripe fruit in a very few minutes. We also crossed the Maxwell ranch and drove on to Fort Union, where we changed back to our own mules, after resting a day, and went on through Las Vegas to Santa Fé where we rested another day, so as to visit the St. Michael's church and other old buildings.[33] There was an old adobe ruin on the road back of Pigeon's ranch, which we visited the day before. After leaving Santa Fé, we crossed the Rio Grande at Piña [Pena] Blanca and drove over a sandy cedar covered trees [*sic*] to San Ysidro where there were many mineral springs and we filled demijohns and bottles, the corks of which began to pop before we had gone far. We passed the Pueblo Santo Domingo and had peaches and grapes. The road then took us to San Mateo, Agua Azul to Fort Wingate and on through the Navajo villages, across the Little Colorado River, over the Mogollon mountains, past Stoneman's Lake, across the Verde River and up its valley to the Rio-Verde Indian Reservation where we arrived about October 10th. Not long afterward, Lieutenant Charles King was wounded by hostile Apache at one of the camps we had made not far from the Little Colorado River.[34] By the time we had reached there we had given out of the fresh meat we had procured from the Navajos, and I could see many antelope near by. I started to get one, but very soon returned, suspecting that Indians were near by watching the camp.

After fording the Rio Grande, we rarely came across a Mexican or Pueblo Indian who could speak English and money was used only to make ornaments of silver, but sugar which they rarely or ever saw, was a luxury and they hastened to take it in exchange for beef, mutton, chickens, eggs and the few vegetables they raised, as they had only a thin syrup made by boiling the bruised and broken stalks of their sweet Indian corn that they raised. They had no milk, although the country teemed with cattle and sheep. They ploughed, or rather scratched the ground with a stick and thrashed their wheat by driving sheep around over it on beaten ground within an enclosure of brush, winnowing it by tossing it up for the wind to drive off the chaff. I haven't written more in detail about this trip, as mother had done so in her "Recollections."[35]

At the Agency we lived in two tents, the largest of which was stretched over a frame and had a floor, a wood door and an adobe fireplace and chimney. A smaller tent back of it had an adobe wall on three sides about four feet high as a bullet and arrow proof. We ate at the Agency mess and were waited upon by Apache boys to whom I had given lessons in English before I brought my family to the Agency. I often called a dozen or more boys into my tent and Cobre, my boy, would explain the pictures in the illustrated papers to them, and I would learn many Yavapai words that they used, and then I taught them the song "John Brown Had a Little Indian," and others. They learned to count up to ten in one sitting and the next day went about calling out the words. We were near the foot of Mount Mingus on the south side of a small stream of water which rose in the mountains, ran underground several miles and came out hot, on which account it was called, "H-ka-roo-ya" by the Yavapai. Twigs of trees left in the water, which soon cooled off, collected lime about them and at length became fossils. I had recommended the removal of the Agency from the river bottom to this more healthful spot, and after Dr. Williams left, the one partly finished adobe house near the river was abandoned and the Indians were brought up here. The first building was a guard-house, which was partly a dug-out and partly of heavy logs, having an entrance on top which was of logs. It rarely had an inmate. A small adobe house was erected and the trader built a rough board store. Vincent, a former enlisted man and later a clerk for the Agent at Date Creek was the first trader.

The next year the Indians were eager to begin work on their farm and asking for more farming implements, when the Interior Department sent out a special commissioner, L. E. Dudley, to take them over to the San Carlos Reservation.[36] After they had been assembled, he told them that he had come from General [now President Ulysses S.] Grant in Washington to move them. He had come out of a tent, thrown a buffalo robe on a step leading from it, sat at the step with one arm resting upon it as he talked. I stood just back of the crowd in order to listen to what might be said by the onlookers, and I heard a buck say in a low tone, "He is drunk," and when he arose and went into the tent, another one said, "he has gone in to get a drink of whiskey," Captain Smook, one of the chiefs, told him they would not go where they would be outnumbered by their enemies, that this was their country and always had been, that their fathers and grandfathers, were born here and had died here, their wives and children were all born here, and he reminded the commissioner of the promises that had been made to them when they were assembled here that the country along the river and ten miles on each side should be theirs for-ever.[37] Then he pleaded to be allowed to remain. Why did the commis-sioner call the Indians Brothers? The white man when he meets his brother always asks him to take a drink, but the commissioner hadn't asked him to take one. Then he begged the commissioner not to drink any more whiskey until the conference the next day so that he might know what he was saying to them. Others pleaded in like vein. I had been with them so long, and they were so accustomed to come to me to talk about their affairs in their own tongue that they came to me and asked me to intercede for them with the government, as the commissioner was crazy or drunk[.] But when I told them that the order did come from General Grant and they must obey it, they agreed to go quietly, providing I would accompany them to see that they were properly treated and not attacked by their enemies. I recommended that the tribes be taken by wagon-road around the mountains and he replied that they were Indians and were used to the mountains. He was going the shortest way; he had moved Indians before and he would accomplish things that army officers could not and they were trying to make this task as difficult as possible.[38]

On February 27, 1875, he started 1400 Indians from the Rio-Verde Agency, all on foot, to tramp about 150 miles by rough trails over high mountains and across numerous streams that were liable at any hour to rise many feet and become impassable. I had seen the Verde come raging down, tearing away every thing before it, great trees and even rocks carried along. They had to carry all of their belongings on their backs in their V-shaped baskets—ku-thaks—old and young with heavy packs. One old man placed his aged and decrepit wife in one of these baskets with her feet hanging out, and carried her on his back supported by a band over his head, an average of eight and a half miles a day for some ten days. The fifteen cavalrymen who were along as a guard for the commissioner and the agency employees, carried as many as possible of the cripples, weaker ones and foot-sore children, on their horses. One day, at least two babes were born on the trail. These were wrapped in blankets and carried to the next camp, before any other covering could be provided, the mothers, after a short rest, following on foot. No wonder the Indian women looked old so soon.

Their progress was slow; the cattle that were driven along to be slaughtered as needed for food, soon became foot-sore on the rough, steep trails and many had to be left behind. At length the beef and flour gave out and the Indians ate the stems of canada thistle and such other greens as they could find, and then the women and children began to cry with hunger. One evening a deer ran along the side of the mountain above our camp and many shots were fired by the Apache-Yuma and Apache-Mojave from the creek below us. As it came opposite our tents, Al Sieber fired and it fell. Then the Indians from below and the Tontos who were above us, ran to claim the carcass, but the Tontos gained possession and the other hungry ones were driven away very angry. The next day—March 8, I think—

Lieutenant George O. Eaton, Fifth Cavalry, who was in command of the escort, and rode ahead and a short way up the hills when we sighted a deer which I killed.[39] We cut off enough for ourselves and hung the rest of the meat in a tree for the Indians to get, but there wasn't enough for so many hungry people, and just after we had made camp on the east branch of the Verde River, the A-Yumas and A-Mojave, who had come in hungry and in an ugly frame of mind, and whom we always located behind us, began to yell excitedly and their women cried out "Kill the Tontos!" Very shortly the men charged past us, and the commissioner, who limped a little from a wound he had received during the Civil War, ran to intercept them and drive them back but they passed him and the agent and his employees who also tried to stop them. They ran up a measa [sic] about twenty feet, upon which the Tontos were camped, dropped on their knees and bellies and began to fire. The commissioner was helpless, so called for the assistance of Lieutenant Eaton, who, with his men stood waiting his authority to interfere. As the troops ran past the Agent and his employees, they were under a tree on their knees praying and singing. This was all they could do, as they had no arms with which to protect themselves. The firing stopped as soon as the cavalrymen reached the top of the mesa and advanced to the front, when they drove the excited Indians and interpreters were told to inform both sides that if there was any more shooting, the soldiers would take part against those who started it. While I was standing guard over the boxes of ammunition, some of the bucks pressed around me and tried to steal cartridges from the thimbles in my belt and laughed when I drove them back. I collected ten wounded men, whose wounds I dressed, and found four dead, shot through the head. These we buried and on my way back to Camp Verde, I disinterred the heads and sent the skulls to the Army Medical Museum, as they showed the so-called explosive action of a bullet passing through the skull which it broke into many pieces.

We crossed Salt River shortly afterward, and one morning on scanning the Indians, as I always did, I saw that the Apache-Mojave and some of the Apache-Yuma men had their faces painted, their noses red and the rest of the face black with galena as when they prepared for war, so I went over and spoke to Captain Charley—Nya-wha-la-wha-la—(Long black Man) a chief, who said "Kwa-wa o-pi" talk no.[40] I returned at once to our bivouac and was telling the commissioner that the Indians were ready to fight, when a bullet came whistling over from there as a warning. I told him to get busy or the next bullet might be for him and he then told the interpreters to call out that he would go ahead and send back food which would soon reach them. He could see the looks of hate beneath the paint that the men cast at him, nor had he understood what the men and women had said to him when on the trail, and when he asked me what they were saying I wouldn't tell him, as most of it was not fit to be translated. Once one of two young bucks, as they passed us, shook his fist in the face of the other and called him a vile name in English, and then looked up into the commissioner's face and grinned and then looked at me with a grin, as if I knew to whom the name was really applied. After the whiz of the bullet over our heads, he lost no time in starting, and that afternoon, at the next camp, beef and flour met them and all were in good humor again. There was plenty of game in the country, but the Indians were not allowed to hunt, and, when not furnished with rations, had to subsist on what greens they could gather, as the stalks of canada thistle, the so-called miners' cabbage and the young stalks of the American Aloe, which they roasted for a short time in an open fire.

The rest of the way now was by easy trail, down grade to the San Carlos River, on the north banks of which was located the few Agency buildings. The Indians were turned over to the San Carlos Agent and the Commissioner felt very much relieved that the most difficult task he had ever undertaken was accomplished, but it was one that might have been easy, if he had not thought he had nothing to learn from the army officers and other men who had been among the Apache for some time, and had taken the very worst route instead of going around the mountains by a regular road. As I left San Carlos to return to Camp Verde, where I had left my family, the Indians begged me to remain with them and I could hear the wailing of the women and children as I passed their oo-wahs, a cry that remained with me for many a day.[41]

¶A few of the Yavapai were allowed later to return to their own country, but the best land had nearly all been located by white men. In the fall of 1921—October 13–31—I was at the San Carlos Agency and met some of the Yavapai who were children when I assisted in removing them over there. Very little had been done for them, and they were only a little better off than they were in 1875. Most of them were living in round huts made of poles thatched with grass or the bows [sic] of cottonwood trees,

sleeping on the ground, cooking mostly in tin cans in an open fire. They
had learned to speak English and a few of them had some schooling. Their children, however, had been to school long enough to learn the three R's and their grand children were receiving a common school training.

Missionaries had come among them late and they said had done but little for them, so they had organized a church of their own. I went to their open air meeting twice. They assembled in a grove of cottonwoods, about two and a half miles above the Agency, every Saturday afternoon and remained until Sunday afternoon, dancing, singing, praying and listening to exhortations. A committee of six men conducted the services and they met me when I arrived with Rob Roy, an Apache-Mojave, who ran a small store and who had brought me in his automobile. They conducted me to a fallen tree on the trunk of which there was a curved depression, forming a very easy seat. While the women were in a long line dancing towards a man who held one hand out, most of the men crowded about me. To my inquiries, they replied that they met there to "Pray to Our Father in Heaven, to dance and sing to Him and to listen to the advice given by their leaders." They were anxious to hear what I believed and I talked to them as I had done forty-six years before, when they first heard of the Almighty God from the white men, one of whom was that Christian gentleman, Dr. Josephus Williams whose gentle kindly ways appealed to them, and he influenced them for their own good. When he broke down in health and had to go east, "Inside," hadn't enough money to pay his expenses home. If men like him had been in charge of Indian affairs, all of the Apache tribes would now be self supporting on the best land in Arizona, instead of the poorest. Those who went back to the Verde River found the best land in possession of the whites.

I also visited old Fort McDowell in 1921, November 6–12, where I found the Indians a little more prosperous, but there were old, nearly blind women who had lost their men folks during the wars and were trying to get money with which to buy food by making baskets, but they received only a pittance for them. Possibly seventy-five cents for one that sold for eight or ten dollars in the stores. Here I met Mike Burns—Hoo-mo-thy-a, or Wet Nose, who was captured in 1872, when a small boy by Captain James Burns, and lived for many years with the whites. He was a scout, etc., and has written an account of the Indian wars in Arizona for which I have tried in vain to find a publisher.[42]

We were at Camp Verde until May 2, 1875, and Mother has told about the kindness of Brevet Major George M. Brayton, the commanding officers and others to her while I was away.[43] When we left, we drove through Copper Canyon to Prescott in one day and there secured seats in a stage that was to make a trip to Los Angeles, about 450 miles, over the new route which a regular stage line was preparing to run. Mr. Hussey drove his stage only in the day time and we made camp where there was water. We passed through old Camp Walapai, crossed the Colorado River at Hardyville and thence crossed the Mojave Desert, camping at Marl Springs and Soda Lake. As we approached the latter, while still on the hills it looked like a vast sheet of water with trees on the far side and a group of very large buildings, but it was a mirage in which small bushes loomed up like trees and the low houses like castles. One of our camps was at old Camp Cady and one in Cajon Pass in which the hills on each side were covered with yerba santa.[44] We passed through San Berna[r]dino and Cucamonga Ranch. We slept in the open, without tents and ate our meals on the ground, without any of the conveniences that we had when crossing the country from Los [Las] Animas to Camp Verde. From Los Angeles to Wilmington we traveled by railroad and then by steamer to San Francisco.

William Henry Corbusier, from an ambrotype taken in 1860
Photo courtesy Pierson Kerig Collection

Mahala Myers Corbusier, from a daguerreotype taken in 1851
Mahala Myers Corbusier was the mother of William Henry Corbusier

Photo courtesy Pierson Kerig Collection

William Henry Corbusier
in 1869, age 25
Photo courtesy Corbusier
Family Collection

Fanny Dunbar Corbusier, April 1869,
after her marriage on March 22, 1869,
at "Dunbarton" in Amite, Louisiana
Photo courtesy Arizona Historical Society / Tucson

William Henry Corbusier, Assistant Surgeon, United States Army, July 1875

Photo courtesy Henry E. Huntington Library

Picnic outing at Fort Mackinac, Michigan, August 1884.
Dr. Corbusier (*top row, second from right*) and his sons
Harold (*middle row, far right*) and Claude (*front row, center*).

Photo courtesy Roy L. Goodale

Post hospital building at Fort Grant, Arizona, 1884–88

Photo by Colonel Anson Mills

Corbusier family on porch, 1885. *Mounted, left to right:* Harold D. Corbusier, Philip W. Corbusier, Francis A. Corbusier, William T. Corbusier, and Claude R. Corbusier. *Top, left to right:* Mrs. Fanny Dunbar Corbusier, Miss Ida Teed, and Dr. William Henry Corbusier.

Photo courtesy Arizona Historical Society / Tucson

William Henry Corbusier and family, Fort Wayne, Michigan, 1893.
Top, left to right: Harold Dunbar, William Tremaine, Philip Worthington.
Bottom, left to right: Francis Addison, Fanny Dunbar Corbusier,
William Henry Corbusier, Claude Romeyn.
Photo courtesy Arizona Historical Society / Tucson

William Henry Corbusier's quarters,
Zamboanga, Philippines, March 22, 1899.
"My bedroom, Jacobo in dining room,
olla in room beyond that."
Photo courtesy Arizona Historical Society / Tucson

Fanny Dunbar Corbusier, September 1899

Photo courtesy Arizona Historical Society / Tucson

Mike Burns
(Hoomothya), scout
at Fort Grant,
Arizona, about 1901
Photo courtesy Arizona
Historical Society / Tucson

William Henry Corbusier and Fanny Dunbar Corbusier
on ship bound for Manila, 1898

Photo courtesy Arizona Historical Society/Tucson

William Henry Corbusier with Harold's daughter,
Barbara Corbusier, Plainfield, New Jersey, July 20, 1909
Photo courtesy Corbusier Family Collection

On facing page, left to right: Major,
Medical Corps, Harold D.
Corbusier; Lieutenant Colonel,
Medical Corps, William H.
Corbusier; Captain, First Antiaircraft
Battery, Claude R. Corbusier;
July or August 1919
Photo courtesy Arizona Historical
Society/Tucson

William Henry Corbusier, Colonel, United States Army, Retired, November 1924

Photo courtesy Arizona Historical Society / Tucson

Yavapai Indians at church service, Sunday, October 30, 1921,
San Carlos Agency, Arizona

Photo courtesy Arizona Historical Society/Tucson

William Henry and Fanny Dunbar Corbusier's monument,
Arlington National Cemetery

Photo courtesy Judy Baber, Navy Recruiting District, Richmond, Virginia

CHAPTER SEVEN

The Old Army

We went out to South San Francisco where I engaged in the practice of my profession and I bought four vacant lots, which I held for many years and then sold for a very small advance, but not enough to pay taxes and a low rate of interest on the money invested.[1] Our son, Philip Worthington was born here on July 4, 1875. I saw very soon that the city would be slow in growing out that way and I was not contented, so, as the Medical Board was in session in New York, I did what I should have done months earlier. I went to New York and prepared for the examination.[2] The first time I reported to the Army Medical Board, one of the members was sick—about April 10, 1876—and to forget my disappointment, I went that night to Booth's Theatre where I saw the great cast in Julius Caesar—Edwin Booth, McCullough, Barrett, Ward, etc.[3] During my examination, some of the questions were about Caesar and I knew him well.[4] I have since then seen many stars in Shakespearian plays, as Adelaid [sic] Ristori, Fanny Janauschek, Medjeska, and visited Shakespeare's home.[5]

After I had passed the Board, I was given a contract May 1, 1876 which I held until August 5, 1876, on which day I was appointed First Lieutenant and Assistant Surgeon, U.S. Army.[6] I was Post Surgeon, Fort Macon, North Carolina, from May 9, '76, to April 29, '77, when the fort was abandoned. Our son Francis Addison was born here on March 15, 1877. We experienced a terrific storm during which the water from the ocean on the east and Bogue Sound on the west was driven to the very foundation of our quarters and we were cut off from the main land several days.[7] I was on duty at Charleston, South Carolina, from May 1 to June 7, '77. Post Surgeon Chattanooga, Tennessee, June 9 to July 24, '77. At the Quartermaster Depot, Jeffersonville, Indiana during the great railroad strike, July 25 to November 3, '77.[8]

¶Post Surgeon, Camp Sheridan, Nebraska, November 23, '77, to April 27, '80.[9] On Beaver Creek, a short distance above the Post, was the site of the old Brulé Agency, which had been removed north to the Rosebud. We witnessed a cloudburst which looked like a great copper scroll at the head of Beaver Creek and a torrent of water came down carrying everything before it so fast that the bridge over the creek couldn't be saved, although many men went with ropes to tie it fast. We had several heavy hail storms, one of which broke several hundred panes of window glass, and killed young chickens, the separate stones as large as turkey's eggs. Once the whole command had to be turned out to fight a prairie fire and burn a fire guard all around the post, except on the west side which was protected by the creek and a high bluff. Captain Emmet Crawford, Third Cavalry, and I went to the sand hills down on the Niobrara on several hunts and always returned with several black-tail deer, but on the second year, after the Brulé had been removed, there were deer nearer by.[10] He and I had fine vegetable gardens after we had lost our first by the flood. Pin-tail grouse were thick and we killed many, and kept some always hanging on the north side of our quarters.

After the Oglala Indians came from the Missouri River and settled down at the Pine Ridge Agency in charge of their Agent, Dr. [Valentine T.] McGillicudy [sic], I inspected their annuities and their cattle—those for stock and for slaughter—from November 25, 1877, to April 27, 1880, when probably for the first time they received all that was due them under the treaties that had been made.[11] The cattle that were intended for beef were penned over night and were weighed the next morning without watering them. They were then branded with cross arrows and issued to the head of each family, who, with his relatives simulated a buffalo hunt with the long horn Texas steer. The blankets, clothing, etc., went directly to those for whom they were intended. Among the prominent chiefs were Red Cloud, Mah-pi-ya-sha, American Horse—or Wasichuunka shunka—Young Man Afraid of his horses—or more accurately: Young man even his horses are feared—Ta-shun-kako-pi-ya.[12] I treated some of the Indians for disease and among them old Red Cloud, who had tape-worm which was quite common among them due to eating raw beef. I also treated the wounded Cheyenne prisoners, when they were on their way to the Pine-Ridge Agency in 1877, after the fighting at Chadron Creek and Fort Robinson.[13] I was able to learn much of interest about the Sioux and they gave me many pictures which they had painted depicting their religious beliefs and also gave me several Counts-Back, or Winter-Counts, which are pictographs which assist them in recalling the names of the years or winters, which they count backward. Mother, the boys and I saw one of their Sun-dances in which they do penance for favors received or requested.[14] We each of us ate a small piece of dog meat. The description of the dance and many pictures made by the dancers were lost in the San Francisco conflagration, April 18, 1906.

The telephone had come into use and I had one from my quarters to the hospital in 1877. I heard the first phonograph in 1880. The dictophone [sic] came later. [Louis] Pasteur made his wonderful experiments, and antiseptic surgery was practiced by [Joseph] Lister and other surgeons. The discovery of the dissemination of disease by insects and the identification of the many germs, led me to take a course in bacteriology at the University of Michigan later and still later I was in New York where I assisted in raising antidipht[h]eritic serum in a horse—the second to be used for the purpose—and watched the first cases of diphtherid [sic] treated with serum at the Willard Parker Hospital, New York. We were very comfortable at Sheridan and could send once and a while to the rail-road to bring butter, eggs, canned fresh oysters, etc.

I received orders to go to Fort Laramie and join two troops of the Third Cavalry to accompany them to Fort Washakie, Wyoming.[15] Going over to Fort Robinson in our own ambulance, we there changed to a larger and more comfortable one with six horses. The driver ran the front wheels up onto an embankment of the White River, after having crossed many times—eighteen or twenty—Frank was thrown into the water under the vehicle and I fell under a front wheel, the reins under me, which I grabbed and held as the six horses moved forward and dragged me out. Mother and our maid Louie hurriedly unfastened the heavy leather curtains and the driver underneath pushed them up with his shoulders, one hand under Frank's head holding it above the water.[16] We sat in the sun to dry off and I sent Louie bareback back to the post for assistance—about eighteen miles.[17] Colonel [Frederick] Van Vliet came out with the surgeon and some enlisted men.[18] We changed to their ambulance and drove on to our camping place to which I had sent the wagon carrying our baggage and camping outfit the day before. The next day we drove to Fort Laramie where I had a plaster cast put on my ankle which was badly bruised. The two troops of cavalry had left some days before I received the order, but it was thought that we might overtake them, so we were given transportation to Fort Fetterman.[19] At the latter we were given ambulance and wagon to Rock Creek and then went by rail to Green River. Here an ambulance, etc. met us to drive us to Fort Washakie where we arrived on June 2, 1880, having been snow bound on May 31 at old Fort Stambaugh for a day.[20]

I was Post Surgeon at Fort Washakie, Wyoming Territory, to November 9, 1881. I inspected and witnessed their issue to the Shoshones [sic] under their chief Washakie—Shoots the Buffalo Running—and the Arapahos under their chiefs Black Coal and William Friday in October 1880.[21] I also treated many of their sick and wounded. The Arapahos held a buffalo dance and I wished to get possession of a head-dress, etc., worn by one of their medicine men on that occasion, and who invited me to come and see it at his camp on the south side of Little Wind River about four miles below the post. Lieutenants Frank Cummings, Third [Cavalry] and Homer W. Wheeler, Fifth Cavalry, now—in 1923, a retired colonel and author of "The Frontier Trail," drove down there to the medicine man's tepee.[22] He invited us to take a sweat-bath with him so we left our clothes and went naked to a low structure about eight feet in diameter, formed of the branches of trees heavily covered with buffalo robes, the hairy side out, in front of which a squaw was heating a lot of stones, each of which was about four inches in diameter. The entrance faced the east and was so low that we had to stoop to get in. The medicine man motioned to the three of us to sit on the ground south of a shallow circular depression, and then seated himself cross-legged on the north side. After he had given each one of us a small piece of ginseng root and cut a piece off for himself, the squaw brought him the heated stones, one at a time, using two sticks to handle them, and the Indian formed a small pyramid about a foot high, with a base of about two feet, after which he began to sprinkle the stones with a white hair switch, dipping it into a vessel of water at his side. The squaw then dropped a robe over the opening, making the little hut almost air-tight, and the man in a guttaral [*sic*] groaning voice began to chant as he sprinkled more water on the stones. The confined air was soon filled with steam and ashes and we gasped for breath.

Cummings had told me that we must sit up as the Indian did to get the full benefit of the bath, but I felt him squat down and then rise up again, when he in a choked voice asked me if I was up, and then duck down again. I replied "Yes," and then also ducked and rested my nose and mouth close to the ground where the robes touched and I could breath[e] more freely, while the sweat rolled down our faces and off of our bodies and ashes gathered in our hair. This play was repeated several times, but we were in for a sweat-bath and we got it. I had taken many Turkish baths, but this was a novel experience and I wanted to hold out to the end. It seemed a long time before the Indian called to the squaw to raise the flap and asked if we wanted any more. Needless to say, we didn't, so he led us down to the river and we all plunged in. It was mid-winter—1880–81—but the water was tempered somewhat by the overflow from the hot spring about two miles higher up, and it had a grateful feeling after the steaming we had undergone. We were a sight for the women and children who looked on as we dodged back to the tepee to dress. The medicine Man and I were now purified and he was in condition to bring out the skin of an unborn calf which held the buffalo-dance outfit. He blew on his fingers and then took out of it the dried skin of a buffalo head which had the tips of black buffalo horns about four inches long fastened to it in place. There were also a belt, armlets and anklets made of thin strips of wood from a quarter to half an inch wide wrapped with thinner colored strips. I paid ten dollars for the bath and the undress costume. On our way back to the post we stopped at the hot spring near the river and about two and a half miles below the post, where we had left a change of clothes in our comfortable bath-house of two rooms at the west margin of the spring or pond, which must be at least two hundred feet across and in the middle of which the water boils up, but is not over 115° Fahrenheit, and on very cold days we could swim across. In the bath-house the water was about 110° Fahrenheit and we usually came here twice a week. This time we came to wash the ashes out of our hair and what was left of them on our bodies. The Indians bathed at the outlet where [it] was not above 100° Fahrenheit.

We witnessed the Sun-dance of the Shoshone Indians in 1881, near Fort Washakie a short distance north of the Little Wind River. The participants did not make incisions in the skin of their chests and tie themselves to the pole in the center of the arena and try to break loose, as we saw the Sioux do, but looked up at the sun and danced, each one blowing a whistle in time with their feet, until they fainted and saw visions, while fasting three days and three nights, not even drinking any water. After the dance, I procured the buffalo horn from which the dancers drank the first water after their fast, and which had been used many years. I also secured the figure of a man cut in wood about six inches long, which probably represented the Sun-God, that hung to the pole, some feathers worn by them and a strip of cotton cloth on which were painted the figure of a horse and one of a buffalo. My son William T. has the buffalo horn.

Fort Washakie was on the south side of the Little Wind River and about 180 miles from Green River, our railroad station from which we received our mail daily by buckboard by the way of South Pass and Miners' Delight and some times in winter over forty feet of snow, which had to be crossed at night when the snow was frozen. One morning in the winter of 1880–81, when the sun was far south, the air was filled with a snow-mist in which I saw four sun-dogs, one east and one west of the sun connected by a snow-bow over the sun, of spectrum colors, and opposite to these were two others, one of them northeast and the other northwest, also connected by a spectrum bow, and all four of them were in a horizontal circle of the spectrum colors. Two sun-dogs were frequently seen, one on each side of the sun and the Indians would say "The sun is warming his ears."

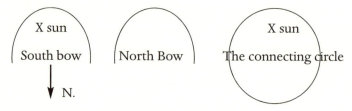

I hunted a great deal and one winter started to hunt buffalo, but our guide, an enlisted man who had come across the country, didn't know it when he went back, so led us up Poison Creek, the water of which was like epsome [sic] salts and there was only a very dwarf sagebrush for fuel. The salts had the usual effect, and we didn't feel like going on into a strange country, so I gave orders to harness up and start back. I rode to the top of a hill to look over the country and saw in the valley beyond a great herd of antelope. I killed one and dragged it back to camp and when the men saw me on the brow of the hill some of them came riding up and all ten of them were soon on the other side and it was not long before we had our two wagons loaded and we were on our way back to wood and water. In two days we were at the post with enough meat for the whole garrison. The thermometer had been 37° below zero, but Lieutenant George Morgan Third Cavalry and I had kept warm by sleeping together under buffalo robes and blankets.[23] During the warm weather, I went fishing over to Bull Lake, so-called because of the noise made by the water under the ice in winter. Salmon [and] trout were numerous in the lake and smaller trout in the outlet. We ate all we could and carried many back to the post.

Having been informed that I was to be relieved from duty at Washakie, I sent my family east early in October, 1881, before winter set in, and went with them one drive on their way to Rawlins on the railroad, to see that they were well started, but they were caught in the first snow of the season, which happened to be a light one. I followed in November and drove day and night in a stage to Green River, where I took a train and went to Elmira, New York, to visit my mother and join them. I was on leave of absence from November 27, 1881 to March 27, 1882, spending most of it in New York City, doing special work with men eminent in my profession in order to keep up with the great advances that were made in medicine and surgery, as Flint Sr., Stephen Smith, Bryant, Wyeth, Welch, Vaughn [sic] and others.[24]

¶My son William Tremaine, was born January 31, 1882, Washington Street, Elmira, New York.[25] On the expiration of my leave we went to Fort Mackinac, Michigan, where I was Post Surgeon from April 23, 1882, to September 30, 1884. We enjoyed the society of many of the people who spent the summer here and had pic nics, dances, drives, sails in sail boats and on the fine yachts fishing and berry parties. In winter we had skating and coasting. When the ice was too rough for fine skating, we used sails of various shapes to drive us. We had to lay in our supplies for winter and store them in our cellar which we boarded up and then entered it by a trap-door in the kitchen. About the middle of April, steamers began to run and we could get every thing we wished for our table from Detroit and the towns along the southern peninsula of Michigan. Fish we always had in abundance. All of our water was hauled by wagon. The people in the village hauled their water from the straits in barrels set on sleds which were drawn by dogs. All of their wood was also hauled by dogs, usually from Round Island across the straits. The inhabitants were a mixture of Indian, French, English and American, owing to the garrisons of different nationalities that had occupied the fort. The old blockhouses, built in 1780, were a source of interest to every one, and old buttons, French, English and American, were found by our boys and Frank found a spike which once topped the palisade which once surrounded the post. On the melting of the enormous quantity of snow early in April, the air was very damp and throat and lung troubles were frequent. Phil contracted pleurisy on his left side and the effusion was slow in being absorbed, so I requested to be ordered to Arizona. While at Mackinac, I practiced my profession among the summer visitors and in the village.[26] Many of the villagers kept opiates in their homes and some of them were addicted to their use. At least one mother caused the death of her babe by giving paregoric and taking it herself. She was what our boys called "Quarters," and she was of mixed blood.[27]

While on our way to Arizona, I received a telegram at Albuquerque to go to Fort Bowie, and I was there from October 23 to November 10, 1884 to replace the surgeon who had broken a thigh bone.[28] After I was relieved, we drove to Fort Grant, Arizona Territory where I was Post Surgeon, from November 10 '84 to October 23, 1888. Claude did not go with us, but went from Mackinac to the school at Lawrenceville, New Jersey, and after the Christmas holidays contracted the measles [and] lost some time, so I went for him.[29] In the mean time I was ordered into the field, May 19, '85 against hostile Chiricahua Indians under their chief Geronimo and on the third day out, while camped at the railroad station San Simon, I saw Claude when the west bound train stopped a few minutes. I was away from the post until June 19, and again from July 26 to August 1, '85, with a squadron of the Tenth U.S. Cavalry under command of Major Frederick Van Vliet.

¶I had been trying to get a teacher for our children and at length occurred the services of Miss Ida Teed, who came to us from San Jose, California, in October 1885 and was with us until July, 1887, when Mr. William Cairns, a student at the University of Wisconsin, took her place.[30] The boys led an ideal life here, and when not in school or at their studies were on their burros, frequently camping out and cooking their own meals near the post or in the Graham mountains. Week ends were spent in camp, their mother and teacher with them, and I, when I could get away. Once when at an elevation of about 9000 ft. above the sea level in the mountains east of the post, we saw below us a thunder storm, while overhead the sky was perfectly clear. When Colonel Anson Mills, Tenth Cavalry assumed command, he let me have men to build a log house near a small clear stream of cold water.[31] At one time there were at least forty-five men, women and children up there in the bracing air. At the very summit of Graham mountain, Phil while sitting and scraping up some very small pieces of broken pottery, saw a piece imbedded in the ground and on scraping around it took out a piece of pottery in the shape of a turtle a little over four inches in diameter and nearly an inch thick, having a hole on the under side leading to a hollow interior. Along the creek below the post there were many stones in quadrangles of about six or eight feet in one layer as if they had been the foundation of a hut, and not far away was a mound which the boys and I measured and then cut a trench across down to the level of the surrounding ground and took out many stone implements making diagrams as we worked. Afterward Claude, when he graduated at the Hays City, Kansas, High School, May 23, 1889, wrote a description of this mound in his graduating essay "The Mound Builders." We collected at least a wagon load of stone implements while at the post and many pieces of pottery, from which could have been almost restored the complete vessels, but nearly the whole collection was lost in the great San Francisco fire.

¶Miss Teed taught the boys to read music, which gave them a good start when they took up instrumental music. She also taught them drawing. We had weekly hops during the cool weather and the young ladies visiting relatives or friends taught them to dance. The boys became expert in the use of bean shooters and air-guns and then I taught them how to handle firearms. After Claude became a pretty good shot with a shot-gun, I let him have a rifle and go hunting with Montgomery, who had been an enlisted man and now made a living by hunting, and who consented to show him how to get a deer. Claude returned in three or four days with his first deer. Not long afterward, snow on the mountains drove the game down and I roused him from his bed quite early and pointed to a grove of oaks in which I was sure there were deer. I told him to go on foot and look sharp. After breakfast the other boys began to watch for him and it wasn't long before they saw him on a bowld [burro] waving his hat. They jumped on their burros at once, saying "He has one." It was only a mile or so to the trees where he had shot a fine fat buck. We were all sorry to leave Grant. We had been there so long that the boys looked upon it as home.

We went to Fort Hays, Kansas, where I was Post Surgeon from October 29, '88 to November 12 '89.[32] Hays City, about three-quarters of a mile and north of Big Creek, once a frontier town and during the building of the railroad the rendezvous of tough gun-men, was now populated by law abiding people, with churches and a fine school, and only "boot hill" to remind them of its one-time reputation.[33] The surrounding low hills were bare of trees, except a few patches that had been recently planted. I had a very good practice here, mostly a consulting one, and patients came from east and west along the railroad. The boys all did well in the school and Claude graduated from the high school. Harold drew maps that were placed on exhibition and Phil and Frank had lessons on the violin. They all had drawing and vocal music, singing by note. The post had outlasted its usefulness and was abandoned, and as the troops left, taps were sounded and we sorrowfully left.

Our next station was Fort Lewis, Colorado, from November 15, '89 to April 9, '90.[34] Claude was left behind to enter the University of Kansas. The other boys attended the Post School the teacher of which was a drunken Roman Catholic priest who didn't last long in the army. Harold and I once went down the mountains west where I had a patient, and returning were caught in a heavy snow storm. There were no houses so we kept on, Hal in front most of the times with a lantern picking out the road. In places the wheel of our buckboard sank down to mud, which caught between the spokes of the wheels and made our ascent of the mountain very slow, so we didn't reach the post until about seven o'clock the next morning, just in time to keep a rescuing party of cavalry to go after us as Little Mother told Major [Tullius] Tupper that I had said I would be back in time for sick call and I had never failed.[35] Hal was pretty tired as he had waded through many miles of snow. We were fortunate in having two strong horses which never wavered. The total distance was about thirty miles, but we were well on the road before the snow began to fall.

Influenza became epidemic in January, 1890, the first cases occurring at the east end of the line of officers' quarters on the fifth and I treated about 120 cases. I had approved of a month's leave for my assistant as he was very restless and seemed home sick, but he was allowed to go to another post, although I had expected him back. I had a mild attack, but didn't have any time to rest. When the epidemic came to an end, I found that I was losing my strength and at length became so weak that I had to remain in my bed, but I kept on prescribing for the sick in hospital and quarters, not realizing my condition until I could scarcely raise my head and thinking about the cases [was] no longer possible. Little Mother then went to Major Tupper and told him that I could no longer go on with my work, so he telegraphed for another surgeon. But there were twenty feet of snow on the railroad and no trains could get through. Assistant Surgeon [Carter N. B.] Macauley at length arrived at the post, having to go around the Mountains and come from the west.[36] Early in April Major [Henry M.] Cronkhite whom I had relieved at Hays, came, and on the 10th I was started for Fort Leavenworth, Kansas under the care of Dr. Macauley, on a spring bed placed in an ambulance to go down about 2000 feet to Durango twelve miles, our railroad station.[37] Early the next morning I was placed in the division Superintendent's car, who happened to be there, and had a comfortable bed through to Leavenworth. My family stopped at Lawrence, Kansas, where Claude was, and remained there until I was assigned to duty at Detroit, Michigan. I left the hospital at Fort Leavenworth, on July 7 '90, and went to Fort Wayne, Detroit, Michigan, where I remained to July 21, when I was given a sick leave to November 21, '90, which I spent with my mother at her home and in Newport with my uncle John Myers and, after that with my cousin Alice Whitson in New York.[38] My family remained at Fort Wayne, except Claude who transferred from the University of Kansas to the University of Michigan.

I was on duty at Fort Wayne from November 21, '90 to July 18, '95 except a month at Mackinac in 1891 with the Nineteenth Infantry for target practice and a few days at Whitmore Lake, Michigan, with the Michigan State Troops, and except June and July, '92, again at Mackinac with the Nineteenth Infantry.[39] My family spent some time at Mackinac after I left in the tent I left for them in the government field. May Addison was with them, as she had come from Amite to attend school, taking the place of her sister Maud who had been with us for about a year for the same purpose. I marched with the Nineteenth Infantry from Fort Wayne to Island Lake, Michigan, August 15 to 17, '92, for duty there from August

18–23 as Instructor and Inspector of the Medical Department and Hospital Corps of Michigan State Troops. I was also at Columbus Barracks, April 4 to June 3, '93.[40]

I was ordered to Fort Supply, Oklahoma Territory, and was Post Surgeon there from July 23, '93 to September 17, '94.[41] My family went to Ann Arbor where Harold entered the University of Michigan. In September 1893, I drove to Woodward, on the railroad about thirteen miles, to witness the arrival of the people from the border to locate land and town lots on the opening of the Cherokee strip.[42] I saw the first man as he appeared on the distant hill top and watched him approach and jump from his horse and drive a stake on 160 acres of land near the station. Others soon followed him, some on horses and others in buggies and other wheeled vehicles. They located town lots, as they supposed, on his claim, but the town site was a mile south along the Railroad, which the train from the south reached at about one o'clock, and the passengers rushed to locate town lots. Wagons and horses were unloaded from the train, followed by lumber which was hauled to the lots and work on buildings was begun. I was there three or four days afterward and stores were doing business, restaurants were furnishing meals, a newspaper was in press and the town had extended its limits and was approaching the town at Woodward station. Many people, when they went to record their land, learned that their claims were miles away from the town, having had no maps or other means of knowing what section they had located on. Men who [were] supposed to be on a lot in the town, were in the middle of a street or possibly on a school lot. I was an important witness in the suit respecting the claim of Frank Morgan, the first to arrive, and my testimony probably gave him the land on which I saw him drive the stake. The thermometer was running up to 110° Fahrenheit, when my relief came. He was Major Curtis E. Price, whom I first knew when he was the surgeon of the Twelfth Tennessee Cavalry during the War of the Rebellion.[43]

I went to Ann Arbor on the month's leave and spent it with my family while I worked in the Bacteriological Laboratory of the University under Vaughn and took the full course. After that, I went to New York City as Attending Surgeon and Examiner of Recruits from October 20, '94 to October 22, '95, and was also in charge of the Medical Supply Depot, July 22 to September 17, '95. Promoted to Major and Surgeon, October 17, '95 I took many special courses to prepare myself for surgical work, and continued the bacteriological work I had done in the University of Michigan, helping to raise anti-diphtheritic serum in a horse, the second one used for that purpose, and saw the serum tried in the Willard Hospital, so successfully, that those who were skeptical as to its effects had to admit that it was saving many lives. I had seen an epidemic of diphtheria while I was at Fort Washakie and had lost two children in an officer[']s family, so had taken up the study of the disease. I attended one of the Old Guard's ball[s] at Madison Square Garden and General Nelson A. Miles and I led the grand march.[44] The applause of thousands of people made me feel that I was a performer in a circus and I seemed out of my sphere.

From New York I went to Fort Monroe and was on duty there from November 12, '95 to October 12, '97 and Little Mother and Will joined me there.[45] Claude had left college and was with Parke, Davis & Co.[46] The other three boys remained at school in Ann Arbor but spent their summer vacations with us. I had a very good practice among the visitors at the hotels, from the north in winter and the south in summer. Old Point Comfort and the Hygeia Hotel were very popular, and our boys had many young people to associate with, and they could dance and swim to their heart's desire. Phil met Ida May Edwards who afterward became his wife. It was too good a station for me to hold long and I was ordered to Angel Island, California, where I was Surgeon from October 18, 1897 to May 17, '98.[47] Will went with us and Phil and Frank joined us to enter the Stanford University, Hal remaining at Ann Arbor to continue his studies. We were well satisfied as Phil and Frank could spend the week ends with us and Will went daily to the Polytechnic High School in San Francisco by the steamer *McDowell* which made several trips a day. The Golden Gate was directly in front of us and we had very little fog.

THE PHILIPPINES

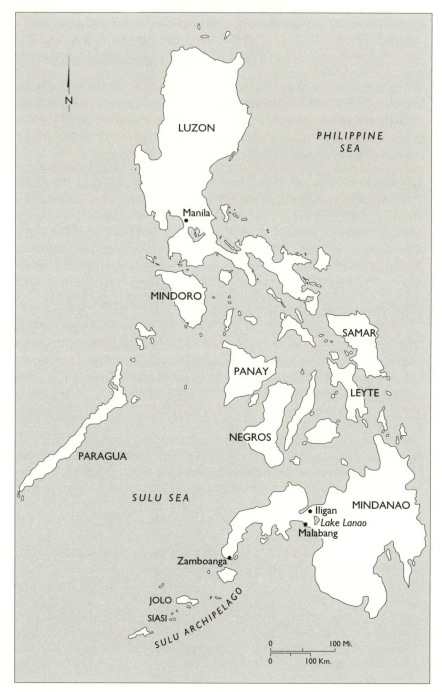

CHAPTER EIGHT

ᏌᎧᏄᎧᏄᏄ

First Tour in the Philippines

W e had hoped that the two at Stanford would complete their college course there, but the war with Spain was forced upon the country and I consented that Frank might enlist in Company K, First Regiment, National Guard of California, May 4, 1898, anticipating the President's call for volunteers, and he and 31 other Stanford students were mustered into the service of the U.S. in San Francisco at 2 p.m., Friday, May 6, 1898, and they left for the Philippines on May 25, on the Steamer *City of Peking*.[1] Philip enlisted in Troop C, Fourth Cavalry, U.S. Army, 9 a.m., May 6, 1898, at the Presidio of San Francisco, and embarked on the steamer *Peru* and left July 15.[2]

¶I was made Acting Medical Purveyor of the Expedition to the Philippines, later called the Department of the Pacific and the Eighth Army Corps, May 17, 1898 and held that position until April 30, 1900. The medical Supply depot had on hand supplies for about 2500 troops and I had to secure supplies for nearly 60,000. The merchants could furnish me with what I needed for only one fleet at a time—two or three transports—and every thing had to come from the east, so it was not until August that I could get together [enough supplies to be] four months ahead to take when I left for the Islands. At first there were no hospitals on the transports, but I gave each one an outfit for one. The bunks of iron piping in tiers were not long enough for the California Volunteers, and I recommended longer ones, among other things. When I went to see them off, they were without salt-water soap and I had some rushed down to them.

We and Frank's friends furnished him with many extra articles of diet, which he did not receive, but he saw the boxes which had contained them and bore his name, thrown overboard from the officers' part of the ship. I met every regiment that arrived in San Francisco and told the surgeons to vaccinate their men at once and where to get the vaccine virus. Some neglected to carry out the instructions and, in consequence, there were small pox cases among them in the Philippines. Very few of them wanted to be responsible for any surgical instruments and appliances so applied to the Red Cross Society for them.[3]

I assisted in organizing the City and State Red Cross Societies and became their adviser. There were many attempts, some successful, to get supplies by people who appropriated them to their own use, until I had requests made in writing and sent to me to approve. The first recommendation I made was to furnish each soldier with an aluminum identification badge the size of a silver half dollar bearing his name and organization, to be suspended by a cord around his neck. It was some years afterward before, on my recommendation, the badge was ordered for the whole army.[4] For a time it looked to me as if nearly every one wanted to go to the Islands, having some scheme to make money, and they were referred to me, men and women and some of them managed in some way to get there, and one young fellow applied to me after I had arrived there for a position as clerk who knew nothing about paper work and said he only wanted to stay until he could look around and find something to do after he had learned how. He was one of many such. I was one of the very few officers who approved of taking trained women nurses to the Islands, and the first to accompany our army out of the country, went in my charge, in spite of the attempts made to prevent them from going. It was after this that the Army Nurse Corps was organized.[5]

Having secured all supplies that I was permitted to take with me, I embarked August 20, 1898, on the U.S. Troop steamer *Arizona* and left San Francisco, California, 11.50 a.m., Sunday, August 21; arrived at Honolulu, Hawaiian Islands, 9.20 p.m., August 27.[6] Brigadier Generals Henry Merriam and Charles King, whom I had not seen since we were in Arizona in 1875 and met again on the *Arizona*, remained here.[7] There were orders for the *Arizona* to await the arrival of the *Scandia* and the delay until 5.00 p.m., Sunday, September 11, was a grateful rest for me.[8] I met Mr. John K. M. L. Farquahar who was in the seed and plant business in

Boston, Massachusetts, and he and I visited every place of interest and took many photos in and around Honolulu. We attended a reception at the home of the ex-queen Liliuakalani [*sic*] and saw the native women still wearing their mother hubbard dresses and straw hats with a brim edged with lace and lace around their necks.⁹ We went as far as we could by rail and stepped to get out and walk on the musical sands. It was like walking over frozen snow. On leaving, I occupied the best room as I was then the highest in rank. By the time we arrived at Manila, I was in fine shape for hard work and I had it a plenty. We arrived 3.30 a.m., Wednesday, September 28, 1898.

On crossing the 180° meridian to or from the Philippines, on the date line, we lost a day or part of a day going and gained one returning, so that going westward Sunday would become Monday, and going eastward two days having the same date, or, when the change was made at noon, we would have the half of two days.

I had some difficulty in finding suitable buildings for my supplies, so took possession of the Arroceros, the grounds and buildings formerly occupied by the Spanish Engineers, and here I established the Medical Supply Depot on the Pasig River, between it and Calle Conception [Concepción], [and] used the School of Arts as one of my storerooms near by. My grounds were a jungle, and it took nearly three months to cut out the tropical growth in which there was enough bamboo to nearly enclose the Botanical Garden. And enough monkeys to furnish the laboratory with them for research work for at least a year. I took for my office and quarters the stone building formerly occupied by the Spanish Colonel of Engineers, and the three other long building[s] as storehouses. They were all very damp until I had the growth cut out to let in the sun and get rid of the mosquitoes. When the Pasig rose, after a downfall of some seven inches of rain, the roadway out to the street was a foot under water, and I waded through to the Red Cross Hospital, where I spent the night with Frank who lay very low with typhoid fever. I had found him, when I arrived, at the Quartel Fortin on the river, in the same room with Sergeant Chester Thomas, next to the bath rooms, the waste water from which ran under the floors and was retained by the solid stone wall of the foundation of the building. The surgeons of the First California Volunteers seemed to have no knowledge of sanitary matters, and permitted the men to occupy the Quartel. At length holes were broken in the walls to let out the filth.

I left some of the bamboo clumps along my drive way, a few hardwood trees and some bananas. A young python—a house snake—about twelve feet long, lived in the bamboo and frequented the space under the roof of my quarters, where I often heard it or the young monkeys and rats in their death struggles. Bats were numerous and my exercise was at night, when in my pajamas, to knock down a few of them with a long strip of bamboo about an inch and a half broad. My furniture was of bamboo, and at night it would draw up and move on the floor, so that when the insurrection broke out, my sleep was at first very much disturbed by the bats against the walls, large roaches against the floor, and the bamboo on the floor and outside producing all sorts of noises rubbing together, and the wind blowing over the open broken or cut ends forming sort of pan pipes. One night I thought I heard the trotting of a troop of cavalry and on opening a window, found it was bamboo. The sentinals [sic] out in the bosquis [sic] in the night heard these sounds, and the strain was so great that in places they had to be doubled, as they heard what might be an insurrecto creeping up to make a spring and cut them.

My quarters were of two stories and I drove under the house to enter by a broad stairway about midway, along which were potted plants. The lower story on the right had rooms for servants the floors of which were about two feet above the ground and the ceiling about eight feet high. On the other side were the stable and carriage house, above which [were] the kitchen, pantry, diningroom and toilet. The grounds in front were laid out in beds which were filled with flowers, among them the san piguete, a small white flower much admired by the natives who, with my consent, came to cut on feast days. The windows of my bedroom had sliding shell sashes which, when closed, admitted but little light. Inside of them were sliding blinds made of strips of wood two inches or so broad and having an upright notched piece with which to open them. I looked out on my issuing storeroom and the landing place of the cascos—huge canoes cut out of huge trees, which brought my supplies from the transports which anchored out in the harbor. The cascos were covered with woven bamboo movable roofs to keep the cargoes dry. A huge tamarind tree was within reach and I could gather the large pods with ease. I had a guard of nine soldiers, and a sentinel watched the river at a slough which was a backwater and extended nearly a hundred yards into my grounds, as any one could creep along the river bank when the tide was

low [and] could cross the slough and get to my quarters, office and issuing storeroom.

I usually had one hundred Chinese coolies at work. They lived mostly on rice and it took four or five of them to handle a box that two white men could pick up, but those who worked inside were paid more, and on a peso a day were able to buy meat which gave them strength to lift the heavier boxes. I had great difficulty in keeping soldiers, as the hours were long and, when the troops left the city and went into the country, the rail-road train that carried them supplies left about seven o'clock in the morn-ing, and telegraph requisitions would come in at night, and we had to work until midnight to send the articles called for by that train. After the troops left the main roads, I had to send a man with each lot, to go by train, casco, canoe, and caribea cart until he delivered it.

One morning, when I made my usual visit to my storeroom in the School of Arts, I found nearly all of the glass globes that belonged to the lamps, which I had placed on tables pushed out of my way, broken on the floor as if someone had been rolling them[.] Cotton for surgical dressings had been torn out of some of the bails [sic] and scattered about. The dam-age had evidently been done by monkeys, several of which were in the building, so, after driving them out, I closed the ventilators. White ants riddled the large packages of blotting paper, and boxes that bore stencil marks resting on the tiled floor, were beautifully etched by them. Corks of some of the bottles, even those that contained carbolic acid, were eaten down to their corks. I had to have the beautiful floors of narra and a wood resembling black walnut, polished with coal oil to keep those insects from eating away the ends. Shasta water was nicely cut on the boxes that contained the water. The covers of books had to be gone over with a solu-tion of corrosive sublimate, especially the red covers. On account of the very damp air, all instruments had to be covered with vaseline and par-rafine [sic] and kept in dry chests.

Three clerks, who had passed the Civil Service examination, were sent to me and I found them incompetent to type-write letters, make out invoices, receipts, return of prop[e]rty or any other kind of clerical work, so I had to continue to teach enlisted men to make out my papers. I was offered an assistant, but it would require more time to teach him than to do the work myself. The work became so great, that I requested the Chief Surgeon to let me issue expendable articles and use the requisitions as both invoice and receipt, which he did. As the Army extended its territory, I established sub-depots, with six months['] supply, in various parts of the Islands, and the work gradually became easier. Not long afterward, I was relieved by Major Merrit [*sic*] W. Ireland.[10]

Before leaving San Francisco, I had purchased an ice plant and had a dozen enlisted men go to the Vulcan Iron Works to see it erected and knocked down, so as to be able to erect it in the Islands. It was sent to Cavite, and I went over there to learn why it was not producing the amount of ice that it should. I learned that the civilian engineer in charge wanted to have it condemned so that he might buy it in himself, but he didn't get it. I had another one erected in Manila, but until it was completed, the hospitals had to get their ice from the San Miguel Brewery, which suddenly ran out of ammonia and I was the only one in the Islands who had any. As the hospitals had to have ice, I loaned the brewery the ammonia to tide it over until it could receive another supply. I also loaned some to the Quartermaster for us on a transport, as its supply had run out.

During the fight at Caloocan and other engagements near Manila, I drove out with supplies of dressings.[11] The first wounded men were brought in from the front by rail. Only one hospital Corps man was on the train, and no transportation from the First Reserve Hospital met them. On that day—March 24, 1899—after the fighting at Malabon, etc., I happened to be at the terminus of the road at the river getting transportation for Frank to return by transport which was to leave the next day, when I heard that the men needed looking after. I sent Frank in my Quilez with a message to my hospital Steward who was my chief clerk, Radetsky, to send me fifty cots and the same number of mattresses and blankets to replace the little green grass which lay on the floor of the small box cars, and all that the wounded had to rest upon. I assumed charge of the wounded as no provision had been made for their care and no one else seemed to have had any war-time experience. I had beef tea made in a house near by and redressed the men badly in need. I then went and borrowed a steam launch and a large flat boat which I filled with the wounded and started them up the river to the hospital. By the time that the ambulances arrived, there were only a few men left to be cared for. Frank, although in a very poor physical condition, was of very great assistance in this emergency.[12]

My supplies ran pretty low and I had to purchase in Manila many articles, but as I knew that those I brought with me would last only about four months, I had made a requisition for every thing that I might need as soon as I arrived in Manila. It seemed to be an immense one, as nine tons of subgallate and subnitrate of bismuth were among the articles I asked for. Only about half were sent to me and were mostly lost on the *Morgan City* in the Japan Sea.[13] But at length I received all, as the President directed that the soldiers in the Philippines should receive everything that they needed. I told the merchants in Manila from whom I had been making purchase[s] that I would probably require very little from them in the future, but advised them to lay in a good stock of bismuth and quinine. One of them cabled, and, when I heard of the loss of the transport I went to Zobell and Co. to learn whether they had any advice respecting these very necessary drugs, and heard that the ship with them then lay in the harbor, so I didn't run short of anything, much to my great relief.

The American Soldier for the first time wore pajamas, as I had thousands of them made, many of them falling into the hands of the insurrectos when they broke out, or rather were in their hands, as many of them were sewing on them when they left for the bosques and the contractors['] pajamas helped to clad the Filipino army.[14] At one time I not only had many of them on hand, as well as thousands of sheets, pillow cases, pillows, slippers, etc. on hand, when a woman tourist wrote home that all of these articles were badly needed by the hospitals. Some of the Army women heard about what the woman had said, so came together to sew. Two of them came to me to learn where they could buy outing flannel. There was none in Manila, as the contractor had bought all. I invited them to accompany me to one of my storehouses and there I pointed to a great pile of pajamas and tier upon tier of the other articles. The sewing-circle disbanded. I expected to hear further of the matter, so made a memorandum of what I had on hand, and was able to so state when a letter came from the Surgeon general telling about what the woman had reported. Based on her letter, an appeal was made for the soldiers in the Philippines to the Congress of the Daughters of the American Revolution, then in session in Washington. Then Mrs. [Charles H.] Alden, the wife of Colonel Alden, read the endorsement I had made on the letter I had received from the Surgeon General giving the number of the articles in question that I had on hand after furnishing the hospitals all that they required, when the appeal fell flat.[15] The only articles which at any time were short, were dishes for the table. I had supplied them with good white enamel ware, and I saw some men drinking from tin cans that had been emptied of their contents, and, on inquiry, the Surgeon in charge told me that many of them had disappeared and the men, when returned to duty, must have carried them away, so I gave the hospitals china ware, which the men might break, but wouldn't carry away.

I had to scan my money accounts very closely, as I hadn't a clerk competent to make them out properly, and when I left, for home, there were about eighty mistakes on my abstracts of property, and I was about six months correcting them. The cots, etc., that I sent to the front, I never saw again, but was relieved from responsibility by a board of survey, whose proceedings were approved by the Surgeon General, as it was an emergency that had to be met. One night, after a hard day's work, I heard some one cussing in my issuing storeroom, and I learned that a special requisition had been received by telegraph and it was the cause. It asked for a sheet of blotting paper and one or two similar articles to be sent in haste.

I messed by myself, so that I could have Phil and Frank visit me an[d] I could have the food I wished and cooked to my taste. At first I had two Tagales [Tagalogs], but my cook said there wasn't enough work for two, so I let the house boy go and kept Jacobo who lived in some rooms at the near end of one of my storerooms with his old uncle who had been a watchman under the Spaniards and for whom I secured a job as a foreman of a street gang.[16] Jacobo's wife and a negrita did my washing, as they didn't beat the clothes to pieces on stones, as most of the lavenderas [lavanderas] did, hung them on a line to dry and ironed them on a clean shoot. I could buy fish, chickens, eggs, etc., at the markets. Beef was for sale in pieces laid out on tables upon which women and children sat, while the vendors frequently turned them over, so I bought none of it. There were snipe, small doves and occasionally venison from the small deer. After the insurrectos had been driven from the city, chickens and eggs were rarely to be found, and I ate duck eggs brought from Hong Kong. I had the many Filipino vegetables, and, when I couldn't get potatoes, ate the boiled roots of the lotus which were plentiful. The meat of the kid is the favorite of the Filipino, and I had it frequently. Water from the Pasig River was piped into the house and I had a huge bathtub of tiles down stairs and twice I killed a snake in it. I had a filter of charcoal and gravel, which I cleaned once a month, and, after filtering the river water, I boiled it, let it cool in a large olla, put it in quart bottles and then set them in my ice chest which I took the precaution to bring with me. I scalded the olla out once in awhile with a boiling solution of permanganate of potassa. There was disease in the food, water and the clothes returned by the lavenderas, so I had to take every precaution to prevent contagion.

The horses I had were stallions about twelve or twelve hands and a half high, and my cochero was a Tagalo[g] who knew only a few Spanish words. I usually drove in a quilez, a two-wheel covered vehicle, having seats for two people on each side and drawn by one horse, and sometimes in a carromette, which has two high wheels and [a] seat for two persons facing forward, with the driver in front. There was also a calesa, a very light vehicle, and I once saw two heavy Americans who entered one, go over backward as the pony was raised in the air by their weight, and, as they rolled out, the pony suddenly dropped to terra firma. I changed horse[s] in the afternoon, unless I drove out in the country and then I took two. They were at first fed on palay (unhulled rice), green grass and molasses or sugar and water. One would take [a] mouthful of rice, poke his mouth into the sweetened water to wet the rice and then chew it. They were subject to colic until the quartermaster began to feed them on the forage used for [our] own horses at home.

The Filipinos were some time preparing to break out, and several times had set the day and changed it, but at last Steward Radetsky told me that he had heard that the day had come, and when I heard the church bells ringing unusual calls and at night saw an unusual light in a church steeple, I strongly suspected they were signals. Sure enough, the next afternoon about dusk February 4, 1899, I heard shots and many bullets fell on the corrugated roof of my issuing storeroom. I went to the Bridge of Spain and there were guards already on patrol duty. My men came from the Tondo district and took quarters on my grounds, and not long afterward the nipa huts in Tondo were all destroyed.[17]

My son Philip came to Manila to undergo his examination for a commission and he was with me on Christmas day in 1899, when I took him and Douglas Potts, who had enlisted when Phil did in San Francisco, to turkey dinner on the *Escolta*.

In May, 1900, I took a trip to Mindanao on the steamer *Uranus* of the Compañía Marítima of which the master was a Biscayan [Bisayan]. He took me to the ship on his launch and told me to order whatever I wanted.

I couldn't move without having a Filipino boy jump to wait on me. We had our meals on the huge transome [*sic*], the master at the head, the first mate on his left and I on his right. Along the sides were a captain of volunteers, several Spaniards, a hospital corps man, two young educated Chinamen, and several meztizoes [*sic*] and lastly several Filipinos. We had four meals a day, coffee and sweet cakes first, then breakfast, tiffin and dinner. Five large plates and two smaller ones were placed for each one. Soup was served and one plate removed, fish came next, followed by beef or kid, then a stew of vegetables and various kinds of meats and even fish and after that prawns or other sea food. The small plates were for a dulce—pudding or cake and fruit. Various kinds of fruits were hanging handy to eat between meals. Thick chocolate was often served instead of coffee after dinner.

At Ilollo I visited some of the factories in which piña was woven—a fabric made of fibre from the pineapple. The people here speak a different language from the Tagalo[g]s—i. e., Visayan.[18] There were many natives in water up to their waists fishing with cast-nets. We were to replenish our supply of ice here, but salt water had been used in the boilers of the ice-plant and the tubes were filled with salt, so that the machine was out of commission. I lay in a good supply of green coconuts to have the water in them to drink. Later at Tacloban I bought more, paying three centavo for each—one cent and a half of American money. Number one—the head waiter—said I had been cheated and he would supply me in the future. After cutting away the end of the husk with a bolo, the small blade of a penknife could be used to cut into the shell which was lined with a thin layer of a jelly-like substance and held the water before it was converted into a milk. It quenched one[']s thirst as well as plain water.

There was considerable coal to unload at Tacloban and natives were engaged for the week. They demanded some pay in advance and receiving it, left to get drunk on tuba, which is the sap from the fruit branch of the cocoanut [*sic*] tree which is cut and a bamboo tube about four inches in diameter and twelve or fourteen inches deep, is fastened to it to catch the sap during the night. When fresh, it is a very pleasant beverage, but after it ferments is mildly intoxicating and in larger portions makes the drinker stupid and sleepy. After sleeping off the effects of the tuba, the men returned to carry off the coal. A native woman in an American costume, shoes, parasol and all, happened to pass them and the fellows jeered at her, but she was happy, as she was the only one out in the latest style. That night we went over to the house of a Biscayan by the name of Rodrigues for a dance. The women appeared in shoes, to which they were unaccustomed, and, when they tried to waltz with us, failed. I then suggested to Rodrigues that they put on their chineles [chinelas]—slippers with only a toe piece—and dance their own steps. The old polka redowa was the first and then the versouovienne [*sic*] which we knew, and afterward some of the Spanish dances.[19]

During some of our stops, I could see down deep through the clear, smooth water great patches of coral of everlasting colors, forming sea gardens of great colored flowers, above which were schools of fish, and while sailing, we would come across spanish mackarel [*sic*] [that] rose many feet out of the water, and there were fish that would come up and at an angle of about forty-five degrees skull [*sic*] along on the surface, using their tails to propel them. The *Uranus* took on abaca—Manila hemp—which is taken from the midrib of a plant that resembles the banana and of which we saw many plantations and the process of converting it into hemp. Most of it was brought on board in bundles and when the hull of the ship was full, it was stored on deck. Between two large islands we saw raps [rips]—water agitated by the meeting of the tides. We saw many old forts on prominent points as we sailed along. There was very little rain at this season, so we could sit under the awning on deck and sleep on a cot, of course under a mosquito bar.

I embarked for the U.S. at Manila, on the U.S. Transport *Hancock*, formerly the *Arizona*, on June 15, 1900, and after a typhoon, sailed at 2.30 p.m., Tuesday June 19. On the twenty-first of June I stood by the master of the ship while he was making his noon observation of the sun. Eight bells struck as he said to me, "We are on the Tropic of Cancer," and I reminded him that it was the 21st of June. There we were without a shadow. We stopped at Nagasaki for coal and were there from June 23 to the 26th, so I had time to go aways into the country. It was about sunset when the transport anchored and another officer and I took the first sanpan [*sic*] that came out. As we landed, a Jap met us and said, "Me speak Englis[h], you want rickshaw" and we did. I told him to take us to a theatre, and after hauling us, each in a light two large-wheeled buggy of one seat, through many very narrow streets, stopped at a one-story house, having a narrow gallery in front onto which we stepped. We there took off our shoes and put on slippers which were furnished us. Then we entered a room per- haps fourteen feet square, in the middle of which was a table a foot or so high, having cushions on the floor around it, upon which we seated our- selves. Cigarrettes [sic] and cigars were brought in and a small dish hold- ing sand on which were small pieces of burning charcoal. In a short time five geishas—accomplished ones—with samisens and other instruments, came in and danced, or rather posed for us, as they moved their feet very little, and waved around and above their heads to form clouds, water-falls, etc., strips of some white fabrick [sic] a foot or so wide and eight or ten feet long. Afterward they put on false faces resembling cupid and heavily whiskered men and gave us some of their ancient dances or acting. We learned afterward that we had the best in the city. I had been told by a naval officer where to buy something I wanted and not be cheated, as the shop-keepers were as a rule not to be trusted, so the beautifully carved turtle shell combs, the satsuma and other articles I bought were genuine.

After we left Nagasaki, we had a kimono party at which we wore our handsomest. Number One, who was a Chinaman, dressed our heads. I suggested a Court of Love to try one of the fourteen young surgeons, on their way home, for breaking the heart of a bud from weeping Kansas, aged thirty years or thereabouts. Neptune ordered the court which was composed of men and women. Cupid, a boy about six years old, was the president and a naval officer was the judge advocate who asked the wit- nesses, and especially the accused and the maiden, the most absurd ques- tions in order to create laughter. When asked her age, she replied that she was old enough to vote, and X-ray found her heart twisted a little, but not broken. The doctor was found guilty of trifling with the young thing[']s affection and ordered to treat the Court to champagne, or, if there was none on board, then to beer.

We were at Honolulu to coal and the Royal Hawaiian Band, Prince Cupid—Jonah Kuhio Kalanianaole—one of its members, entertained us and played most, if not all of their native music, using some of their native instruments.[20] At night there was a hulu hula [sic] dance outside the city limits, as it was not allowed inside, and a party was made up to see it. Men beat long narrow drums with their fingers and hands, while half a dozen women in kilts, apparently made of grass or bast, nude above and below, made various gestures and motions at the hips, stamped their feet, keeping time with the drums and singing of the men. No admittance was charged, but we were told to throw silver money on the floor, which we did. After the dance, gin was offered us which we declined, but the performers were drinking pretty freely when we left, and had gin enough for a big carousal.

WILLIAM HENRY CORBUSIER'S MINDANAO

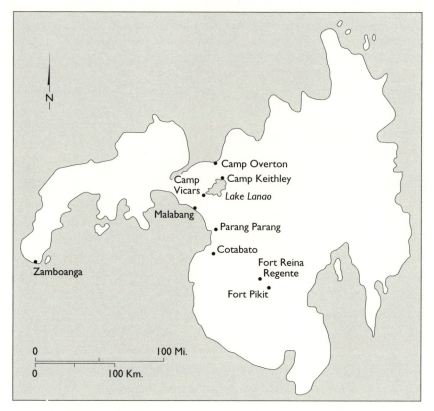

N

Camp Overton
Camp Keithley
Camp Vicars
Lake Lanao
Malabang
Parang Parang
Cotabato
Fort Reina Regente
Zamboanga
Fort Pikit

0   100 Mi.

0   100 Km.

CHAPTER NINE

❧◎❧

Second Tour in the Philippines

We landed in San Francisco, Saturday, July 14, 1900, where Little Mother, Frank and Will met me, and Harold arrived with the First Battalion, Fifteenth Infantry, on his way to China, for which they left on the *Sumner*, July 17th. I left for Washington on the 20th where I reported to Surgeon General [George M.] Sternberg and afterwards to the Secretary of War, Elihu Root, to whom I made two very important recommendations[.][1] One was to have the convalescent sick brought home where they would recuperate faster, and not keep them in the Islands, as had been done with so many cases[.] Another was to shorten the tour of duty to two years and not allow the enlisted men to stay longer, as some of them wished to do in order to receive credit for double service. The Surgeon General asked why we had used such large quantities of certain remedies. Apomorphia [apomorphine] was one of them, and it was given hypodermically to men who were poisoned by drinking vino—an impure alcohol made by distilling the nipa plant—which made them crazy. The emetic brought up the alcohol and then the stomach could be washed out.

Since I began the study of medicine there had been many advances. The hypodermic syringe had come into use, the clinical thermometer, the grafting of skin and bone, the counting of blood cells.

I was on duty at Fort Columbus, Governors Island, New York Harbor, from September 30th 1900 to December 15, 1902, and while there Will was with us and Hal returned to the U.S. and visited us November 1, 1902.[2]

Mother and I went to Fort Crook, Nebraska, and was [*sic*] there from January 17, to July 24, 1903, when having received a rush order, she and I left for the Philippines, I [doing so] again.[3] Philip was fortunately visiting us and helped us to hurriedly pack and get off. Our furniture had to be rushed, and it reached San Francisco the day before we sailed from there on the U.S. Transport *Sheridan* for Manila, August 1, 1903.[4] I had very little time to look for a storing place for our household effects and left them at the medical supply depot. While at Crook, one night about bedtime the greatest electric storm I ever saw came up and lasted about half an hour. The whole firmament was filled with sheets and flashes of lightning by which one could read a newspaper. Our voyage was a delightful one, and at Honolulu, August 9–11, Mr. Walter Dillingham, a friend of Phil and Frank, placed his carriage and driver at our disposal, and we drove many miles.[5] We stopped at Midway, August 15, which was the next relay station of the cable across the Pacific, and also at Guam, August 24–25, which the men at the relay station called, "The land of pus and blood," as they had suffered with numerous boils, and one of them had to leave. We drove over to Agaña on bullock carts, landing from the transport on small boats, which nearly touched the reef of coral which formed beautiful sea gardens of many colors.

We arrived at Manila, August 30 and left there September 8, on the U.S. Transport *Seward* for Zamboanga, Mindanao, where we landed, September 11, 1903, and where I was Chief Surgeon, Department of Mindanao, Attending Surgeon at Headquarters and in charge of the Medical Supply Depot until it was discontinued August 6, 1905.[6] Promoted to the grade of Deputy Surgeon General, with the rank of Lieutenant Colonel, April 26, 1904. Little Mother was badly stung by mosquitoes while on a trip to Jolo on the little steamer *Sabah*, and was so badly poisoned by malaria that we thought she better return to the U.S. where she remained some months and then came out again. We lived in quarters rented from a Portugu[e]se Malay and it was not until some time after she had left that my quarters were completed farther west and between the canal and the sea wall, and I moved into them.

Besides my duties in the army, I had charge of the health of the natives in the town and surrounding barrios, probably 12,000 people. I appointed an East Indian, who was a graduate of an English medical university, as health officer, but he didn't last long, as he was accused of grafting. Tuberculosis was common and the people expectorated on the floors of the churches. The holy water, in a tacloban shell at the entrance of the church was also a source of contagion, as the unwashed fingers were dipped into it and the lips of many diseased ones touched, but kneeling on the floors in the dry sputum was probably a greater menace. A medical officer, during an epidemic of Asiatic cholera, used antiseptics in the drinking water, and a native made an oath in one of their courts of law that the doctor had given him a poison to pour into the water and it was the cause of the disease. The doctor had to be followed by a sentry where he went on account of the threats against his life, so we had to be very careful in the use of antiseptics that had an odor, so I had the floors white washed with freshly slacked lime, large cuspidores filled with sand installed and the priests requested to tell the people that it was wrong to spit on the floor of the house of God. After one of the Assistant Surgeons was made health officer, I had thousands of the natives vaccinated.[7]

My new quarters were near the sea-wall, which had steps so that we could go into the water and swim, when so inclined, and return to dress after a shower of fresh water. Filipinos were first employed, but were so slow that at length Japanise [sic] were put on the work and did all except the painting, which the Filipinos did. When the whistle blew, one would lazily get up, light a cigarette, open an umbrella to hold it over one shoulder, and then begin to paint with the other hand. The house was of two stories and the uprights were that long and set in concrete. Cross pieces were fastened to these and the sills of both stories. The rooms were large and the windows of two sliding screens, one of sea-shells about two and a half inches square which admitted very little light, and the other outside of lattice, the pieces of which were about two inches broad and were raised to open them by a notched upright. All sides of the house could be opened by pushing back these shutters which were five feet or more high. A broad veranda ran the whole length of the east side and beautiful orchids and huge ferns hung all along. Moros brought them to us, as well as sea-shells, of which mother made a large collection, to which I added while she was gone, but it was lost in the great fire in San Francisco. I cannot estimate its money value, but it was considerable.

Larie, a Moro boy, whose elder brother was a messenger for the civil governor and rode a bicycle, went to the Moro school across the river in Maguy, [and] came with the Moros to interpret for them and help sell

sea-shells, orchids, ferns, brass utensils, etc. in order to receive a commission. The rice crops on the Island of Basilan were very poor and many of
the carabaos had died, so they had to part with some of their brass, of
which most of their wealth consisted, and I secured nearly fifty pieces,
vases, jars, kettles, cuspidores, buyo boxes, etc., some of them inlaid with
copper and german silver. I saw many pieces in sort of bamboo crates
arranged along the walls in the houses of those who were well off. Often
the houses were large enough to hold several families, and in one was a
platform, or bed, large enough to hold twenty people. This was in the
home of young Datto Alli [sic], aged about sixteen years, whose father
had been killed in a fight.[8] The sea shells were in size from that of a pin
head to the tacloban three feet in length. Great bats, with bodies a foot
long and a spread of wings of four feet, came in large flocks about sun-
down from across the Straits of Basilan, to feed on the fruit of the almen-
dro trees—a kind of almond—which marked the two sides of the drive-
way to the fort, and kept up a chattering all night. My new quarters were
in their line of flight, and for some time they would approach and then go
back some distance before going around, but one of them did strike a
building and fall dead.

The hospital at Zamboanga and the one at Parang were designed by me
and built under my direction.[9] I once made the rounds of the posts to
inspect the hospitals, and the sanitary condition of the posts, going by
transport to Cagayan, Camp Overton, where Phil was stationed as First
Lieutenant of Cavalry.[10] While superintending the clearing of the jungle
near the post, he saw a python about forty feet long, the head of which
was nearly a foot across. It was killed later and found to be half a foot
longer than his estimation. I drove from Overton to Camp Keithley on
Lake Llanao [Lanao], where the Moros frequently attacked the sentries
and had killed several.[11] I visited the outpost across the lake, around which
was a barbed wire fence on which were strung empty tin cans to alarm the
guards. Not infrequently a Moro would run juramentado—run amok—
and kill as many Christians as possible before he himself was killed.[12]
Some times he was a man sentenced to death and allowed to meet it in
this manner. After my visit, I had some Army Corps nurses ordered here
on the request of the Surgeon, but one of them had to be replaced, as she
saw a soldier struck down with a campilan about ten feet away as she came
out of her nipa quarters, and [it] caused her a nervous breakdown.[13]

Leaving Keithley, I crossed the lake in a steam launch and was driven from the landing to Camp Vickars [Vicars], where the strictest watch had to be kept and guards had to go around at night to see that there were no Moros in hiding.[14] This was the coolest post in the department, but it rained most of the time. From Vickars, I descended the mountains to camp Malabang on the coast, having two men in the ambulance with me, two mounted men in front and two behind, as this was a dangerous piece of road, the troops being frequently attacked but were not allowed to punish the people along the road.[15] The pack train that carried most of the supplies up into the mountains, however, fired at every Moro who appeared, so were never disturbed. There was a friendly one, Datto Grande, who advised the others to let the Americans alone and trade with them. He said he sold them any old thing he had, brass, knives, etc., and they gave him gold and silver of which he showed a bag full. I saw coffee trees all along and the Moros were gathering some of the beans to sell on the coast. We had wild boar meat for dinner the animal having been killed that morning back of the hospital by one of the corps men.

¶After leaving, I went to Parang Parang by boat and thence again by boat to Cotto Batto [Cotabato] on the Colorado River. On leaving there I ascended the river to Margosa Tubig [sic], Reina Regente and Fort Pikit, stopping a short time just above Datto Piang's fort.[16] Piang was a Chinaman, a friendly enemy, who had a large following of Moros, all well armed. He had lantakas, or cannon[s] of small calibre, with which to defend his village where they manufactured arms, casting the lantakas, also brass helmets and brass utensils of various kinds. All along the lower stretches of the river, the cogon grass was ten to fifteen feet high, into which the hostile Moros could wend their way by water into many hidden nooks, and for miles very little of the land was more than a foot or two above high water until we reached Margosa Tubig, and after that it raised into low hills. Mosquitoes were thick and if one lived in a native house, it had to be lined with cheese cloth or similar fabric and have double doors to keep them out. I returned to Zamboanga on one of our gunboats, sleeping on deck. One of them had a mascot in a young python, which often moved about at night on the deck. A young army officer who was sleeping on a cot under a mosquito bar on deck saw the snake, jumped up very much frightened and at length killed it, while the navy officers lay quiet enjoying the proceeding.[17]

Before I occupied my new quarters, Ida with her baby daughter Phyllis visited me, having left San Francisco in charge of Frank, April 1, 1904, on the transport *Logan* arrived at Manila, April 28 to join Phil at Camp Overton, May 15. The baby was already in a poor condition and she continued to fail, so they were compelled to return to the U.S. leaving Overton, July 27 and Manila August 15, 1904, and Frank, who also visited me, returned with them on the *Sherman*, August 15, 1904. After Mother's return, I visited the southern posts to inspect, going first to Jolo, a small quaint walled-town commanded by Major Hugh Scott, now a Brigadier General Retired, who had lost some of his fingers through the treachery of a datto, whom he had captured and permitted to bid his family adieu, when he was set upon and wounded.[18] He and I had a long talk with Datto Mundi, the Sultan of Jolo's head man, both of whom I met afterward in New York, when General Scott was showing them about the city. Scott was an expert in the use of the Sign Language, and we wished to learn if the Moros used signs, and we watched the datto closely. He used many gestures which enabled us to understand much that he said before the interpreter told us. He knew about the formation of coral rock, and was well informed on other subjects. A hadji is a man who had made a pilgramage [*sic*] to Mecca. I had an escort every time I went outside the walls.

From Jolo I went to Bongao and then on to Siassi [Siasi], our most southern post, where we arrived early one morning, when the water was placid, and we could see down many feet great schools of fish and great coral gardens.[19] Many of the fish came to the surface and skulled [*sic*] along by means of their tales [*sic*] and Spanish mackerel jumped to a great height. On another trip Major George Gale and I went to the Island of Sulu to see the Sultan and then to the island of Paragua, or Palawan, where we had a small post.[20] We had the best oranges here of any place we had visited in the islands, and I took [a] bag full back with me. On our return, we ran into the tail of a typhoon and made very little headway during the night, as we were among reefs in the Sulu Sea. No food could be cooked and Major Gale and I in the only stateroom besides the Captain[']s, had to subsist one day on hard bread, sardines and large red onions, as we lay most of the time in our berths, getting out only to hang on a rail while a deckhand turned the hose on us to cool us off. We were very much relieved when early in the morning our little steamer, the *Gibson*, ran into clear water. That afternoon we were back in Zamboanga.

We were very comfortable in our airy house, through which the south-west monsoons blew during the day and the land breeze at night, and only about sunset were the mosquitoes bad, when the wind was shifting. Our cook, a mestizo, was probably the best in the town and our muchacho, Santiago also a mestizo, was well trained and reliable. Our cook did the marketing and chickens and ducks were plentiful and we could get mound-bird eggs, as well as those of the game chickens which were quite small. We could hear the conchs of the Moro fisherman early in the morning and our cook would then go to the Moro market for fish, often buying crayfish (lobsters) which had been speared and which he would cook at once. I have seen as many as twenty huge turtles there at one time, but while at Simoes, he gave us turtle so often that we tired of the meat. There were also small oysters, which were opened or shelled with a hammer or stone, and small clams. We ate all of the various kinds of Filipino vegetables. Curry and rice with the ten or twelve fixings, as shredded white radish, shredded cocoanut, bits of fried egg and bacon, Bombay duck—a kind of smoked fish—chutney, etc., all piled in a crater of a pile of rice. Pineapples, sour sap, mangoes, mangosteens, from Jolo, various kinds of bananas—lacutan & lacustan [Lactusan] & and [sic] red ones—grape fruit, oranges, the skin of which were yellow and green, lemons and other fruits were plentiful and cheap.[21]

I had rich earth hauled and a thick layer spread over the coral sand, holes dug and filled with it and wood ashes from the ice plant, in which we planted mangoes—called mangos by the Filipinos—which mother brought from Honolulu, also papayas she brought, and "the golden shower" from the seeds of which Mrs. [Anna] Dole, the wife of the governor gave her.[22] We had over a hundred saplings of the papaya, planting all we could around our quarters and giving the rest away, as they were far better than the Philippine varieties. I brought in from the country two or three "Landeras de España [España]," a kind of canna, the flowers of which have the Spanish colors, and from the increase had by the time we left, a bed twelve feet in diameter and two smaller ones, so many that at a wedding not long afterward, the flowers were used to decorate the church. One elephant ears plant grew to be over six feet tall and had a flower with a cap in all a foot high. We also had el coraz[ó]n de Jes[ú]s, coraz[ó]n de Ma[rí]a, alfombra de reina and a plant having large white leaves with splashes of green, the roots of many of which I brought home and were lost in the great San Francisco fires. All along the canal in front of our quarters were cocoanut trees, which were only about ten feet high on our arrival, but grew very rapidly.

I rode a bicycle every afternoon after the sun was well down, while mother was gone, and drove a pony cart when she returned. By this time, the roads had been raised above the rice paddies and cornered with finger coral and we could take longer drives. We went east to the salt ponds, where salt water was pumped by man foot-power on an endless chain sort of stepladder, having wooden boxes to carry the water into ponds and allowed to evaporate, when the salt was shoveled up for shipment. West were groves of cocoanut which extended for miles. When ripe, the meat is taken out and called copra, which is shipped abroad, in great quantities. First the fibre is torn off, the nuts are then broken open, placed on platforms over smoking fibre until the meat shrinks and can easily be shelled out. The oil extracted from the copra is used for many purposes, for cooking illumination, on the hair and the body, etc.

The Filipinos are very musical and play mostly on stringed instruments. The night after our first arrival, we were serinaded [sic], and whenever we had visitors come on the inter-island transport, we had a band of five or six play for them at the club, and when they left, the band would lead the way to the boat, where, as the transport slipped away, it would play, "No te vayas de Zamboanga" which we joined in with our voices. The aria by which we marched to the boat was usually one I first heard in Tennessee, during the War of the Rebellion called, "The Pirates Serenade," ["]Then awake lady wake, I'm waiting for thee, This night live or never my bride thou shall be." Other popular aria[s] were "El beso de amor," "La noche serana," "Pasea de la Alameda" and others. While Frank was with me, he delighted the Filipinos when he took first a mandolin and then a guitar, followed them for a time to catch the aria, and then led them as they had never been led before, playing the above arias as well as others. The Moro "Bee Dance" was one we had for our guests. In this a Moro hunts for bees, finds them, takes off his turban catches some, when he expresses his delight. Afterward they escape, and begin to sting him, when he tries frantically to drive them off until he drops down exhausted.

Datto Mandi, or Raja Muda, Chief of the Samal Lauts—People of the Sea, who are Islamites, was the head Moro, and controlled many people.

Datto Sacularan, Chief of the seas, formerly Panglima Gondoon was his head chief. Some of the followers on islands near by were still eager to kill Christians and one morning several dead Filipinos, one a woman, were brought in. The head of one had been split open down to the chin, and the chest and about half of the abdoman [*sic*] of another one had been split open apparently with one stroke of a knife, probably a campilan, a long knife, broader at the end, having a light piece of thin light wood on each side tied together with very light string. It is held on one shoulder ready to be thrown forward with both hands and deliver a terrific blow. It as well as the kriss [kris] and borong a shorter heavier weapon are kept very sharp and ready for instant use.

¶All of the Moros are Islamites. The Maguindanaos—People of the Isle of the lakes. Maninging was the Sultan of Mindanao and had jurisdiction over the tribes from Sindangan on the west coast to Glan on the east coast. Datto Daculat (Great?) was his war chief and prime minister, and Datto Manna was one of his head men. The Kalibuganas, Samal Lauts—People of the sea—Yacans, Joloanos, or Tau Suk—from Tau, people, Samal Lautangans—People of the shore—, Samal Bitali, Samal Batuan—Batuan, stone—, Datto Gumba, Datto Dugan and Hadji Nuno, a datto. These people and their head men, met for a conference with Captain John P. Finley of the Infantry, U.S. Army, the Governor of Zamboanga, many of them arriving, Tuesday, November 24, 1903, in about 35 boats, mostly vintas, bedecked with streamers of many colors, carrying about 250 men.[23] Datto Pedro Cuevas, or Calun [Kulan], came from Basilan, an island on the opposite side of the straits, at 4 p.m., November 26, with about 30 boats, bringing about 200 men. Datto Mandi, who had been a Spanish sergeant, and had married into the Moros, lived at Magay, a suburb of Zamboanga, on the north side of the small river that arose in the mountains near by, and connected by a bridge. I took photographs, 4 x 5 inches of nearly all of their chief men, each one of whom had an umbrella held over him and a guard carrying a knife resting on one shoulder ready to strike, on each side of him. There were also priests, called Panditas and Imaams, and Majarajas, Mandarins, and Panglimas.

¶During their stay, there were dances by women, or rather posing as their hands were thrown well back and rotated. Sham fights between Moros took place and a bout between a cavalryman with his sabre and a Moro with his spear and a shield. The Moro was unable to get at the soldier's body, nor could the latter get to the Moro. We attended the Moro religious services one Friday night, and sat on pillows resting on the split bamboo floor about six feet above the ground, while an Arabian priest read from a Koran which rested on an inclined support of wood. After the reading, or recitation, for the priests cannot all read, it is said, we had chocolate and sweet cakes brought in by the women. I have seen more than one bride sitting in state, with her hands resting on a pillow, each finger having at its end a silver extension of the nail about an inch long.

When we started to return to the U.S., we were furnished transportation on General Wood's little steamer, the *Sabah*, to Manila, December 21 to 24, and as we struck the end of a typhoon, the trip was a rough one.[24] There had been some delay in the receipt of my order, or we would have taken the *Seward* and been tossed about less. There had been many improvements in Manila since I had first seen it. Street cars of a modern type had been installed. The ditch about the walled City had been partially filled in[,] a sea wall erected, the harbor dredged and the sand used to raise the surface behind.

We left Manila, January 4, 1906, and arrived in San Francisco, February 4, making two stops on the way, Nagasaki and Honolulu. I received a leave and went with Little Mother to visit my Mother in Elmira. I was in Washington about April 16, when I wrote to have our household effects shipped to my new station, Vancouver Barracks, Washington, but too late, as the earthquake struck San Francisco, April 18, 1906, and the great fire the next day was only twenty minutes in reaching the Medical Supply Depot, 655 Mission St., and destroying our highly prized and valuable heir looms and our own collection of thirty-five years.[25] There was a set of Canton ware that had belonged to the Dunbars since 1804. Plates, cups, saucers, bowls, etc., of beautiful French china, each worth at least ten dollars. Three or four oil paintings, water colors, daguerreotypes, photographs of the family and about 500 of the Philippines and the insurrection. Many books that are no longer published and were worth 20.00 to $25.00 each, many of them about the Indians of America and many notes of various tribes collected in the course of many years. Two buffalo robes, each worth $100.00, old Navajo blankets. Apache baskets and many other articles of Indian make. A very old Spanish halberd, used in the palace until about fifty years ago, two very long blades and other swords. Moro spears, krisses, shields of wood, two brass helmets and other arms and curios, were burned before Frank could get them out. But we were more worried about him than about our property, as it was three days before he could wire us that he was safe.

CHAPTER TEN

Last Years

I was Chief Surgeon of the Department of the Columbia, May 8, 1906 to March 10, 1908, and from August 1 to September 18, 1906, also Chief Surgeon of the Camp of Instruction, Camp Tacoma, Murray, Washington, where I demonstrated at the maneuvers there the value of the identification badge very fully, and it was after this that it was adopted by the War Department and has been of inestimable value in identifying the severely wounded and the dead.[1] An endurance test for the litter bearers showed their ability to carry a wounded man farther than [had] been done before.

I made a medical and sanitary inspection of the posts in Alaska, June 25, to September 3, 1907, leaving as soon as I heard that navigation was open on the Yukon River. Little Mother went with me by rail as far as Seattle, the hills of which were being washed down instead of by the slow process of digging. I took the steamer *Bertha* and went by the inside passage to Juneau. The steamer's cargo was mostly lumber, which was piled wherever there was standing room and I had to crawl over it to get into my stateroom. A part of the upper deck was taken up with a large gasoline launch to be taken to Valdez. The master of the ship had taken the U.S. transport *Seward* to the Philippines, and, while passing through some straits, he asked me if I had seen any like them before, and we agreed that the Straits of St. Peter and St. Paul between two islands in the Philippines looked like these. We made several landings at salmon fisheries, and at one of them saw an engine that had once run on an elevated road in New

York City. There were no lighthouses to guide us, and we saw a bouy [*sic*]
that had been washed up on shore. We stopped at Juneau long enough to
unload some freight and after leaving, had heavy rains, which the sailors
said were due to the presence of a sky-pilot on board, but it happened that
he had brought his bag on board and then gone back to the church and
had been left behind. There was, however, a bishop of the Greek Church
on board, and whom I treated for tonsillitis. We ran into clear weather at
Valdez, where I was on the fourth of July and saw a parade of a very small
wagon hauled by a black bear, and about a dozen people. The weather
turned very warm and the ice of the glacier back of the town, melted so
rapidly that the river, its outlet, threatened to wash over the town, which
is on a terminal morain[e]. Fort Liscum was opposite the town and I
remained there until the *Bertha* returned from the west, when I returned
on her to Juneau.[2] While wa[i]ting for a boat, I visited the Treadwell mine,
opposite the town where Robert Kinzie was in charge and one of his
brothers with him, son of Major David H. Kinzie of the Artillery, with
whom we had served at Charlestown [*sic*], South Carolina, in 1877.[3] An
excursion boat happened along, so I took a trip on it to the glaciers not far
away. At the town, I saw a new house that had a patched look and was
told that an Esquimo [*sic*], who had become rich had built it and then sent
for furniture. When it came, the carpet was too long and he added to the
end of the house enough to fit the carpet.

The next post was Fort William H. Seward, and I had a photo of a set
of quarters taken at midnight of the 21st of June.[4] After inspecting there,
I was taken by a gasolene [*sic*] launch to Skagway, where I remained over
night at a hotel kept by a woman who had mushed over the Chilcoot Pass
with her husband and driven a dog team since then. On the railroad over
the White Horse Pass, which I took the next morning, were many people
who left the train when a few miles out to gather wild red currants. There
were no tourists on the train, but a few did come as far as the summit and
then returned when they reached the North West Territory, where on the
line we had sentinals [*sic*] posted at our flag and on the other side was an
English post with the English flag flying. We descended to White Horse,
the terminus of the railroad, and waited until about three o'clock the next
morning for the stern-wheel steamer to leave, the passengers all walking
about driving mosquitoes away with branches from bushes, as it was not
possible to sleep until the boat was in motion, and there was light enough

until midnight to ready by. We arrived at Dawson early the next morning and here I met Chester Thomas, who was in charge of the Gugenheim interests, who had looked me up and with whom and his wife I had dinner.[5] He had been the First Sergeant of Company K, First Infantry, California Volunteers, and on October 6th, 1898, was admitted to hospital in Manila with Frank. He died in 1923 of amoebic dysentery contracted in the Philippines and I met his wife and two children in Berkeley, California afterward.

¶I went on that night by steamer to Fort Egbert at Circle.[6] There was a very good garden at the post in which were potatoes and a few other vegetables, although the ground about two feet down was still frozen. After leaving there we continued down the Yukon River and crossed the Arctic Circle, Latitude 66, 32 N. passed old Fort Yukon and on to Fort Gibbon at Tanana.[7] Claude was at Tanana and in charge of the mail route from Fairbanks to St. Michael. He had gone from here to go to Lexington, Kentucky to marry Belle De Long, July 11, 1905. Frances De Long was born here, July 2, 1906. Mrs. Frances H. De Long, Belle's mother, and Daisy, her sister were visiting them, the only tourists I met this far in the interior of Alaska. We were all very comfortable in a log house which had a slab porch on top of which was the only roof garden in Alaska which I had been told about when on the *Bertha*.

Claude, Belle and I went to Fairbanks up the Tanana River, on the government steamer *Jeff Davis* with Major General Adolphus W. Greely, the Commanding General of the Department of the Columbia, who also had as his guests a son, Hon. William Sulser [Sulzer], M. C. of New York, and Mr. [Thomas] Cale, Delegate of Alaska.[8] There we went out on the railroad and visited some placer mines and then to the end of the line. We saw $16,000 in gold dust in a miner's pan, that had just been cleaned up. Mr. Cale remained here. Claude and Belle returned to Tanana with us, and then I went on down the Yukon on the *Jeff Davis* to St. Michael, where General Greely left me and went on to Nome and thence back to Vancouver Barracks.[9] After inspecting at St. Michael, I went to Nome by steamer and drove out to Fort Davis to inspect.[10] Here, as at other posts in Alaska, water for all purposes was kept as ice during the very cold weather piled up on the back porches, to be melted in large galvanized iron boilers in the kitchens as needed and garbage and excreta were usually deposited in empty coal oil cans and carried a long way out on the ice, to remain until the latter broke up in the spring and was floated away. On the road out to the fort we passed a claim for which the old owner had been offered a big price, but he wouldn't sell, as he said that if he did, he would go to a city and spend all of his money, so he remained and took out enough gold each year to buy what he needed, and there was enough to last him the rest of his life. I bought a huge polar bear skin which had been brought from Siberia by some Eskimo and I afterward had it made into a rug for Little Mother, as a Christmas present and Claude at the same time gave her a big Alaska bear robe.

To return to Seattle by steamer from Nome, we first boarded a gaso- lene [*sic*] launch and were taken to a flat boat that lay at the steamer which we jumped upon as the launch rose and fell and from which we had to watch for a chance to spring on the steps at the side of the steamer on which two sailors stood ready to grab us. There were times when a cage had to be used in boarding. We took the outside passage and had a very rough voyage, so that several meals, the captain and I were the only ones at the table, but at length the clouds began to break away and when we were opposite Mount St. Elias, they cleared from its peak and then slowly sank until they left the whole 18,024 feet in sight from the sea level, one of the great sights of the world. I had seen Mt. McKinley, 20,300 feet high, from the Tanana River, but it was farther away and didn't loom up as did St. Elias. A little farther south, we stopped opposite a great glacier from which icebergs had broken away and the captain sent boats to the bergs to lay in a supply of ice. Young whales surrounded our ship in schools and sported in the water and the bergs were covered with great flocks of sea pigeons. The rest of the voyage was a very enjoyable one, and if I had known what an easy trip it was to Tanana and back, I would have taken Little Mother with me. I resumed my duties at headquarters, Vancouver Barracks, September 3, 1907.

On March 10, 1908, I was ordered home to await retirement on account of failing health. I had been following the advice of the surgeons at the post, but as soon as I left to consult the Mayo Brothers, at Rochester, Min- nesota, and treated myself I began to improve, and the Mayos found only excessive acidity which was soon corrected and I was as well as ever.[11] Little Mother and I then started to travel. We first went to Elmira, where my mother had died, August 11, 1907, and then to Bermuda where we spent two winters and springs. We visited Plainfield, New Jersey, [and]

Lexington, Kentucky, where Phil was Professor of Military Science and Tactics at the Agricultural & Mechanical College.[12] At Indian Lake, New York, summer of 1910–11, in California and Grant's Pass, Oregon. In August 1911 we crossed the continent via the Canadian Pacific Railway from Vancouver, British Columbia to Toronto stopping on the way at Sicamous, Glacier, Field and Banff, and then by water to Montreal by water to take the Steamer *Lake Manitoba* to Liverpool, England.[13] We visited Chester, Conway, Carnovan [Carnarvon], Warwick, Stratford-on-Avon, Oxford and London, and then crossed the channel at Dover to Ostend, to visit Liege where there are people who bear our name, also at Brussels, where we spent some days. In October, 1911, we were in the Greenwich Observatory, England, and I placed one foot in west longitude and the other in east longitude then stood on the dividing line one half of each foot was on the east and the other on the west, just as other people probably had done. We wanted to spend the winter in Italy, but, hearing that Asiatic cholera had appeared in some of the cities, we went to Antwerp, to remain until November 4, 1911, on which date we sailed on the Steamer *Lapland* for New York.[14]

We were in Plainfield, New Jersey until June 7, 1912, and then went to Will's at New Brunswick, New Jersey and remained until January 8, 1913 when we went to Alameda, California. There we were from April 15, 1914 and again August 4, 1915 to January 29, 1916. We were in San Antonio, Texas in May, 1914 and again January 18, to May 10, 1915. We saw the San Diego Exposition and the San Francisco Exposition in June, July and August, 1915. Spent the summer and fall of 1914 at Plainfield, Dingman's Ferry, Pennsylvania, and Elmira, the summer of 1915 at Arrow-head Springs, California, and Los Angeles, and three months early in 1916 at Saratoga, California. After that spent some time in Elmira on and off.

¶We went to Florida and were there from January 8, to April 19, 1917, at Miami until the heat drove us away and we went farther north, stopping at several towns until we reached Jacksonville where mother had a breakdown, as at St. Augustine she had contracted the influenza. As soon as she was able, we hurried back to Plainfield and went to 120 Crescent Avenue where we had engaged two rooms, a bath, and a washroom on the first floor and here Claude, on route from San Francisco to France, came to pay us a hurried visit from 10 p.m. Saturday December 1, to 3.15 p.m. Sunday, and then returned to Camp Merritt at Tenefly [Tenafly], New

Jersey to sail, as he told me after the World War, December 12, 1917 at Hoboken, New Jersey on the U.S.S. *Susquehanna* formerly the German liner *Rhein*, as Adjutant of the First Antiaircraft Batallion [sic].[15] Mother failed slowly, but sat up a little every day, losing strength slowly until February 3, when she slept much and we could understand only a few words that she spoke. At 8:20 p.m., Friday, February 8, 1918, she passed slowly and quietly away, in the back room on the north side, from the two windows of which, she had long enjoyed the trees, shrubs and green grass and looked at the moon and stars. On the 9th at 612 Park Avenue about 5 p.m., funeral services were conducted by the Reverend E. Vicars Stevenson, rector of Grace Church, and seven Choir boys sang, "Oh Paradise," "Abide with Me," and "Peace Perfect Peace," accompanied on the piano by Frederick Smith, the choir master. We accompanied the remains of my beloved companion and helpmate of half a century to the Arlington National Cemetery, Fort Meyer [Myer], Virginia, where they were interred in lot no. 2009, Southern Division, Officers Section, on Monday, February 11, the Reverend Colwort K. P. Cogswell, Church of the Incarnation, reading the burial services at the grave. I had a Barre, Vermont granite monument erected on the lot in 1920.

For a more detailed account of some of the events of my life, consult the type written copy of mother's "Recollections" which I made in 1918.

After losing my sweet companion of so many happy years, I wandered around disconsolate. I paid Ida a visit in Schenectady, Phil having gone to France leaving on H.M. Steamship *Cedric* of the White Star Line at 7 a.m. October 3, 1917, and, on returning to Plainfield, I was glad to return to active service, so I volunteered for duty and was detailed and reported for court-martial duty to the Commanding General, Port of Embarkation, Hoboken New Jersey, July 26, 1918, on which duty I continued until August 15, 1919, having served the time required and been appointed Colonel on the retired list, March 28, 1919.[16]

I lived at the Earle Hotel near Washington Square, New York, most of the time, and, while there great efforts were made to sell the Fourth Liberty Loan bonds.[17] One afternoon I went to a vaudeville theatre on Broadway near 29th St. New York when between some of the acts, speeches were made and actresses in their costumes walked up and down the aisles to sell the bonds, but very few were sold and these were of small amounts so to arouse the people, the speaker called upon all of the men in uniform to come up and help him. I was about six seats from the front, and thought that there were enough going up, but the speaker came close to the front and leaning over requested me to come up, so I went up the steps and stood close to the curtain with the footlights almost blinding me. I was introduced and my rank given. I then said that I had saved $1000.00 out of my pay and had bought a bond and asked if anyone in the audience would cover that amount. Almost instantly one of the actresses called out, "here is a gentleman who will." I asked him to come forward and we shook hands. After that bids came in fast, and I learned afterward that we sold $11,000.00 worth of bonds. I also assisted in selling bonds at another place.

¶On Armistace [*sic*] Day, November 11, 1918, as I walked over to Fifth Avenue, Italians came pouring across Washington Square, dancing shouting and singing and on the avenue the work lofts were pouring their thousands of men and women, mostly Jews out on the street. They danced around me, pinned decorations on me and sang, some even hugging me. On a cross street, four French girls threw their arms around my neck and kissed me on both cheeks. When I reached Madison Square, I was seized and lifted up onto the speaker's stand as thousands of men, women and children cheered and sang. Horns were blown, cow bells and others rung and every thing that could be used to make a noise was in evidence. Great pieces of sheet iron were banged. Rat traps with the mark "The Kaiser" were dragged along the streets. I had to walk in the middle of the street in order to get up to the Waldorf-Astoria on 34th Street and on going in heard singing. Following the sound, I fetch up at the bar-room, around the door of which stood many ladies. One of them asked me if it was proper for her to be there. "On a day like this, Yes," I said as I entered. A very large Frenchman met me and hugged me while he kissed on both cheeks as the Marsaillais [La Marseillaise] had just been sung and the Star Spangled Banner begun. A step or two on, a Spaniard met me and wrung my hand, saying "Ninety-eight is forgotten." When near the bar, two Americans stepped toward me, one of them having his hands hidden under his arms, and as he reached me, said "Have one on me," and held out a glass of whiskey which I declined and told him that the hotel would be closed as no intoxicant could be given to anyone in uniform. But the order was ignored this day, and the soldier was treated to drinks wherever he went.

I was at Chevy Chase, Maryland, from August 30, 1919 to January 30, LAST YEARS
1920, until after Phil came home from France on the *Melita*, arriving at
Boston, Massachusetts, January 28.[18] I then went to New York and
remained to March 15 on which day I sailed to Bermuda and remained to
May 8 when I returned to New York and from there went to Amite,
Louisiana, for a short visit and then on to Fort Sam Houston, Texas, arriving June 22.[19] I had been walking about ten miles a day and the side walks
in New York had caused a cal[l]osity on the ball of my left foot at the base
of the great toe which began to trouble me. A corn formed and at length
left a sinus which led towards the bone and I entered the Station Hospital
October 25, 1920 where after some delay, shreds of tissue were cut out
under local anaesthesia.

Not being benefitted, I returned to Phil, who was then living at 424
Jones Street, and was there at the time of the great flood. September 9 &
10, 1921, Phil and Ida were dining out and Phyllis, Billy and I were alone
in the house when [a] raging torrent came down the side street—Cam-
den—from a bend in the river.[20] It carried the servants' quarters and
laundry away, the servants just escaping, but losing all of their belongings. I was in my room with my left foot resting on a chair and unable
to move about without the use of a crutch. The water rose very rapidly
and would soon enter the house when Phyllis took charge and carried
every thing she could lift to bring up to the second floor. She, Billy and
the man cook salvaged nearly every thing on the first floor before it was
covered with over two feet of water, and the floor was at least five feet
above the level of the street. The house was a very large one resting on
a strong concrete foundation, so I felt that it was safe. Phil started for
the house as soon as he heard of the danger, but could get on foot only
to the southeast corner of the street and there the water was nearly to
his arm pits. Phyllis went out on the great veranda and he called to her
that he couldn't get over, but not to be afraid, the house was safe. It was
seven o'clock the next morning before Phil and Ida could reach the
house in their automobile. She put on her bathing suit and had a big job
washing out the mud before the water from the mains gave out. The oil
tank at the old brewery west of the house broke and the oil did much
damage in the city. At the bridge over the river at Jones Street oil could
be seen clinging to the trees six feet up. By the third day gas, water and
electricity were back in the house and I was there from January 21 to

— 157 —

February 14, 1921, and then returned to the hospital to remain until May 28, '21. Then went to Jones Street again to September 29, and it was during that time that the flood occurred.

¶We then went to Camp Travis.[21] After I returned to the hospital, some more shreds were dug out of the minute sinus, and as the pain had become great, massage and electricity were tried, but they gave no relief. I was convinced that the sinus led to necrosed bone, but an X-ray showed nothing, the surgeons did not agree with me, and declined to operate until I insisted that there was necrosed bone and it must be taken out. At length Major Raymond F. Metcalfe cut down and found what was to be expected, necrosed bone on the head of the first metatarsal and took it out, but left the head of the bone.[22] He, however, took out the base of the bone of the great toe. This operation relieved the cramps in the muscles of my leg, and especially the flexor of the great toe. The cut made, healed rapidly, but the sinus remained, indicating that the bone was still affected. The sinus was then cut out, but not the affected bone. Much scar tissue was left, and after I had walked about for some weeks, it began to swell and a bursa formed which enlarged until it was greater in size than a silver quarter dollar.

¶During this time I left Camp Travis, October 11, 1921 and went by rail to Bowie, Arizona and thence to the San Carlos Indian Agency to which I assisted in removing the Apache Indians from the Rio-Verde Agency in February and March in 1875. They had learned to speak, read and write English, but most of them had made very little progress otherwise and were living in wickeups [sic] a little larger, sleeping on the ground and cooking in old tin cans. The best land had been taken by the whites and that which fell to them was of very little use unless irrigated. Most of their horses were still bronchos. I went over a part of my Yavapai vocabulary with Arthur Kitjeyan, aged about 55 years, who had been a scout and spoke very fair English, but had not been to school. His daughter Virginia who was married to an Apache-Mojave, had children who were at the Agency School. She washed some clothes for me and ironed them on a blanket laid on the ground, but had no starch. They said that the missionaries hadn't come among them until late, and hadn't taken much interest in them, so they met every Saturday afternoon in a cottonwood grove about two and a half miles above the Agency and remained until Sunday afternoon.

¶I visited the grove on a Sunday afternoon and they invited me to come again, so I went the next Sunday October 30 with Rob Roy, an Apache-Mojave, who had a small store and owned an automobile. A committee of six men met me and conducted me to a fallen cottonwood on which was a very good seat, and men crowded around. About one hundred feet away were at least fifty women in single file singing while dancing towards a man who held up a hand. I asked what they were dancing for, and the reply was, "To our Father in Heaven," and to the question what else they did, I was told that they prayed to their Father in Heaven, and the six men talked to the people and urged them to be good. Then they asked me what I thought about their worship. I talked to them as I had done over forty-six years before, when they had heard for the first time that there was an Almighty God. On the road back, we stopped and talked with a grandson of Geronomo [sic] who had a small patch of sweet potatoes and corn from which he was driving out some hogs.

From San Carlos I went on by train to Globe and drove out to some of the copper mines. After two or three days, I went by automobile to the Roosevelt Dam, which has converted into a lake thirty miles long the Tonto Basin, through which Lieutenant Schuyler and I chased hostile Indians. On our return to Rio-Verde Agency in May, 1874, we made a camp where there is now many feet of water. While at the Dam, I visited the monument erected to Al Sieber up the Tonto road, two miles northeast from the Apache Lodge, on the spot where he had been killed by a rock that fell upon him. He was a veteran of the War of the Rebellion and had been in charge of Indian scouts in Arizona for a long time. From the Dam the drive by automobile was a very rough one over the mountains, as heavy rains had washed the soil from off the rocks. I could see the old Apache Trail which in May, 1874, I climbed in many places, leading my horse. After descending into the valley, the road was an easy one and we entered Phoenix near sunset, November 3.

¶From there I drove in an auto to old Fort McDowell on the afternoon of November 5, 1921 where Mike Burns—Hoo-mo-thy-ya [sic]—was living. I first saw him at Camp Date-Creek early in 1873, not long after he had been captured by Captain James Burns, Fifth Cavalry, when he was about eight years old. He had received a common school education at Carlisle, Pennsylvania, and elsewhere, had been an Indian scout, and during later years had been collecting material for the Indian side of the history of the

Apache troubles in Arizona.[23] He turned his manuscript over to me to arrange and edit. It was mostly in the form of loose leaves written with an indelable [sic] pencil which had been badly cared for and some of which were partly torn. I was three months placing the leaves and wetting the faded ones to bring out the writing and then type writing them all. I then tried to find a publisher, but eight or nine of them wouldn't undertake to offer it to the public, fearing that it wouldn't sell well enough to pay for the printing. I saw Mike again in Prescott in July, 1922 at the Pioneer celebration.

¶At a meeting of the pioneer Society I met the Governor and the State Historian.[24] On July 6, 1922, I drove over to Cottonwood on the Verde River, the site of the First Rio-Verde Indian Agency and which on my recommendation was moved up to the foot of the mountains—Hoo-wal-ka-ya-na-ya-na, or Pine top—now called Mount Mingus. The Indians called the new site Hakarooya from the hot water that made its exit after running underground for three or four miles. Twigs of trees that fell into the water soon were covered with lime and after a time became fossilized. I used the mud from it in the treatment of external diseases and injuries with much success. I drove from Phoenix to the Casa Grande ruins, November 15, 1921, much of the road running through the ancient irrigating canals that enabled thousands of people to live in that part of the country at the time that the Casa was occupied.[25] While I was at old Fort McDowell, quail were so thick that I ate on an average six a day, making a total of at least sixty.

From Phoenix, I went to Long Beach and was their [sic] from November 17, '21 to March 9, '22 and have spent much time there since then. I went to San Francisco March 10, '22. Early in June, Claude, Will and I drove by auto to Tia Juana [sic], Mexico and visited the Mission San Juan Capistrano, June 9, '22, San Diego and Ramona's marriage place. At Tia Juana evidences of vice were evident along the block of saloons in front of which young women were standing to invite men to treat them to a drink, and drunken women were seen staggering along the street. Gambling was carried on by means of slot machines. At the end of the long block we stopped and I leaned my cane against a hydrant and after taking a [K]odak picture walked away without it. On going a short distance, I said that I had left it. A man who was passing heard me and said "It is at the safest place in town, at the hydrant," and there I found it. Prohibition has driven such dens of vice from our cities and if the laws are properly enforced, there will be fewer crimes committed due to drunkenness.

¶ I returned to Long Beach and hobbled about until the bursa became very painful, so I determined to go to a hospital and have another operation. I wrote to Frank and he came for me and took me in his automobile to the Letterman General Hospital, Presidio of San Francisco, California where we arrived May 15, 1923, and where I remained to March 23, 1924.[26] We were two days making the 480 miles and had lunch with the Walter Cobbs at their beautiful home at Montecito the first day and spent the night of May 12, '23 at Paso Robles. The bursa broke before I reached the hospital and here water dressings were applied and then alcohol. Afterward Major Charles Berle used balsam peru and later Major Dean F. Winn advised the violet rays and they were tried for three weeks.[27] Sloughing went on for a time and then the ulcer began to close in and the edges to harden, but it deepened, as the discharge broke down the granulations as fast as they formed. My general health was good and all of my organs were in good condition, so I urged an operation. Accordingly on August 11, 1923, Major Joseph Casper cut out the ulcer, the greater part of the first metatarsal bone and amputated the great toe, which furnished the tissue to fill in the great hole left from the ulcer. Three stitches were removed on the 20th and the rest on the 25th, when the flap was firmly adherent. At the end of three weeks, I was advised to bear a little weight on the foot and was soon urged to use it. A felt and leather sole, with a depression in it for the stump and I wore it until a swelling appeared at the edge of the flap turned over from the toe which was very sensitive and the whole foot began to ache, so that I could no longer bear my weight on it. The pain was much greater at night and I slept only by spells. A minute corn formed in the middle of the swelling and grew to the size of a silver dime and became exquisitely tender. Massage of the foot and leg gave relief in the day time and lead and opium lotion relieved somewhat the superficial pain. The swelling becoming greater, I asked Frank to bring Dr. Philip K. Gilman from San Francisco in consultation on October 23, and as a microscopical examination of a specimen from the ulcer showed some suspicious cells of an epithelial growth, he advised amputation of all of the toes.[28] I was not told until a month afterward about the result of the microscopic examination, but I suspected and requested that all of the toes be taken off. Conservative or timid surgery and the failure of the Xray to show any caries of the bone, although there was the sinus leading to it, was the cause of my suffering and the loss of the toes of my left foot. If the head of the first metatarsal had been taken off at Fort Sam Houston, there would probably [have] been no further trouble, but I was under an anaesthetic and couldn't direct the operator.

Thursday, October 25, 1923, Major Joseph Casper took off all of the metatarsal bone leaving the tarsals, and on the tenth day, the stump was healed, except the outer end of the flap which looked as if about to slough. There was no pain, but an uneasy feeling and on the fourteenth day it was nearly the size of a silver quarter dollar. At first for some days and nights I was in great pain and had to have drugs to give me relief and it was about ten days before my head was clear. On January 11, 1924 my son Frank took me in his Buick Sedan for my first drive since May 11, 1923, Frances D. L. with us, going to Alameda, Oakland and Berkeley and I had dinner with Frank and Lois. It was a great treat to be in a home atmosphere once more, and see beautiful rugs on [the] floor, pictures on the walls and not eat in a bedroom. Claude came and took me out and drove me many miles south along the coast and after that there were many drives. On March 23, 1924, Claude took me over to Berkeley where I remained at the Hotel Whitecotton and remained until June 7, '24, hobbling around trying to get used to a wooden toe and a steel sole in my left shoe.

While in the hospital and trying to forget the irksome confinement and drive dull care away, I began to make notes about my early life about which my sons and their wives had urged me to write more than I have given in my "Ancestry," and while in Berkeley, I employed a typest [sic], to whom I dictated or read from my notes my Memoirs of 1924 and now at Phil's home, at 370 Terrell Road, San Antonio, Texas, with his copy before me I have rewritten them, doing the typing myself. Much that I have written is of little consequence, as must be expected in the doings of over Eighty-two years.

Many have been the secrets of nature that have been unfolded and put to practical use during my lifetime and advances have been made in all branches of life. In medicine and surgery anaesthetics, as ether, chloroform, nitrous oxide gas and others have lessened misery and pain[.] The experiments of Pasteur have led to the discovery that germs are the cause of many diseases, and to their serum treatment; skin and bone grafting;

the use of antiseptics; the part that insects and animals play in the spread of disease. Clinical thermometers have come into use, the hypodermic syringe, stethoscope and other instruments; the X-ray, ultra-violet rays and the spread of the knowledge of the benefits of fresh air, sunlight, pure water and the proper disposal of excreta. There are health officers and sanitation is more widely practiced. Electricity is put to many uses in medicine as well as in other affairs in life. Electric cars have replaced horse and steam cars. There is electric lighting, cooking, etc., and photographs are not only taken by the camera but also by telegraph, and broad casting by radio is occurring daily. Phonographs, Typewriters, Adding machines, Dictophones [*sic*] are in offices and homes. Sewing machines in home and factory, also knitting machines. Automobiles are in most families, air-planes may be seen or heard every day and night, run by the [power] of gasolene [*sic*], submarines at nearly [every] port. The Young Men's Christian Association, The Salvation Army, and Boy Scouts are doing great work and the Red Cross Society is helping mankind everywhere[.] I have made only a beginning of the list of wonderful advances.

I spent a summer at Hillsdale, New York, with Hal and his family in their summer home, Barnstead, which is an old hay barn converted into a dwelling about three miles from the village. There is a great chimney in the living room and the old hay mow, which is now a bedroom looks down towards it and the whole appearance is antique. On October 1, 2 and 3, 1924, I was at the meeting of our New York State Historical Association in the Hotel Statler, on the corner of which we unveiled a tablet to Ex-President Millard Fillmore, visited the Albright Art Gallery, the site of the shooting of President Mc Kinley, was entertained at a dinner by the President, Frank H. Severance and one by Dr. Lucien Howe and visited Old Fort Niagara at the mouth of the river.[29] One day we crossed the Niagara River to the Canadian side to visit the old battle fields, including Fort Erie, Chippewa, Lundy's Lane, and Queenstown [Queenston] Heights, had dinner at the Falls of Niagara, and was given a reception by Dr. Henry R. T. Grant head of the Victoria Park.[30] On my way back to Plainfield, I stopped a day at Dunbar, Fayette County, Pennsylvania, named after Little Mother's father, George Towers Dunbar, one of the engineers who helped to build the Baltimore and Ohio railroad. I afterward visited Exeter, New Hampshire, where my grandson, William Henry Corbusier was at the Exeter Academy. After that I left Plainfield November 4, 1924, to visit Phil and Ida at the Command and General Staff School at Fort Leavenworth, Kansas, November 22 to December 6.

I took the Santa Fé railroad from Kansas City to Ash Fork, December 6, and thence to Phoenix, Arizona, on the 8th, snow as far as Ash Forks [sic] and then rain. On the 10th Mr. George H. Kelly drove me in his auto to Fort McDowell to see Mike Burns.[31] I gave Mr. Kelly, who is the State Historian, the account I had written of the end of Del-Cha, a noted Tonto chief, and also many Indian geographic names in Arizona. I went to Kingman, Arizona, on the 11th to work on my Walapai vocabulary until the 20th and then went on to Los Angeles, where Will, Mabel and Mary met me and took me to their home, 247 Coronado Avenue, Long Beach, California. Afterward I went to the Hotel De Luxe. In February 1925, I had the influenza and had to go to the Seaside Hospital from February 27 to March 9, where the accommodations were poor and the appliances with which to treat a cold were not to be had.

Will drove me to Riverside, as my cough hung on and here it disappeared. From March 27, to April 2, I spent the time in reviewing my Walapai vocabulary with some boys from the Sherman Institute, one of them being Willie Walker, a cousin of Peter Walker and the grandson of Waki-yoota, the old Walapais at Kingman who had given me most of the words and sentences and the story of Wolf's son. I went to Riverside again, and from June 13 to 28 collected Yuma or Kachan words, but the children had been to school so long that they had forgotten most of their native tongue. The thermometer in my room was usually 84°, but one day was up to 112° in a newspaper office. I drove in an auto, and there was always a breeze and I enjoyed the change from the chilly fogs of the winter and spring on the coast. One drive was to San Bernadino [Bernardino] and back over Smiley Heights and Prospect Mark to Redlands, another drive was up Mt. Roubidoux [Rubidoux]. Mabel came for me and drove back to Long Beach, 67 miles, and I went to the De Luxe again. Many of my meals I took at the Mission Cafeteria which gave the best meals in town.

July 19, 1925, Will and family drove me to Wilmington, where I took the steamer *Harvard* to San Francisco.[32] It was at Wilmington that mother, Claude, Harold and I had taken a steamer in the middle of May, 1875, to the same destination. Claude and Frank met me and Frank drove me to the office of Dr. Philip Gilman whom I consulted about a hard gland in

my left groin and then, July 20 entered the Letterman Hospital where on
July 28, Major Jesse Sloat cut it out under local anaesthesia. It was an inch
long and nearly three-quarters of an inch thick. The incision was healed
by August 6 and on August 17, Frank drove me over to Hotel Whitecotton, in Berkeley where I remained until October 17, 1925.

¶On September 6, Claude and I drove in his car to Rainbow Lodge of
the San Francisco Flycasting Club at Union Mills, a station on the railroad,
208 ½ miles elevation 5623 feet. The Lodge is on the south side of the
Truckee River and six or seven miles from Truckee. We started at 7.15 a.m.,
crossed the Vallejo ferry and were making good time until we entered the
foot hills beyond Sacramento when rain set in when we were near Auburn,
and after passing Colfax, when at the Black Canyon we had a blowout and
Claude had to change tires in a pouring down rain. The road was very slip-
pery and we had to drive very slowly and it was dark when Frank and Lois
met us when we were still about ten miles out, to lead us over the rocky and
steep hills, and it was 7 p.m. when we arrived. There were 15 or 16 men and
women and the men had caught enough rainbow trout to give each one of
us two for dinner, and so it was as long as we were there, and all took some
home with them. We left on September 10. Snow could be seen on the
mountains north and accounted for the cold nights when a huge wood fire
was kept burning in the great fire-place. We had a punctured tire after passing Truckee and Claude had to walk nearly a mile to find a phone to order
a new tire for which we had to wait. When night came on and we turned
on the lights, they soon gave out and had to be replaced and these lasted
only a short time. Then on looking closely it was found that a broken wire
was the cause, but it was after 9 p.m. when we arrived back at Berkeley.

¶On October 29, Will and I drove to Lake Cuyamaca, 147 miles, having
lunch at Escandido—Hidden Valley—105 miles. We slept in one of the
comfortable cabins and had meals at the Lodge. We returned on the 30th
via San Diego, 20 miles, and had lunch at Solano. Sunday, November 1
Will took us to Hollywood where we ascended Magnetic Hill for a short
distance after having turned off the power, and had to turn it on in order
to descend, or we would have gone up hill again. To go back to Berkeley, — 165 —
on October 17, 1925, Claude drove me from the Whitecotton to Oakland,
Belle and Frances with us, and here I took a pickwick autobus at 10.30
a.m., passed San Jose 12.30 p.m., lunched at Salinas 2.45 p.m, and arrived at
San Luis Obispo, 241 miles at 7.50 p.m., went to the Blackstone Hotel for

the night and left there the next morning, Sunday, 8.15 a.m., lunched in Santa Barbara and arrived in Los Angeles, 211 miles farther, at 5.30 p.m. where Will and family met me and took me to the Hotel De Luxe. We then went to the Mission Cafeteria for dinner.

Will, Mabel, and I left Long Beach at 9.10 a.m., November 7, 1925 in his automobile and drove to Yuma, Arizona, 399 miles, via Anaheim, Corona, Riverside, Beaumont, Indio, where we had lunch, Banning along the west side of the Salton Sea, Brawley, Imperial, to El Centro, 235 miles, where we staid [sic] at the Barbara Worth Hotel, and on Sunday, November 8, drove on and passed alfalfa and cotton fields, date orchards, etc., and then fifteen miles over sand dunes on a plank road nearly to old Fort Yuma where we stopped for a short time. Here Little Mother and I spent Christmas of 1872, on our way into Arizona, long before their [sic] was a bridge which we now crossed and went to the Arizona Hotel. Here Will and Mabel left me to return home on November 9. I worked on my Yuma vocabulary until November 19, having William Savilla, aged 26 years, and other Yuma Indians to assist me. After I had received from them all that they could give me, I left for San Antonio, Texas, as the hotel was not heated. The people of Yuma have to go out of doors and stand in the sun to get warm. White, black, red, yellow and brown stand at many of the crossings and spit on the crossings and one cannot easily avoid the sputa which look like sunbursts, and rain so infrequent that the wind drives the contaminated dust into your face.

Phil met me at the railroad station, San Antonio, and drove me about eight miles to his newly built home, a couple of blocks beyond the city limits, 370 Terrell Road, north of the city on the highest ground near it. The house is stuc[c]oed two story high, and they have added two sun-parlors on the east side of 9 ft. by 18ft., one above the other. The lot is 100 ft. by 200 feet and on it they have planted Bermuda grass, fruit and shade trees and many varieties of flowers. Phil was assigned to duty here as Instructor of the Tyth [sic] Cavalry Brigade Headquarters and 112th Cavalry, Texas National Guard, July 23, 1925.

My first great grand child was born at Camp Stotsenburg, Pampanga Province, Philippine Islands on Monday, March 8, 1926, and he was named after William Corbusier Pierson.[33] The announcement of his birth was received from his father, First Lieutenant Millard Pierson, Field Artillery, U.S. Army, by cable on March 7th, the day before his birth, on account of

the difference in longitude. His mother, Phyllis, and Millard were married
in Manila, Philippine Islands on November 9, 1924.

I have written vocabularies of the Yavapai, Tulkepai, Walapai, Mojave, and Yuma dialects of the same language, the manuscripts of which are in the American Bureau of Ethnology, Washington, D.C. The Yavapai and Mojave have been published in the *"Zeitschrifur Ethnologie [Zeitschrift für Ethnologie]*," Berlin, 1883, pages 123–147, and pages 1–18 of 1892. *The American Antiquarian*, September, 1886, pages 276–284, and November, pages 325–339, have my article on the Apache-Yuma and Apache Mojave. Other writing that I have done may be found in "Magic Circle of the Yuma Conjurors" in the *Magazine of American History*, pg. [indecipherable in text], August 1879. "Sign Language among North American Indians," by Garrick Mallery, in the *Annual Report of the Bureau of Ethnology*, 1879–80.[34] "The Dakota Winter-Counts" by Mallery in 1882–83, *Report of the Bureau*, and "Picture Writing of the North American Indians "by Mallery in 1888–89 *Report of the Bureau*.

I am a member of the following societies: Empire State Society, Sons of the American Revolution—No. 54, March 20, 1891; Society of Colonial Wars in the State of New York—No. 1110, 1901; Society of the War of 1812 of Pennsylvania—No. 16, 1891, National Society of the Army of the Philippines; The American Flag Association; The Military Order of the Moro Campaigns—No. 40, April 22, 1905. The Association of Military Surgeons of the U.S.—January 1, 1907. New York Historical Association—1909. Order of Indian Wars of the U.S.—October 1910. Military Order of the World War—September 29, 1924, New York Chapter. Credited with eighteen ancestors in the Colonial Wars. One of them was Simon De Ruine—The Walloon—a corporal in the Third Company, New Harlem, June 12, 1663 and served at Esopus against Indians. I am descended from him and his wife Madlaine Van der Stratten in three lines through their daughters, Jacomina Demarest, Maria Demarest and Jennetie De Pré. I am also descended form Sarah Rapalie, who was born at Fort Orange, now Albany, New York, June 9, 1625, the first child of European parentage born in the New Netherlands, married in 1639 to Hans Hansen van Bergen; and also descended from her sister Jannetje, born, August 10, 1629, who was married December 21, 1642, to Rem Jansen Van der Beeck. They were daughters of Joris Jansen Rapalie and his wife Catalina Trice, who arrived at Manhattan Island late in May 1624. According to tradition,

Joris was a great grandson of Colonel Gaspard Colét de Papalye, or Papallo, who was a nephew of Admiral Gaspard Coligni.

My pedigree in the Corbusier line: 1. William Henry Corbusier, born, New York, April 10, 1844. Son of 2, William Morrison Corbusier, married, October 25, 1841, Mahala, daughter of Stephen Myers of Nyack, New York. Son of 3. James Henry Corbusier, came from Bermuda in 1805, married, October 28, 1818 in New York, Eleanor Catherine, daughter of Alexander Sloat. Son of 4. Thomas Pullein Corbusier, married in Bermuda, February 2, 1782 Alice, daughter of Francis Peniston. Son of 5. James Corbusier, married, in Bermuda, August 11, 1748, Ann, daughter of Thomas Outerbridge. Son of 6. Henry Corbusier, married in Bermuda, before November 19, 1719, his first wife, Miriam, daughter of James Mallagan. Henry came with his father Philip to Bermuda before 1719 from London, England in the sloop Corbusier. He was Colonel of His Majesty's Volunteer Troop of Horse Grenadiers, 1739 to 1755, and member of the Council from 1743 to 1757. He died, April 24, 1764. Son of 7. Philip Corbusier, who came to Bermuda in his ship *Corbusier*, probably in 171[last digit illegible] and died there March 1, 1719/20, and his estate was administered by his wife Catherine in May, 1729, who lived in Stepney, County Middlesex, England. Son of 8. Henry Corbusier of Stepney, Middlesex County, England. Possibly son of 9. Jan Corbisier, baptized December 3, 1620 at L'Eglise Wallone de Norwich. Jan was the son of 10. Jan Corbise, Curbysser Corbese, Corbysyes or Corbigir, or Jean Corbisers, Corbisie or Corbigeir, or Jan Corbisy or Corbisier or Corbizy, as the scribes write the name to a fancied pronunciation. His wife was Judith, baptized March 23, 1660 possibly daughter of Luc Malebranc and the grand daughter of Franchois Mamlbrancq and his wife Crestienne.

NOTES

Introduction

1. Harold Dunbar Corbusier's published diary is *A Boy at Fort Mackinac*. Four of Dr. Corbusier's surviving diaries, spanning parts of the years between 1903 and 1913, are in the private collection of Nancy Corbusier Knox. I have used the copy of Dr. Corbusier's genealogy, "Ancestry of William Henry Corbusier, Lieutenant Colonel, United States Army, Retired, and Fanny Dunbar Corbusier, His Wife" in the New York Public Library, New York. The "Lieutenant" on the title page has been crossed out, presumably after his subsequent promotion to colonel in 1919.

2. I have used the copy of Fanny's "Recollections" in the Center for American History, University of Texas at Austin. Dr. Corbusier's thirty-seven page contribution to the surgeon general's collection, "Record of William Henry Corbusier, Colonel, U.S. Army, Retired," April 10, 1924, may be found in the United States Army Surgeon General's Office. For his "Memoirs," I have used the typescript provided by Nancy Corbusier Knox.

3. This expands on a concept I first heard in Brian Linn's paper "The Long Twilight of the Frontier Army."

For works by or about late nineteenth-century army surgeons, see Kimball, *A Soldier Doctor of Our Army*; Kober, *Reminiscences of George Martin Kober, M.D., LL.D.*; Mattison, "The Diary of Surgeon Washington Matthews, Fort Rice, D. T.;" Byrne, *A Frontier Army Surgeon*; Fitzgerald, *An Army Doctor's Wife on the Frontier*; Garrison, *John Shaw Billings*; Buecker, "A Surgeon at the Little Big Horn;" and Luce, "The Diary and Letters of Dr. James M. DeWolf." Especially noteworthy among unpublished collections are the Lauderdale Letterbooks, Beinecke Rare Book and Manuscript Library, Yale University.

Among contemporary accounts by surgeons in the Philippines, see Heiser, *An American Doctor's Odyssey*; Abbott, "Acting Assistant Surgeons in the Philippines;" Anderson, "Notes of an Army Surgeon in the Recent War;" Banister, "Medical and Surgical Observations During a Three-Year Tour of Duty in the Philippines;" Seamen, "Some Observations of a Medical Officer in the Philippines;" and Turnbull, "Reminiscences of an Army Surgeon in Cuba and the Philippines."

The best secondary works include Olch, "Medicine in the Indian-Fighting Army, 1866–1890;" Gillett, *Army Medical Department*; and Ashburn, *History of the Medical Department of the United States Army*.

4. Thrapp, *Encyclopedia of Frontier Biography*, 1:323.

5. United States Army Surgeon General's Office, "Record of William Henry Corbusier." Notations of Corbusier's contracts as acting assistant surgeon (including his Civil War service) are in Station Cards, Acting Assistant Surgeons, 1862–68, 1898–1901, RG 94, National Archives. For acting assistant surgeons during the Civil War, see Adams, *Doctors in Blue*, 45–49, 174–75.

6. The eldest son, Claude, went into the insurance business. Harold, Philip, and Frank joined the army at the outbreak of the Spanish-American War and served in the forces that eventually occupied the Philippines. After a stint in China with the Boxer Relief Expedition, Harold opened a civilian medical practice, rejoining the army during World War I. Philip made a career of the army and was buried with his father at Arlington National Cemetery. Frank became a safety engineer and insurance manager; William T. also became an insurance man, blending this profession with his work as a construction engineer.

7. The Corbusier family mounted an unsuccessful campaign to secure his promotion to brigadier general upon retirement. They based their claim on an act of April 23, 1904, which granted such advancement to officers who had served during the Civil War. Unfortunately, the War Department ruled that service as contract surgeon was not included in the act and therefore denied the petition. See materials in 4565 ACP 1876, Appointments, Commission, and Personal Branch Papers, RG 94, National Archives.

8. For an obituary (which contains several errors), see the *New York Times*, February 9, 1930, sec. 2, p. 6. A diary entry for July 13, 1903, (W. H. Corbusier, Diaries), gives the number of boxes the family had packed for their sojourn to the Philippines. An undated typescript page in this collection mentions José. The latter document also reveals an intriguing side of Corbusier's personality:

> After a man has lived four score years and over five months he may think that he stands tall with his fellow man whom he has tried to serve all through life as I have, but on Saturday, September 15, 1928, I received a great shock and all conceit was wrung from me.
>
> I have been striving to keep on my feet and not take to a wheeled-chair, so walk a little every day by using a cane with my right hand and hanging to one of Jose's arms with the other. I went to Oakland by street-car on Saturday and walked two blocks to Maxwell's Hardware store, 1320 Washington Street to have a hole in [an] aluminum cup soldered to get a new one. As I leaned against a counter, Jose took the cup from his pocket and handed it to me and as he did so a clerk came up and dropped a nickel into it. I was so confounded and ashamed that I could say nothing, but took the nickel and handed it back to him. Both Jose and I were better dressed than he was, and what prompted him to give a piddling nickel to a gentleman tramp or beggar, was a puzzle to me, a customer using aluminum ware. I must try to keep on walking in spite of such degrading experiences.

I let Jose read the above, as a valet's view-point is not always that of his master, and he laughed —which he rarely does—that I, a colonel, should be thought a beggar, and I then laughed with him.

9. Eaton is quoted in W. T. Corbusier, *Verde to San Carlos*, 6. W. H. Corbusier, officer's individual report, February 19, 1894, Personal Papers of Medical Officers and Physicians, RG 94, National Archives.

10. See 4565 ACP 1876, Appointments, Commission, and Personal Branch Papers, RG 94, National Archives.

11. On Corbusier's contributions, see Mallery, "Sign Language Among North American Indians" and Gifford, *Northeastern and Western Yavapai*. Other miscellaneous Corbusier materials on the cultures of the Yavapai, Kawia, Shoshoni, Walapai, and Yuma may be found in the National Anthropological Archives, Washington, D.C.

Among various copies of Mike Burns's manuscript still in existence is a typescript, edited by Robert D. Sullivan, in the possession of Nancy Corbusier Knox. A fictionalized version has been published by Elaine Waterstrait as *Hoomothya's Long Journey, 1865–1897: The True Story of a Yavapai Indian*.

12. "On my recommendation," insists Corbusier, "the badge was ordered for the whole army." He may have suggested such a policy, but the idea was neither a new one nor entirely his own. Civil War soldiers, for example, often pinned name tags to their uniforms for identification purposes in case they fell in battle. They did so with good reason, for as a post-Civil War study by Clara Barton later revealed, about 45 percent of the 315,000 Union soldier graves were marked "unknown." In 1905, an army board (which Corbusier's suggestion indeed may have influenced) was detailed "to investigate the various systems of personal identification now in use." The army made dog tags standard issue the following year. See Linderman, *Embattled Courage*, 248–49; *Washington Post*, June 1, 1998, p. F5; and the United States Army Surgeon General's Office, "The System of Personal Identification by Finger Prints Recently Adopted for the U.S. Army," vol. 3, pp. 55–61.

13. W. H. Corbusier, "Ancestry," 1–2A.

14. Ibid., 6–7.

15. Ibid., 1–6; W. H. Corbusier, Diaries, 1903; "Addenda" to F. Corbusier, "Recollections."

16. E. H. Greene to Corbusier, February 15, 1918, and Frank to "My Dear Father," February 28, 1918. Both letters are in the private collection of Nancy Corbusier Knox, who explained, "They were a very devoted family—all because of her [Fanny] I think." Personal interview, June 15, 2001.

— 171 —

Chapter One: Boyhood in New York

1. Antebellum militia units were often more ceremonial than functional. Fanciful though they undoubtedly were, even the resplendent Lafayette Fusiliers

could not match the Swartara Guards of Middletown, Pennsylvania. The Guards wore blue trousers with wide yellow stripes and blue swallowtailed uniform coats, faced with yellow and trimmed with yellow cords, bullet buttons, and huge yellow epaulets on each shoulder. High, stiff caps with brass fronts and one-foot-high scarlet feather plumes topped off the garish outfits. Mahon, *History of the Militia and the National Guard*, 79–96.

2. The first American-born star of the stage, Edwin Forrest (1806–1872) boasted a muscular build and resonant voice, capturing the public imagination during an era in which the theater attracted audiences from a cross section of American society. He married the actress Catherine Norton Sinclair in 1837. During scandalous divorce proceedings in 1851, Forrest and his wife both accused each another of infidelity. He nonetheless remained a popular performer until his death. Garraty and Carnes, *American National Biography*, 8:259–61.

3. Built in 1795, the Park Theatre (located on Park Row), was New York City's preeminent theater from the 1810s through the 1830s. Its fare deteriorated somewhat after that, and it burned in 1848. It was replaced by commercial buildings. Wilmeth and Miller, *Cambridge Guide to American Theatre*, 366–67.

4. Stephen Myers is listed as head of a thirteen-member household (six males and seven females) in the 1840 census for Clarktown Township, Rockland County. Four persons living there were employed in "manufactures and trade." Rockland County, N. Y., 1840 Manuscript Census.

5. Haskins, *Argonauts of California*, 436, confirms that the elder Corbusier was aboard the ship but lists the sailing date as February 1.

6. Published in 1848, Stephen C. Foster's "Oh! Susanna" was soon adopted as their own by many forty-niners. Ewen, *American Popular Songs*, 291.

7. Taken from the Dutch "zee" (sea or ocean), the Tappan Zee is the expansion of the Hudson River to a width of nearly three miles near Tarrytown and Ossining, New York.

8. A Stephen Myers served in the Eighty-third New York Militia during the War of 1812. Index to Compiled Service Records of Volunteer Soldiers Who Served during the War of 1812, Microfilm M 602, National Archives.

9. The 1850 census lists Jane Tasman, a forty-four-year-old native of New York, as living with her husband, Thomas, age forty-two, and five children in Rockland County. A carpenter, the English-born Thomas Tasman claimed property valued at $500. Rockland County, N. Y., 1850 Manuscript Census.

10. Founded in 1625 by the Dutch West India Company on present Governors and Manhattan Islands, New Amsterdam had a cosmopolitan population of about one thousand in 1656. It fell into English hands in 1664 and again in 1674 when it became New York City. *Dictionary of American History*, 5:40–41.

11. In 1850, New York-born Catherine R. Remsen, age seventy-three, lived in New Town, Queens County, New York. Mary Lawrence, age fourteen, lived with Remsen. They claimed no property. Queens County, N. Y., 1850 Manuscript Census.

12. On August 19, 1850, federal census takers found one Mahala Corbusier, age twenty-six, in New York City's Eighth ward. She and four other boarders (one male and three females) were rooming with William Downing, an Irish-born clerk, and his wife. New York County, N. Y., 1850 Manuscript Census.

13. In 1860, Rachel Myers, age sixty-five, lived with Elizabeth A. Myers, age thirteen, in Rockland County. A native of New York, Rachel claimed $1500 real and $4000 personal property. In the next household was fifty-year-old Catherine Myers, a milliner, who claimed $4000 real and $1500 personal property. Rockland County, N. Y., 1860 Manuscript Census.

14. Plagued by an inadequate and polluted water supply, New York City dammed the Croton River. Masonry aqueducts and tunnels carried the water some forty miles into New York City. One of the era's great engineering feats, the seven-year, $13 million construction project was completed in 1842. Shumsky, *Encyclopedia of Urban America*, 2:867–68.

15. Hungarian revolutionary Lajos Kossuth (1802–1894) had fled the continent to England in 1849 following a long, unsuccessful battle against oppressive Austrian rule. His periodic tours of the United States were generally met with great enthusiasm. Magnusson, *Cambridge Biographical Dictionary*, 839.

16. The anti-Catholic, anti-immigrant American Party of the 1850s briefly served as an alternative to the newly emerging Republican Party. When asked about their intent, some members allegedly responded with a noncommital "I know nothing," thus giving the party its informal name. Foner and Garraty, *Reader's Companion to American History*, 622.

17. The city's dominant political machine, Tammany Hall, assiduously courted the Irish vote. See Burrows and Wallace, *Gotham*, 512–15, 629–35, 823–27.

18. George N. Christy (1827–68) ranked among the most popular blackface minstrel stars of the era, often as the featured performer in the "Christy's Minstrels" troupe. Garraty and Carnes, *American National Biography*, 2:856–57.

19. Belief in supernatural manifestations has long been a part of American popular culture. The "Rochester rappings" of 1848–49 in Hydesville and Rochester, New York, are sometimes cited as having marked the beginning of spiritualism in the United States. *Dictionary of American History*, 6:157. See also Carroll, *Spiritualism in Antebellum America*.

20. Leonard Wood (1860–1927) won the Medal of Honor as a contract surgeon during the Geronimo campaign of 1885–86. He became a close friend of Theodore Roosevelt and helped to organize the Rough Riders at the outset of the Spanish-American War. Appointed military governor of Santiago, Wood implemented Progressive Era reforms, such as rejuvenating schools, implementing a massive public health campaign, and overseeing elections. Named commander of the Department of Mindanao in 1903, he coupled an ambitious reform program with a savage counterinsurgency campaign against the Moros. Linn, *Guardians of Empire*, 37–39; Beede, *War of 1898 and U.S. Interventions*, 599–603.

21. Washington Irving, whose short stories included "Rip Van Winkle" and "The Legend of Sleepy Hollow," had purchased in 1836 an old Dutch house overlooking the Hudson River near Sleepy Hollow, New York. At the time of Corbusier's visit, Irving was editing a collection of his earlier works and was about to launch a five volume biography of George Washington. Garraty and Carnes, *American National Biography*, 11:686–89.

Chapter Two: The California Gold Fields

1. New York and California Steamship Line advertisements promised that passengers would find steamers such as *Prometheus* to be "unsurpassed in their ventilation and accommodations." *New York Times*, July 5, 1854.

2. Born in Tennessee, William Walker (1824–60) established a short-lived Republic of Lower California in Mexican-held Baja California in 1853. Driven back to the United States the following year, he was acquitted of charges that he had violated his nation's neutrality laws. In 1855, he and several hundred mercenaries, raised in the United States, took control of the Nicaraguan government. Walker promptly legalized slavery and planned to build an inter-ocean canal there. Overthrown in 1857, he returned to the United States and outfitted another expedition to Central America. He was executed by a Honduran firing squad. Garraty and Carnes, *American National Biography*, 22:521–23.

3. Launched in 1837, the sloop U.S.S. *Cyane* served along the California and Mexican coasts during the war against Mexico. It bombarded Greytown on July 13, 1854, in response to depredations against United States citizens in the region. The *Cyane* was decommissioned in 1871. Office of the Chief of Naval Operations, *Dictionary of American Naval Fighting Ships*, 2:226.

4. "Ometepe" means "between two hills" in Nahuatl, a Central and South American language indigenous to Nicaragua. The island of Ometepe contains two volcanoes, Concepción (still active) and Maderas.

5. Displacing 2,141 tons, the oceangoing paddle wheeler *George Law* was launched in October 1852 for the United States Mail Steamship Company. Its name was changed to *Central America* in 1857, but the ship sank that September while en route from Havana to New York. Four hundred twenty-three persons died, and eight million dollars in gold was lost. Swiggum and Kohli, "Panama Route Ships," website.

6. Launched in 1850 from New York, *Pacific* entered the San Francisco-Panama route the following year. Following the Civil War, it was largely involved in California and Pacific Northwest traffic until 1875, when it sunk. Over 250 persons went down with the ship. Ibid.

7. Lieutenant Edward Russell Theller was actually killed during the Nez Percé conflict in 1877 at White Bird Creek, Idaho, as Fanny Corbusier correctly explains in her "Recollections." Theller was appointed captain of the Second California Infantry in 1861. Mustered out as a brevet major in 1866, he was commissioned as

a second lieutenant in the regular army in 1867 and promoted to first lieutenant four years later. F. Corbusier, "Recollections," 13; Heitman, *Historical Register and Dictionary*, 1:952.

Edward Otho Cresap Ord (1818–83), a West Point graduate, fought in Virginia, Mississippi, Louisiana, and North Carolina during the Civil War, service which was eventually rewarded with brevet promotions to the rank of major general. Following the Civil War, Ord commanded the military departments of Arkansas, California, the Platte, and Texas. McHenry, *Webster's American Military Biographies*, 303.

8. German-born Johann August Sutter (1803–80) moved to California in the late 1830s and was at the vanguard of non-Indian penetration into the Sacramento Valley. His fort dominated the region. Following the Mexican War, he built a sawmill up the American River. His overseer, James Marshall, found gold there in January 1848, sparking the California gold rush. But Sutter was no businessman, and he soon lost his California empire. Phillips and Axelrod, *Encyclopedia of the American West*, 4:1531.

9. The site of a gold mining camp of three or four tents, Auburn was named in 1849. Census takers the following year found 1,032 persons in the vicinity. A post office was established there in 1853. Gudde, *California Gold Camps*, 22–23.

10. Pushed by poverty at home and pulled by opportunities in America, thousands of Chinese migrated to California during the gold rush period. Here they faced severe racial discrimination and bigotry; the many who made their way to the gold fields faced a "foreign miners' tax" of three dollars per month and were usually relegated to abandoned or poorly producing placer claims. Typically, they remained socially isolated from other miners and lived in city ghettos. The California census of 1852 found that 3,019 of Placer County's 10,784 residents were Chinese. Phillips and Axelrod, *Encyclopedia of the American West*, 1:302–07; Bancroft, *History of California*, 483.

11. "Digger Indians" was a derogatory term used to describe Indians who exploited roots as a food source, particularly in California. Here Corbusier is probably referring to the Nisenan tribe. Heizer, *California*, 397.

12. "Alkalied" was a slang term that meant "experienced in living in the west." Cassidy, *Dictionary of American Regional English*, 1:36.

13. Here Corbusier may be referring to the Brulé Indian Winter Count, 1230–1907. The Brulés used significant events to mark each year, or "winter," in their tribal calendars. Battiste Good, a Brulé elder, copied his winter count onto paper for Dr. Corbusier in 1879–80. Presumably, the original "Corbusier 'Winter Count'" was destroyed with most of the doctor's possessions in the San Francisco fire of 1906. Good made another copy in 1907, which is now housed at the Library of Congress, Washington, D.C. Library of Congress, "Epilogue," website.

14. Auburn was nearly destroyed by the 1855 blaze. Bancroft, *History of California*, 483.

15. Historian Hubert Howe Bancroft described Sunday as "the harvest day for the gamblers, who raked in regularly the weekly earnings of the improvident." Ibid.

16. The son of an actor, Edwin Booth (1833–93) was born in Maryland. He performed in California mining camps and San Francisco from 1852 to 56 before returning east, where he began to attract national attention. Although his brother, John Wilkes Booth, was the assassin of President Abraham Lincoln, Edwin Booth remained a popular Shakespearean actor and theatrical manager until his death. Garraty and Carnes, *American National Biography*, 3:191–93.

17. Born in Ireland, Maria Dolores Eliza Rosanna Gilbert (1813–61) adopted the stage name Lola Montez during the early 1840s. She became a popular dancer and stage figure in England and on the European continent. Following her sensational and much publicized dalliance with Ludwig I, she debuted on the New York stage in 1851. Montez eventually made her way to the California gold-mining region. Her home included an imported bathtub, a marble fireplace, and a menagerie of animals. Her dances in California featured the provocative "spider dance," which apparently blended elements of the polka, waltz, jig, and mazurka. She later moved back to New York, where she lived the rest of her life. Phillips and Axelrod, *Encyclopedia of the American West*, 3:1026; Wilmeth and Miller, *Cambridge Guide to American Theatre*, 323.

18. The 1852 California census reported only 343 white females among Placer County's population of 10,784. Bancroft, *History of California*, 483.

19. Exotic displays of "western" life and people had long been popular in Europe and the United States, but the most spectacular "Wild West Shows" would not come until the 1880s. As many as 1,500 Indians performed in the dozens of touring troupes of the late nineteenth and early twentieth centuries. Phillips and Axelrod, *Encyclopedia of the American West*, 4:1745–49.

Chapter Three: On Both Coasts

1. Determined to avenge the murders of General William Richardson and newspaper editor James King, many San Franciscans formed a Committee of Vigilance. A number of prominent Californians, including future Civil War general William T. Sherman, believed the Committee went too far. As Sherman later wrote: "As they controlled the press, they wrote their own history, and the world generally gives them the credit of having purged San Francisco of rowdies and roughs; but their success has given great stimulus to a dangerous principle, that would at any time justify the mob in seizing all the power of government; and who is to say that the Vigilance Committee may not be composed of the worst, instead of the best, elements of a community?" The Vigilance Committee eventually fortified its headquarters building, which became known as "Fort Gunnybags." Yankee Sullivan, a noted prizefighter, committed suicide while under the committee's "arrest." Phillips and Axelrod, *Encyclopedia of the American West*, 3:1425; Sherman, *Memoirs of General W. T. Sherman*, 150.

2. Alvin Adams founded the Adams Express Company in Massachusetts in 1839. It rapidly expanded into a national shipping powerhouse and came to hold huge shares in many transportation concerns. However, the 1854 failure of its California subsidiary, Adams and Company, caused a regional economic panic. *Dictionary of American History*, 1:9–10.

3. In 1841, showman P. T. Barnum bought Scudder's American Museum, enlarged it, and renamed it Barnum's American Museum. For twenty-five cents, patrons could view a cornucopia of curios, relics, and novelties. Among its chief attractions was Charles Sherwood Stratton, a three-foot-tall comedian and impersonator known as Tom Thumb. Thumb starred in several successful world tours before his death in 1883. Barnum's Museum was destroyed by fire in 1865. Ibid., 1:268; Garraty and Carnes, *American National Biography*, 21:743–44.

4. Authorized by the city's board of education in 1847 to provide free secondary and college schooling for talented students, the Free Academy evolved into the College of the City (and later University) of New York. Spann, *New Metropolis*, 259–60.

5. During the 1850s New York City used its powers of eminent domain to displace some 1,600 people and build Central Park. Sparked by the imaginative landscape design of Frederick Law Olmsted and Calvert Vaux, the park developed into one of the most important urban public places in the United States. Shumsky, *Encyclopedia of Urban America*, 1:132–34.

6. Edward H. "Corbysier," age twenty-seven, lived with "Hester Corbysier," age twenty-five, in the third district of New York City's Nineteenth ward in 1860. They had two children and lived with one Anna Ellis, age sixty. All were born in New York. New York County, N. Y., 1860 Manuscript Census.

7. Soon after their introduction, horse-drawn passenger cars on rails in city streets came to provide the foundation for American urban public transportation in the latter half of the nineteenth century. The model for early horsecar lines was provided by the New York and Harlem Railroad, established in 1852 to serve lower Manhattan. The older horse-drawn omnibuses did not have rails. Shumsky, *Encyclopedia of Urban America*, 1:351–52.

8. During the 1830s, the Bowery Theatre rivaled the prestigious Park Theatre as New York City's top showplace. Walt Whitman remembered its audiences in those days as "alert, well dress'd, full-blooded young and middle-aged men, the best average of American-born mechanics." Whitman wrote that by the 1840s, "cheap prices and vulgar programmes came in. . . . Slang, wit, occasional shirt sleeves, and a picturesque freedom of looks and manners, with a rude good-nature and restless movement, were generally noticeable." Whitman, *Complete Poetry and Prose*, 2:439–44.

George Washington Lafayette Fox (1825–77) was a noted comedian and mime famed for his Shakespearean burlesques and hugely successful production *Humpty Dumpty*, which ran for over 1,200 performances. He was physically removed from the stage during the middle of a performance in 1875 and taken to an insane asylum. Wilmeth and Miller, *Cambridge Guide to American Theatre*, 189–90.

9. Here Corbusier probably confuses his chronology. Scottish soprano Euphrosyne Parepa-Rosa (1836–74) debuted in Malta in 1855. Following engagements in many European cities, she embarked on a lengthy U.S. tour after the Civil War. Boasting a two-and-a-half-octave range, her opera, concert, and oratorio performances were legendary. Hitchcock and Sade, *New Grove Dictionary of American Music*, 3:470.

Located on Fourteenth Street, the Academy of Music began offering operatic concerts in 1854. Lankevich, *American Metropolis*, 76–77.

10. Tycoon Cyrus W. Field spearheaded American involvement in the transatlantic telegraphic cable project. After a failed effort in 1857, the ships, each carrying half of the needed cable, finally succeeded in making the connection on August 5. Unfortunately, the cable deteriorated rapidly and had failed entirely by October. A new cable was finally completed in 1866. *Dictionary of American History*, 1:400–01.

11. The 1860 census for Rockland County, New York, lists William H. Corbusier as the eldest of twenty-three boys at the Nyack Classical and Commercial Academy. The youngest student was nine years old. English-born Christopher Rutherford, forty-seven, had a wife and six children and an estate valued at $1,000. Four female servants, all Irish immigrants, also lived there. Rockland County, N. Y., Manuscript Census.

12. American children had been playing various adaptations of the modern game of baseball for years when in 1845 a Manhattan team, styling themselves the Knickerbocker Base Ball Club, wrote down the rules by which they had been playing. Foner and Garraty, *Reader's Companion to American History*, 86.

13. From his home in Springfield, Illinois, President-elect Lincoln took the train through Buffalo, Albany, and New York City en route to the capital. Corbusier may be referring to a suspected assassination threat south of Harrisburg, Pennsylvania. Against his better judgment, Lincoln took the advice of detective Allan Pinkerton and arrived in Washington in the middle of the night. Donald, *Lincoln*, 273–79.

14. The first Northern regiment to reach Washington when the war began, the Sixth Massachusetts was attacked by a secessionist mob in Baltimore on April 19. The Seventh New York arrived in the capital via Annapolis on April 25. The Ellsworth Zouaves, colorfully dressed in baggy trousers and short jackets, were recruited by Elmer Ellsworth in New York City that month. Most had been volunteer firemen. They arrived in the capital on May 2. Much more effective when it came to fighting were the men of the Fifth New York, known as the Duryee Zouaves in honor of their colonel, Abram Duryee. Boatner, *Civil War Dictionary*, 263–64, 593–94; Donald, *Lincoln*, 297–99.

15. Corbusier could be confused here, depending on the actual date of his voyage. Captained by Raphael Semmes, the C.S.S. *Sumter* captured eighteen ships in

the Gulf of Mexico, the Caribbean Sea, and the South Atlantic before being aban- NOTES
doned at Gibraltar in January 1862. The *Alabama* was launched in May 1862. TO PAGES
Under Semmes's able leadership, it enjoyed even more success in the North and 36–46
South Atlantic, the Gulf of Mexico, and the Indian Ocean, sinking or capturing
nearly seventy Federal ships before being sunk in June 1864 off the French coast.
Current, *Encyclopedia of the Confederacy*, 1:19–20; 4:1562–63.

16. Bancroft notes that the fertile Santa Clara Valley was, next to Los Angeles,
the most densely settled region by non-Indians before the California gold rush.
Bancroft, *History of California*, 524–25.

17. Born in Nice, Giuseppe Garibaldi (1807–82) began his long quest for freedom and Italian nationalism as early as 1834. After years of exile in South America and New York, he returned to Italy at the invitation of King Victor Emanuel
of Piedmont and Sardinia. Garibaldi's victories over Naples paved the way for the
unification of Italy. Magill, *Dictionary of World Biography*, 5:879–92.

18. The 1860 census for Santa Clara County, California, lists one "J. J. Bramann,"
a thirty-seven-year-old native of New York. A physician, he claimed an estate of
$3000 and lived with a woman (probably his wife), E. C. Bramann, twenty-two, a
native of Ohio. Santa Clara County, Calif., 1860 Manuscript Census.

19. The exploits (or depredations) attributed to California folk hero and social
bandit Joaquin Murieta (1829?–53) are widespread. Some scholars suggest that the
Murieta of popular culture may have actually been based upon a composite of
Hispanic leaders who battled racial prejudice in gold rush-era California. Whatever the case, the head of a bandit called Murieta was displayed to audiences
across much of the state. Garraty and Carnes, *American National Biography*,
16:123–24.

20. *Manada* is Spanish for "herd."

21. The Federals' destruction of the Confederate supply train during the Battle of Glorieta Pass, New Mexico (March 28, 1862), ended the South's dreams of
expanding into the Southwest. Alberts, *Battle of Glorieta*.

22. The Disciplines, or Christian, movement emerged from the Second Great
Awakening. Alexander Campbell was one of its leading theorists. Controversies
about slavery had split the Methodist church in 1843–44. *Dictionary of American
History*, 2:352–53; 4:318–19.

23. Spanish Franciscans established San Juan Bautista in 1797 in the San Ben-
ito River valley. The present church was completed in 1812. The mission was
secularized in 1835, but the church continued to serve the local parish. Lamar,
New Encyclopedia of the American West.

Chapter Four: The Civil War

1. Previous attempts to stimulate enlistment produced disappointingly small
numbers, and on July 17, 1862, Congress issued a draft for three hundred thousand militia. Conscription came the following March, but a draftee could still

avoid military service by hiring a substitute for $300. Substitutes received federal bounties of $100. Boatner, *Civil War Dictionary*, 74, 858.

2. Assisted by a large French army, Ferdinand Maximilian Joseph was established as emperor of Mexico in 1864. Although he never fully extended his authority into the state of Guerrero, French naval forces did for a time occupy Acapulco, the state's largest port and long a major source of supplies to the anti-imperialist cause. Dabbs, *French Army in Mexico, 1861–1867*, 143, 148, 168.

3. Officially named *Memphis* but generally referred to as *Belle Memphis*, this 645-ton side-wheel packet was built in 1860. It frequently served as a river transport during the Civil War. It sunk in January 1866 after being completely frozen in solid ice. "Steamers," website.

4. Born in 1830, Christy became assistant surgeon of the Thirty-second Illinois Infantry in early 1862. He joined the Ninth Illinois Cavalry in March 1863. After the war, he practiced in Chicago and Dunlap, Iowa. *History of the Ninth Illinois Cavalry*, 208–09; Illinois USGenWeb Project, "Roster of Field and Staff, 9th Illinois Cavalry," website.

5. A former music teacher and clerk, Benjamin Henry Grierson (1826–1911) joined the Sixth Illinois Cavalry as a major in 1861. Promoted to colonel the following year, he led a daring cavalry raid through central Mississippi during the Vicksburg campaign. Brevetted to major general during the Civil War, he commanded the Tenth Cavalry during the wars against the Indians, serving in the Indian, Arizona, and New Mexico Territories. He retired as a brigadier general in 1890 and died at Omena, Michigan. Leckie and Leckie, *Unlikely Warriors*.

6. This is probably "A. DeFoe," listed in the 1860 census of Hamilton County, Illinois, as a thirty-six-year-old physician who claimed $1000 in property. Index to Compiled Service Records of Volunteer Union Soldiers Who Served in Organizations from the State of Illinois, Microfilm M 1539, National Archives; Hamilton County, Ill., 1860 Manuscript Census.

7. Here Corbusier is uncharacteristically confused. On June 10, 1864, Nathan Bedford Forrest defeated a Union force twice the size of his own, commanded by Samuel D. Sturgis, at the Battle of Brice's Cross Roads, Mississippi. This humiliating Union defeat is sometimes referred to as Guntown, after a small village near the site. Sturgis's command included Grierson's cavalry brigade. Major General Andrew Jackson Smith (1815–97) had just been transferred back to Tennessee from Louisiana, where he had fought in the Red River campaign. In Tennessee, Smith was then given command of a large force tasked with blocking Forrest's efforts to cut Union supply lines as William Sherman moved against Atlanta. Boatner, *Civil War Dictionary*, 85, 289–91, 768, 816–17.

8. A resident of Olney, Illinois, Edward Ball enlisted as a sergeant in October 1861. He was promoted to first lieutenant in February 1862 and to captain in November 1863. He was killed on July 22, 1864. Ancestry.com, *Civil War Research Database*, website.

9. Mathew H. Starr was commissioned as a second lieutenant in May 1862 and reached the rank of full colonel on July 19, 1864. As Corbusier later explains, Starr died of his wounds on October 1, 1864. Ibid.

The Robert Tyler mentioned here was probably Edmond W. Tyler, a hospital steward from Pope County, Illinois. Tyler was mustered in on January 9, 1862, and was discharged for disability on June 21, 1865. United States Army Surgeon General's Office, "Record of William Henry Corbusier;" Illinois USGenWeb Project, "Roster of Field and Staff, 6th Illinois Cavalry," website.

10. Whitset entered the service as a second lieutenant in Company I, Sixth Illinois Cavalry. Index to Compiled Service Records of Volunteer Union Soldiers Who Served in Organizations from the State of Illinois, Microfilm 1539, National Archives.

11. Tennessee-born Nathan Bedford Forrest (1821–77) was one of the Civil War's most controversial figures. His daring raids confounded Union efforts in the West for most of the war, but his role in the slaughter of black troops at Fort Pillow (1864) and his postwar assistance to the Ku Klux Klan tarnished badly his reputation. Hurst, *Nathan Bedford Forrest*.

12. Born in Indiana in 1836, Stacy Hemenway moved with his family to Oregon as a boy. After graduating from the Chicago Medical College, he was mustered in as an assistant surgeon in June 1863. He was promoted to surgeon of the Forty-first U.S. Colored Infantry Regiment in December 1864. After the war, Hemenway was a contract surgeon for the army and a physician at the Asylum for the Insane, Washington Territory. *History of the Ninth Illinois Cavalry*, 209–10.

13. Edward Hatch (1832–89) ranked among the North's best cavalry commanders in the West. He would receive brevet promotions to brigadier and major general for his efforts in the Battles of Franklin and Nashville. Following the Civil War, he commanded the Ninth Cavalry. Boatner, *Civil War Dictionary*, 384.

14. Former Republican Congressman Cadwallader Colden Washburn (1818–82) raised the Second Wisconsin Cavalry and was appointed its colonel in 1862. Eventually appointed major general of volunteers, he resigned from the army at the end of the war and was later elected governor of Wisconsin. Ibid., 892.

15. George F. Root's "The Battle Cry of Freedom" included the words "we'll rally round the flag boys"; he also wrote "Just before the Battle, Mother." Charles Sawyer wrote the words and Henry Tucker wrote the music for "Weeping, Sad and Lonely," often known as "When This Cruel War Is Over." "John Brown's Body," author unknown, was another favorite among Union soldiers. See Watson, "Music of the War between the States," for an accessible mixture of historical text, words, and music.

16. William A. Duer enlisted as a hospital steward in the Sixth Illinois Cavalry on March 10, 1864. He was mustered out in November 1865 at Selma, Alabama. Ancestry.com, *Civil War Research Database*, website.

17. Following the loss of Atlanta, John Bell Hood (1831–79) led his Army of Tennessee in a daring counterstrike. By threatening Union supply lines in Tennessee, he hoped to force William T. Sherman's triumphant armies out of Georgia. Rather than taking Hood's bait, Sherman embarked on his legendary March to the Sea. He did, however, dispatch troops under John M. Schofield to reinforce Union positions in Tennessee. The ensuing campaign, described in the text that follows, resulted in the Battles of Franklin and Nashville.

18. On November 30, 1864, Hood hoped to catch his foes before they crossed the Harpeth River. He launched a series of costly attacks against Major General John M. Schofield's Union troops at Franklin. Confederate casualties were about seven thousand (out of about twenty thousand engaged). Schofield, whose losses were roughly a third of Hood's, crossed the river that night. McDonough and Connelly, *Five Tragic Hours.*

19. At the Battle of Nashville, Major General George H. Thomas's fifty thousand Federals delivered a crushing blow to Hood's twenty-three thousand Confederates, who were deployed in a concave line south of the city. The two-day battle forced Hood's shattered troops back to Mississippi. Granny White Pike ran south from Nashville, bisecting the battlefield. Boatner, *Civil War Dictionary,* 579–81.

20. George Anderson, a resident of Kinderhook, Illinois, had been commissioned as a second lieutenant in September 1861. As Corbusier notes, he was killed on November 22, 1864. Ancestry.com, *Civil War Research Database,* website.

21. A resident of Belvidere, Illinois, merchant Joseph W. Harper joined the army as a lieutenant colonel in December 1861. The Ohio-born Harper was promoted to full colonel three years later and was discharged the following year. Ibid.; Boone County, Ill., 1860 Manuscript Census.

22. Formed shortly after the war began as an auxiliary to regular government agencies, the U.S. Sanitary Commission provided supplementary donations of food, clothing, medicine, doctors, and nurses to Union soldiers. Its inspectors also did much to improve sanitary conditions in Union camps. The Commission sometimes clashed with official army bureaucracy but was extremely popular with the troops. McPherson, *Ordeal by Fire,* 385–86.

23. Born in Maryland, John Wilkes Booth (1838–65) was a popular actor but never achieved the critical acclaim accorded his brother Edwin. Sympathetic to the Confederacy, Booth had organized two previous attempts on President Lincoln's life before finally succeeding at Ford's Theater. Booth was killed twelve days later. Wooster, *The Civil War* 100, 70–72.

Canadian-born Alexander Grant Skene (1838–75) enlisted in the First Artillery (dropping his last name) at the outset of the Civil War. Promoted to sergeant on August 17, 1865, he was commissioned as a lieutenant in the First Cavalry Regiment the following year. Grant campaigned against the Indians in Oregon and Arizona and died at Camp Halleck, Nevada. Altshuler, *Cavalry Yellow and Infantry Blue,* 143.

1. Stephen Smith (1823–1922) was one of America's leading surgeons of the latter half of the nineteenth century. Author, editor, and teacher, Smith would later help to promote the use of antisepsis in surgery, and he was a successful advocate for public health. Unknown to Corbusier, Smith had died at Montour Falls, New York, on August 26, 1922. Kaufman, Galishoff, and Savitt, *Dictionary of American Medical Biography*, 2:699–700.

Austin Flint, Sr. (1812–86) has been described as "possibly the most influential and distinguished American physician of the midnineteenth century" for his efforts to elevate the quality of medical education. He helped to found the Bellevue Hospital Medical College and was especially noted for his advocacy of listening ("auscultation") to the sound of internal organs to aid diagnosis and treatment. Ibid., 1:253–54.

2. René Théophile Hyacinthe Laënnec invented the stethoscope in 1816. In 1852, George P. Cammann developed a binaural version that featured a tube for each of the physician's ears. McGrew, *Encyclopedia of Medical History*, 318.

3. Corbusier's dissatisfaction with civilian medicine was not uncommon, as the twelve to fifteen hundred dollars paid to contract surgeons equaled or exceeded the average civilian doctor's income. Gillett, *Army Medical Department*, 15.

The post at Amite, Louisiana, was established in February 1868. Located on the New Orleans, Jackson, and Great Northern Railroad, it lay about sixty-eight miles north of New Orleans. Amite, Louisiana, Feb., 1868, Returns from U.S. Military Posts, 1800–1916, Microfilm M 617, National Archives.

Robert Hilton Offley, born in New York, served as a midshipman in the U.S. Navy from 1850–51 before being commissioned as a second lieutenant in 1857. Promoted to first lieutenant and later to captain in the first year of the Civil War, Offley won a brevet promotion to major for meritorious service in the Vicksburg campaign in July 1863. In March 1891, Colonel Offley retired. Heitman, *Historical Register and Dictionary*, 1:756; *Records of Living Officers*, 320.

4. The 1870 census lists George Terriberry, a thirty-year-old physician claiming $1000 in property, as a resident of Paterson, Passaic County, New Jersey. In 1904, he filed for a pension for his Civil War service as a contract surgeon. Passaic County, N. J., 1870 Manuscript Census; Ancestry.com, *Civil War Pension Index*, website.

Dr. Henry C. Van Giesen also appears in the 1870 census as a resident of Paterson. He valued his estate at $500. Both Van Giesen and Terriberry lived in households headed by wealthier men. Passaic County, N. J., 1870 Manuscript Census.

5. Residents of the region hardly could have been pleased with the arrival of the Northerners. In fall 1864, editors of the *Amite Daily Wanderer* urged fellow Confederates to engage in guerilla warfare against the Union. Hyde, "Bushwhacking and Barn Burning," 181.

6. New York native Charles D. Viele (1841–1916) joined the army in 1861 and received his promotion to first lieutenant the following year. A veteran of the Vicksburg campaign, Viele was one of the postwar army's most notable raconteurs. Assigned to the Tenth Cavalry, he served in the Red River War of 1874–75, the Victorio campaign of 1880, the Geronimo campaigns of 1886, and the Spanish-American War. In 1899, Colonel Viele was transferred to the Philippines but was forced to retire from active duty for medical reasons the following year. He died in Los Angeles. Altshuler, *Cavalry Yellow and Infantry Blue*, 343.

Shadrach Hubbell, appointed from Ohio, was commissioned as a second lieutenant in the 186th Ohio Infantry in February 1865. He was mustered out that September but secured a regular army commission in May 1866. He died in September 1867. Heitman, *Historical Register and Dictionary*, 1:551.

7. A native of Ireland, John Joseph O'Connell enlisted in the army in 1865 under the name of A. Eng. Commissioned as a second lieutenant in the First Infantry in October 1867, O'Connell served at numerous western posts, fought in the Spanish-American War, and had a tour of duty in the Philippines before retiring as a brigadier general in 1904. He died in Atlantic City in 1927. Altshuler, *Cavalry Yellow and Infantry Blue*, 251–52.

8. Although he attended the U.S. Naval Academy for three years, Florida-born Allen Smith was commissioned as a second lieutenant in the First Infantry in 1866. Transferred to the Fourth Cavalry in 1881, Smith fought in the Geronimo campaigns of 1885–86. Following a tour of duty in the Philippines, Brigadier General Smith retired in 1905. He died in Spokane, Washington, in 1927. Ibid., 307.

Madame Clements is probably Desiré Clements, listed in the 1870 census as a resident of Amite City, Tangipahoa Parish. Born in Belgium, the fifty-two-year-old Ms. Clements claimed an estate of $6000 and ran a "coffee house." She headed a household of five others, including George T. Dunbar, who was by that time Corbusier's brother-in-law. Tangipahoa Parish, La., 1870 Manuscript Census.

9. For George Dunbar's military record, see Fenner's Battery, Light Artillery, Index to Compiled Service Records of Confederate Soldiers Who Served in Organizations from the State of Louisiana, Microfilm M 320, National Archives. Boasting two twelve-pounder howitzers, two six-pounder rifled guns, and two six-pounder howitzers, Captain Charles E. Fenner's Battery was formed in May 1862 from men of the disbanded First Louisiana Infantry Battalion. After being stationed in Louisiana, eastern Mississippi, and Alabama, it joined the Army of Tennessee and fought in the Atlanta and Nashville campaigns. Late in the war, elements of the battery manned the defenses of Mobile, Alabama. Bergeron, *Guide to Louisiana Confederate Military Units*, 30–31.

10. Set during the Napoleonic Wars, *Charles O'Malley* ranks among Irish novelist Charles James Lever's (1806–72) best works. Hogan, *Dictionary of Irish Literature*, 375–76.

11. Clay eating, sometimes known as geophagy (the deliberate consumption of soils), has been practiced for centuries. It is especially associated with the

South, where specific clays, identified locally as food, were extracted and some-times baked before being eaten. Wilson and Ferris, *Encyclopedia of Southern Culture*, 1368–69.

12. Born in Baltimore, George Towers Dunbar (1811–50) married Caroline Eliza Robinson (1811–69) on July 11, 1837. After working as an engineer for the Baltimore and Ohio Railroad, Dunbar moved to Louisiana, where he served as assistant surveyor for the New Orleans and Jackson Railroad and engineer of the Second Municipality of New Orleans. He was in the process of surveying a railroad line through the Isthmus of Tehuantepec when he died. A naturalist and friend of John J. Audubon, Dunbar painted Louisiana fishes, but the paintings were destroyed in the San Francisco earthquake and fire of 1906. Conrad, *A Dictionary of Louisiana Biography*, 1:266; F. Corbusier, "Recollections," 2; Knox, "The Longer View."

13. The adopted daughter of a noted actor and theatrical manager, Mary Runnion McVicker gave some stage performances herself before marrying Booth in 1869. At his request, she then retired from public performances. Garraty and Carnes, *American National Biography*, 3:192; Wilmeth and Miller, *Cambridge Guide to American Theatre*, 295.

14. See also Corbusier to Randolph, October 22, 1868, Personal Papers of Medical Officers and Physicians, RG 94, National Archives.

15. *New York Herald*, April 3, 1867.

16. Launched in 1864, the Pacific mail steamer *Henry Chauncey* carried eight hundred passengers. Fanny Corbusier remembers being "seasick most of the time" while on board. The Corbusiers paid $225 each for passage on their "honeymoon voyage," which lasted twenty-three days. The ship burned at sea in 1871 off the Carolina coast. F. Corbusier, "Recollections," 5–6; Swiggum and Kohli, "Panama Route Ships," website.

17. Established in August 1865 to help control the Paiute Indians, Camp McDermit lay just south of the Oregon border in the Santa Rosa Mountains. The military abandoned the post in 1888 and turned the buildings over to the Interior Department the following year. Frazer, *Forts of the West*, 93.

18. Sarah Winnemucca claimed to be the daughter of Chief Winnemucca of the Northern Paiutes, although her lineage is disputed. She learned English and became an interpreter for various government officers. Her assistance was crucial in bringing about a peaceful conclusion to the Bannock wars of 1877–78. Critical of most Indian agents, she traveled widely as a popular lecturer for Indian causes and wrote *Life among the Piutes: Their Wrongs and Claims* (1883). In his description of Camp McDermit for the War Department, Dr. Corbusier described her as "an educated intelligent girl, who was brought up amongst the whites, and is a fair example of the civilization of which the Piute is capable." Fanny Corbusier, however, was fairly critical of Sarah, claiming that "she sometimes drank to excess, poor creature, and caroused with the men." Winnemucca died in Monida, Montana, on October 16, 1891. Thrapp, *Encyclopedia of Frontier Biography*, 3:1583;

Camp McDermit, Descriptive Commentaries from the Medical Histories of Posts, Microfilm M 903, National Archives; F. Corbusier, "Recollections," 9.

19. Born in present-day Nevada about 1805, Chief Winnemucca, also known as "Old Winnemucca" or "Po-i-to," was chief of the Northern Paiute Indians. Despite numerous provocations, Chief Winnemucca advocated peaceful relations with whites. Thrapp, *Encyclopedia of Frontier Biography*, 3:1582–83.

20. In her much lengthier descriptions of life at Camp McDermit, Mrs. Corbusier explained that they shared a house there with Lieutenant James M. Ropes and his wife. "The Post was a lonely, desolate place," she recalled, adding that "it was a very healthful place and father had but little work to do." She also provides what seems to be a comprehensive list of the officers they encountered while stationed there. Of the coyote hunt, she noted that "everyone turned out to see the end of the exciting chase." F. Corbusier, "Recollections," 7–16. Another army officer's wife, Martha Summerhayes, agreed that Camp McDermit was "a colorless, forbidding sort of a place." Summerhayes, *Vanished Arizona*, 225.

21. Henry A. Reed enlisted in the Twenty-fourth Wisconsin Infantry Regiment on August 14, 1862. Participating in the Battles of Perryville, Stones River, Chickamauga, Missionary Ridge, the Atlanta campaign, and Nashville, he rose through the ranks and secured his officer's commission in February 1865. Reed graduated tenth in his U.S. Military Academy class four years later. After his service at Fort McDermit, he graduated from the artillery school at Fortress Monroe and became an instructor at West Point and at the School of Application for Infantry and Cavalry at Fort Leavenworth, Kansas. *Records of Living Officers*, 208.

22. Built in 1862, *Newbern* served as the *United States* during the Civil War. Renamed following the war, it plied the West Coast trade between California and Mexico. Allegedly, it was often used to smuggle Mexican silver into the United States. It sunk off the coast of California en route from Ensenada to San Francisco in 1893. Lawson, "*Newbern*," website.

23. Mrs. Corbusier, however, remembered that the shredded dry salted codfish and champagne provided by the ship's captain also worked effectively in treating her seasickness. F. Corbusier, "Recollections," 17.

24. Fanny explains that "mark twain" was the slang term for "two feet" of water depth. Ibid.

25. In describing a similar journey of her own, Martha Summerhayes called Mellon "the Wizard of the Great Colorado" for his prowess in river navigation. Summerhayes, *Vanished Arizona*, 41, 45.

26. Established in 1850 near the junction of the Colorado and Gila Rivers, Fort Yuma guarded the southern emigrant route to California and served as a supply depot for posts in Arizona. The expansion of railroads into the Southwest rendered the post obsolete, and it was abandoned in 1883. The site was later used as an Indian school and mission. Frazer, *Forts of the West*, 34–35.

27. In 1870, forty-two-year-old Isaac Polhamus, superintendent of the Colorado Steam Navigation Company, claimed an estate of $15,000. A native of New

York, he lived in Arizona City, Yuma County, Arizona, with his wife, Sacramento, and their two children. Yuma County, Ariz., 1870 Manuscript Census.

28. Born in Pennsylvania, Wieting enlisted in the Pennsylvania Light Artillery in 1864. Following the end of the Civil War, he attended the U.S. Military Academy, graduating in 1870. He served briefly with Corbusier at Camp McDermit before resigning his commission in December 1870. Wieting rejoined the army a year and a half later, reaching the rank of captain. He died at Fort Sam Houston, Texas. Altshuler, *Cavalry Yellow and Infantry Blue*, 367–68.

Chapter Six: Life among the Yavapai

Corbusier divided the Yavapai Indians of central and western Arizona into three subgroups: the Apache-Yumas (Tolkapaya); the Apache-Mojaves (Yavapai or Yavepe); and the Apache-Tontos (Kewevkapaya). Modern ethnographers commonly subdivide the Apache-Mojaves into the Wipukpaya and Yavepe. Minor differences in dialect separate the groups, whose subsistence economy was based primarily on hunting and gathering. They enjoyed fairly close relations and often intermingled with their neighbors to the east, the Apaches. On December 27, 1872, an army patrol cornered and killed many of the Kewevkapaya in the Salt River Canyon in an episode known as the Skeleton Cave Massacre. W. H. Corbusier, "The Apache-Yumas and Apache-Mojaves"; Gifford, *Northeastern and Western Yavapai*, 248; Khera and Mariela, "Yavapai"; Malinowski and Sheets, *Gale Encyclopedia of Native American Tribes*, 2:376–81.

1. In January 1867 the army established a temporary post on Date Creek, about sixty miles southwest of Prescott, Arizona. Initially known as Camp McPherson, it was moved two months later to a position closer to Prescott. That May, it was returned to Date Creek and officially renamed Camp Date Creek in 1868. Roberts, *Encyclopedia of Historic Forts*, 36–37.

2. Ochocama was suspected of having taken a leading role in an unsuccessful effort to assassinate General George Crook in a tense 1872 encounter. Thrapp, *Al Sieber*, 97–100.

3. Captain John G. Bourke recalled that Agent Williams steadfastly attempted to ensure that the Indians at his agency received proper supply shipments, despite attempts by nefarious contractors to cheat him. "Williams was a very honest, high-minded gentleman," continued Bourke, "and deserved something better than to be hounded into an insane asylum, which fate he suffered." Bourke, *On the Border with Crook*, 235.

Eschetlepan later broke from the reservation and proved one of the most difficult Yavapais to catch. Thrapp, *Al Sieber*, 147.

4. One of the army's most renowned western campaigners, Ohio-born George Crook (1828–1890) graduated from West Point in 1852. Five years later, he was wounded by a poisoned arrow during the Rogue River War (Oregon). Brevetted to major general during the Civil War, he once again proved his mettle

fighting Indians in the Pacific Northwest during the late 1860s. Transferred to command the Department of Arizona in 1871, Crook launched a series of successful campaigns against the Apaches. He was promoted to brigadier general in 1873 and went to the Department of the Platte two years later. There Crook participated in the Sioux wars. Escalating violence in Arizona led his superiors to transfer him back to his old southwest command in 1882. He clashed with General Philip Sheridan over the proper means of dealing with Geronimo, and Crook's 1886 request for a transfer was quickly accepted. Promoted to major general of the regular army in 1888, he died in Chicago two years later. Altshuler, *Cavalry Yellow and Infantry Blue*, 87–88; Boatner, *Civil War Dictionary*, 209.

5. Mrs. Corbusier explains that she and the children left Ehrenberg about September 12 on a three-day stagecoach trip to Los Angeles. From there, they caught a steamer to San Francisco and then took the railroad to Elmira, New York, where they stayed with the doctor's mother. During their visit east, the family also visited Fanny's sister in Amite, Louisiana, and met Samuel Clemens (Mark Twain). F. Corbusier, "Recollections," 25–30.

6. Delshay (ca. 1835–74) became distrustful of government authorities following the Camp Grant Massacre of 1871. Initially eluding Crook's columns, he and his followers later surrendered when their wives and children were at risk. They were then taken to Fort Apache on the White Mountain Reservation. Delshay then fled to Camp Verde before making a final break. Waldman, *Who Was Who in Native American History*, 97–98.

7. The appointment as surgeon for the Rio Verde agency netted Dr. Corbusier an extra $1000 per year in addition to his army pay. F. Corbusier, "Recollections," 39.

8. In 1871, regular troops relocated Camp Verde, which New Mexico volunteers had established seven years earlier, to a site one mile west of the Verde River below the mouth of Beaver Creek. The army abandoned the post in 1890. Frazer, *Forts of the West*, 14.

9. Born in Ithaca, New York, Walter Scribner Schuyler (1849–1932) graduated twentieth in his U.S. Military Academy class of fifty-eight in 1870. In May 1872 he oversaw the removal of the Yavapais from Camp Date Creek to the Rio Verde Reservation. He would in 1890 receive a brevet promotion for his actions fighting the Apaches. Schuyler saw action during the Spanish-American War and later served in the Philippines, Arizona, Hawaii, Kansas, and as military observer to the Russian army. He retired as a brigadier general in 1913 and died in San Antonio. Altshuler, *Cavalry Yellow and Infantry Blue*, 294–95.

10. Corbusier describes the process the pasemache, or medicine man, underwent to secure this status in his "Apache-Yumas and Apache-Mojaves," 333.

11. Originally known as Fort Fauntleroy and later Fort Lyon, this post was established in 1860 in McKinley County, New Mexico, on the road from Albuquerque to Fort Defiance. Renamed Wingate in 1868, it became an ordinance

depot during World War I. Some of the military buildings were used as a Navajo school. Roberts, *Encyclopedia of Historic Forts*, 534–35.

12. Irish-born John J. Coppinger served as an officer in the papal guard before immigrating to the United States. Securing a captaincy in the Fourteenth Infantry, Coppinger was wounded at Second Bull Run and brevetted for his actions at Trevilion Station and Cedar Creek, Virginia. He remained in the regular army and commanded the post at Camp Verde from December 1872 to July 1874. In 1883, he married Alice Blaine, daughter of former Secretary of State James G. Blaine. Coppinger was retired as a major general of volunteers in 1898. He died eleven years later. Altshuler, *Cavalry Yellow and Infantry Blue*, 78–79.

13. Humorous, colorful, and anti-Indian, John Huguenot Marion (ca. 1836–91) purchased the *Arizona Miner* in 1867 and became the best-known newspaperman in central Arizona. He died in Prescott. Thrapp, *Encyclopedia of Frontier Biography*, 2:942.

14. Eskiminzin (ca. 1825–95), an Arvaipa Apache chief called "Skimmy" by some whites, was one of the best-known Apaches of the mid-nineteenth century. In the Camp Grant Massacre (1871), about one hundred members of his community were butchered by a posse of Tucson militants while he and most of his warriors were away. He and his followers left San Carlos following the murder of Almy, but he returned following the departure of the inept agent, C. F. Larrabee. Eskiminzin later visited Washington and established a ranch but was arrested in 1891 and sent to join a group of exiled Chiricahuas at Fort Marion, Alabama. He was released three years later. Non-Indians differed about Eskiminzin's role as a war leader; George Crook called him "the 'head center' of the cut-throats" and boasted of having put him in irons for "his rascalities." Ibid., 1:467–68; Crook, *General George Crook*, 168–75.

Established in 1872 in southeastern Arizona along the Gila River, San Carlos was the center for some of the most controversial reservations in the American West. The Indian Bureau hoped to concentrate the western Apaches and Yavapai there; historian Robert M. Utley describes it as "a hot, barren, malarial flat" and "a terrible place to live." Utley, *Indian Frontier of the American West*, 193–96.

Born to Quaker parents, Jacob Almy (1842–73) joined a Massachusetts volunteer regiment in 1862 but soon thereafter accepted an appointment to the U.S. Military Academy. He graduated forty-first in his class in 1867. After fighting Indians in Kansas, Nebraska, and Wyoming, he arrived at Camp Grant in February 1872. From there Almy patrolled the nearby San Carlos Reservation, whose agent, C. F. Larrabee, soon lost control of his supposed charges. Responding to Larrabee's request for assistance, Almy was shot dead by an unknown assailant. Altshuler, *Cavalry Yellow and Infantry Blue*, 7.

15. Born near Heidelberg, Germany, Albert Sieber (1844–1907) ranks among the army's most legendary scouts. Sieber enlisted in the Union Army in 1862 and fought in the Peninsula campaign and at Antietam and Fredericksburg. Severely

wounded at Gettysburg, he moved west after the Civil War. George Crook named Sieber his chief of scouts soon after his transfer to Arizona, and in that capacity he participated in virtually every major campaign against the Apaches. He was badly wounded in the Apache Kid outbreak of 1887. Sieber died in a construction accident near Roosevelt Dam, Arizona. Thrapp, *Encyclopedia of Frontier Biography*, 3:1305–07.

16. Kelho, classified by the army as an Apache-Yuma, enlisted as a scout several times between 1873 and 74. Descriptions of his height and age varied; on March 1, 1874, when Corbusier was the examining officer, he was listed as standing five feet, seven inches tall and twenty-three years of age. Enlistment Papers, U.S. Army Indian Scouts, RG 94, National Archives.

17. Established in 1865 seven miles from the junction of the Rio Verde and the Salt River, Fort McDowell was designed to control the Yavapai and Apache Indians. The army left in 1891, and the reservation was turned over to the Interior Department. Frazer, *Forts of the West*, 11.

18. The black felt folding campaign hats adopted in 1872 were "universally despised." A better black campaign hat was adopted four years later, but only in 1883–84 did the army officially move to a lighter colored hat that better reflected the heat. McChristian, *U.S. Army in the West, 1870–1880*, 45–46, 55, 166, 248.

19. Also known as Camp Infantry or Camp Picket Post, the temporary Camp Pinal was only occupied for a few months in late 1870 and early 1871. Summerhayes described it as a "blighted and desolate place" that "might have been the entrance to Hades." It was later the site of a mining camp. Roberts, *Encyclopedia of Historic Forts*, 44; Summerhayes, *Vanished Arizona*, 215–16.

20. Located on the San Pedro River in Graham County, Arizona, Fort Grant was established in 1872 to threaten the nearby Apaches. Its garrison was withdrawn during the Spanish-American War, and the land was ceded to Arizona in 1902. It was later used as a state industrial school. Roberts, *Encyclopedia of Historic Forts*, 38.

21. Ohio-born George Morton Randall (1841–1918) enlisted in the Union Army during the Civil War, earning brevets for gallantry at Antietam, Petersburg, and Fort Stedman. He accepted a captaincy in the much-reduced postwar army. During Crook's Apache campaigns, Randall, who sported a huge mustache and was respected as a strict but fair disciplinarian by Indians and whites alike, won recommendations for two more brevets. Randall commanded Crook's Indian scouts during his Rosebud, Big Horn, and Yellowstone campaigns of 1876. He served in Cuba during the Spanish-American War and later commanded the Department of Luzon, Philippines, before retiring as a major general in 1905. Heitman, *Historical Register and Dictionary*, 1:814; Thrapp, *Encyclopedia of Frontier Biography*, 3:1191; Altshuler, *Cavalry Yellow and Infantry Blue*, 272–73.

Born in Louisiana, John Breckinridge Babcock (1843–1909) nonetheless fought for the Union, earning brevets for his gallantry at the Battles of Mansfield, Pleasant Hill, and Cane River Crossing, Louisiana. He resigned from the army as a major in

1865 but then rejoined as a second lieutenant a year and a half later. Babcock would eventually be awarded the Medal of Honor for his actions against the Indians at Spring Creek, Nebraska, in 1869. Transferred to Arizona in 1872, he was wounded the following year. He remained in the army, retiring as a brigadier general. Of his actions with the Apaches, John Bourke described Babcock as "the man for the place," one who "performed his duties in a manner remarkable for its delicate appreciation of the nature of the Indians, tact in allaying their suspicions, gentle firmness in bringing them to see that the new way was the better, the only way." Altshuler, *Cavalry Yellow and Infantry Blue*, 14–15; Bourke, *On the Border with Crook*, 217.

A native of France, Joseph Basil Girard (1846–1918) joined the army as an assistant surgeon in 1867. He served in Colorado, Wyoming, Nebraska, and Kentucky before coming to Arizona in 1872, where he remained for four years. Stints in Michigan, Texas, California, Hawaii, and the Philippines followed. He died in San Antonio. Several of his Arizona watercolors are in the Huntington Library. Altshuler, *Cavalry Yellow and Infantry Blue*, 140; *Records of Living Officers*, 57–58.

22. Maryland-born William Henry Brown enlisted in the army in 1858. Commissioned as an officer in 1861, he earned brevets to major for gallantry in the Piedmont and Five Forks campaigns. Emerging from the Civil War as a captain of the Fifth Cavalry, Brown won high marks from George Crook for his service in the 1872–73 Arizona campaigns against the Apaches. While on leave in New York, he died after cutting his throat with a razor. Ironically, the Corbusiers would later inhabit the quarters known as "Brown's Folly" for a short time during their tenure at Fort Grant. Mrs. Corbusier described it as "a large ugly stone structure," which Brown had constructed in his belief that all the officers should live under the same roof. Altshuler, *Cavalry Yellow and Infantry Blue*, 46; Heitman, *Historical Register and Dictionary*, 1:254; F. Corbusier, "Recollections," 89.

23. Something of a legendary figure in the army, Charles Morton (1846–1914) fought in several volunteer Missouri regiments during the Civil War before graduating twenty-fifth in his U.S. Military Academy class in 1869. He arrived in Arizona the following year and was presented a set of commemorative pistols by appreciative citizens following the June 1871 scout described in the text. He later took part in the Sioux wars of 1876–77 and in the Spanish-American War before retiring in 1910. During his long service, Morton successfully sued the army for additional longevity pay (a case that eventually went to the Supreme Court) based on his years as a cadet. His complaints to a Chicago newspaper that the army was "hidebound and topheavy" nearly resulted in his court-martial. Altshuler, *Cavalry Yellow and Infantry Blue*, 240.

24. The *Arizona Miner* asserted that the patrols had marched fifteen hundred miles and accounted for eighty-three killed and twenty-six prisoners. Official army records set Indian casualties at a more modest thirty-eight killed and twelve captured. Thrapp, *Al Sieber*, 145; Adjutant General's Office, *Chronological List of Actions*, 57.

25. Educated at the Kentucky Military Institute and Shelby College, Pennsyl-vania-born Julius Wilmot Mason (1835–82) joined the cavalry at the outset of the Civil War. Securing brevets to major and lieutenant colonel for his services at Beverly's Ford and Brandy Station, Virginia, he emerged as a captain in the regular army. Mason also took part in Crook's Arizona campaigns of 1872–73. When Dr. Williams, the regular Indian agent at Camp Verde, went insane, Mason was appointed temporary agent, and it was in this capacity that he initiated the agricultural program. He later participated in the Sioux campaigns of 1876. Major Mason died at Fort Huachuca, Arizona, where he was serving as commander. Altshuler, *Cavalry Yellow and Infantry Blue*, 223–24; Heitman, *Historical Register and Dictionary*, 1:695.

26. A second head reputed to be that of Delshay was also brought in. Crook paid bounties for both; one was displayed at Camp Verde, the other on the San Carlos River. Waldman, *Who Was Who in Native American History*, 98.

27. This agent was Oliver Chapman, who quickly clashed with Lieutenant Schuyler over the most appropriate means of dealing with the Yavapai. See Chapman to Smith, December 21, 1874, C-26, Letters Received by the Office of Indian Affairs, 1824–1880, Microfilm M 234, National Archives.

28. Originally known as Fort Fauntleroy and then Fort Wise, Fort Lyon was renamed in 1861 for General Nathaniel Lyon, who was killed in the Battle of Wilson's Creek, Missouri. Colorado volunteers from Fort Lyon participated in the Sand Creek Massacre of 1864. When the Arkansas River endangered the foundation of the fort, Fort Lyon was moved to a new site near Las Animas in 1866. Abandoned by the army in 1889, the site was converted into a Veterans Administration hospital in 1934. Roberts, *Encyclopedia of Historic Forts*, 862–63.

Irish emigrant James Burns (ca. 1837–74) joined the army in 1858. Commissioned as a second lieutenant in August 1865, he was promoted in 1866 and again in 1872. During the Arizona campaigns of 1872–73, Crook recommended him for no less than three brevets. To save him the expense of moving his wife and two children back east, Crook arranged for Burns, who was mortally ill, to go on leave in Washington, D.C. Altshuler, *Cavalry Yellow and Infantry Blue*, 50.

29. Philip Reade attended West Point in 1864–65 and 1865–67. Commissioned in May 1867, he saw service as a volunteer during the Spanish-American War before returning to the regular army in 1901. Heitman, *Historical Register and Dictionary*, 1:819.

30. Established in 1851 northwest of Las Vegas, New Mexico, Fort Union long served as the supply depot for New Mexico. It was abandoned by the army in 1891 and eventually was declared a national monument. Frazer, *Forts of the West*, 106.

31. A more commonly used explanation held that "shave-tails" were new mules whose tails had been clipped to more readily distinguish them from veteran "bell sharp" mules. The former had to be watched carefully. Essin, *Shavetails and Bell Sharps*, xvii.

32. Mrs. Corbusier described her husband in this fashion: "His beard had grown and he was covered with dust and looked like a tramp, not having had time to clean up. Mother and I cried about his looks, but we were glad to be with him again." F. Corbusier, "Recollections," 30.

33. Lucien B. Maxwell's claim to ninety-seven thousand acres east of the Sangre de Cristo Mountains was validated by U.S. courts in 1869. He sold his interests to Jerome Bonaparte Chaffee and Stephen B. Elkins, whose Maxwell Land Grant Company evolved into one of the Southwest's largest economic enterprises, expanding its claims to over 1.7 million acres of mining and ranch lands. Phillips and Axelrod, *Encyclopedia of the American West*, 3:946–47.

34. Born in Albany, New York, Charles King (1844–1933) grew up in Wisconsin and graduated from the U.S. Military Academy in 1866. In the fight at Sunset Pass, Arizona, he took a bullet in his right arm, a wound that would plague him for the rest of his life. Though troubled with various ailments, King was credited with seven decades of active military service that included campaign badges from the Civil War, the Indian wars, the Spanish-American War, the Philippine Insurrections, and World War I. He also wrote sixty-two books (fifty-two of which were fiction), most of which dealt with the Indian wars. King died in Milwaukee. Russell, *Campaigning with King*.

35. Fanny's seven-and-a-half-page single-spaced typed account of this journey provides a richly detailed description of the geography and people found between Las Animas and the Rio Verde Reservation. "It was a journey, the like of which very few army women have taken and not many officers," she explained, "but we are glad that we took it and wish that all of our sons could go over the same road." F. Corbusier, "Recollections," 31–38.

36. A Civil War veteran, Levi Edwin Dudley (1842–1913) helped organize the Grand Army of the Republic and was superintendent of Indian Affairs for New Mexico from 1872–74. After managing the removal of the Indians from Verde to San Carlos, he served in several government positions, including U.S. consul in Vancouver, British Columbia. Thrapp, *Encyclopedia of Frontier Biography*, 1:427.

37. "Captain Smook" is probably "Snook," who served at least two six-month stints as an army scout in 1873–74. Listed as an Apache-Yuma, the thirty-year-old Snook stood five feet, six inches tall. Enlistment Papers, U.S. Army Indian Scouts, RG 94, National Archives.

38. Captain Bourke labeled the decision to remove the Yavapai to San Carlos as "outrageous;" Crook believed it stemmed from greedy Tucson merchants and real estate interests. Bourke, *On the Border with Crook*, 217; Crook, *General George Crook*, 183.

39. After graduating twenty-sixth in his U.S. Military Academy class in 1873, George Oscar Eaton (1848–1930) joined the Fifth Cavalry in Arizona later that year. Here he met author Charles King and was said to have been the model for the hero of King's novel *The Colonel's Daughter*. Eaton fought in the Big Horn and Yellowstone campaigns of 1876 and was promoted to first lieutenant three years

later. He retired from active duty in 1883; in civilian life, he was a rancher, mining engineer, and surveyor general of Montana. He died in Florida. Altshuler, *Cavalry Yellow and Infantry Blue*, 116–17.

40. Captain Charley served as an army scout in 1873–74. Standing about six feet tall, he was described as an Apache-Mojave between twenty-seven and thirty years of age. Enlistment Papers, U.S. Army Indian Scouts, RG 94, National Archives.

41. For different accounts of the perilous journey, see Chapman to Smith, March 20, 1875, C-487, and Dudley to Smith, April 3, 1875, D-200, Letters Received by the Office of Indian Affairs, 1842–1880, Microfilm M 234, National Archives; and Eaton, "Stopping an Apache Battle," 12–18.

42. Born in the mid-1860s, Mike Burns was sent to school in Carlisle, Pennsylvania. He returned to the Yavapai, where he served at least three six-month stints as an Indian scout for the army. He died in 1934. Among various copies of his manuscript still in existence is a typescript copy, edited by Robert D. Sullivan, in the possession of Nancy Corbusier Knox. A fictionalized version has been published by Elaine Waterstrait as *Hoomothya's Long Journey, 1865–1897: The True Story of a Yavapai Indian*. See also Enlistment Papers, U.S. Army Indian Scouts, RG 94, National Archives.

43. With the outbreak of the Civil War, Massachusetts native George Mitchell Brayton (1834–1911) was commissioned as a first lieutenant. In 1863, he was promoted to captain and was awarded a brevet for gallantry at Missionary Ridge, Tennessee. Transferred to Camp Verde in 1874, Brayton engaged in several scouts. He retired in 1892 as a colonel and died in Washington, D.C. Altshuler, *Cavalry Yellow and Infantry Blue*, 42. Fanny remembered Brayton in much more personal terms. "Everyone was very kind to us. Col. Brayton came every evening to exercise and play with the boys as father always did. He was very jolly and I think enjoyed the play as much as the boys." F. Corbusier, "Recollections," 42.

44. Located in San Bernardino County, California, Camp Cady was established to meet expected threats from the Shoshoni and Paiute Indians. The army occupied it sporadically between 1860 and 1871. Roberts, *Encyclopedia of Historic Forts*, 64.

Chapter Seven: The Old Army

1. The Corbusiers set up housekeeping at 1735 Fourteenth (now Newcomb Avenue) between Phelps and Newhall Streets in south San Francisco. He bought four lots on Fifteenth and Sixteenth Avenues. "The same amount of money invested elsewhere in San Francisco would have brought a large profit," rued Mrs. Corbusier. F. Corbusier, "Recollections," 45.

2. While Corbusier was in New York City, his family lived with his mother in Elmira. Ibid., 46.

3. Irish-born John McCullough (1832–85) immigrated to the United States at age fifteen and became a noted Shakespearean actor. Lawrence Barrett (1838–91)

was probably best known for playing the role of Cassius in *Julius Caesar*; Booth played Brutus in the same production. Hartnoll, *Oxford Companion to the Theatre*, 58, 511.

4. Less than a third of those taking the exams usually passed. Questions covered not only medicine, but science, literature, history, and geography. Gillett, *Army Medical Department*, 15. See also Hume, "Admission to the Medical Department of the Army Half a Century Ago."

5. Adelaide Ristori (1822–1906) was a renowned Italian actress. Dr. Corbusier probably saw her during one of her four U.S. tours, the first of which came in 1866. Czech actress Francesca Romana Maddena Janauschek (1830–1904) began her first tour of the United States in 1867, frequently playing opposite Edwin Booth. She retired in 1900. Hartnoll, *Oxford Companion to the Theatre*, 432, 697–98.

6. Congressional budget cuts had left the army with more surgeons than available positions, thus necessitating the delay in Corbusier's official appointment. Gillett, *Army Medical Department*, 17.

7. One prescient doctor at Macon had warned that the post, a pentagonal masonry work capable of mounting sixty-two guns located on the west end of Bogue Island at the outlet of Pamlico Sound, was "in imminent danger from the encroachment of the sea." Abandoned in 1877, it was regarrisoned during the Spanish-American War and World War II. Fort Macon, Descriptive Commentaries from the Medical Histories of Posts, Microfilm M 903, National Archives; Roberts, *Encyclopedia of Historic Forts*, 619–20.

8. For the railroad strike, see Foner and Garraty, *Reader's Companion to American History*, 910. Fortunately, Mrs. Corbusier left a much more detailed account of this period. The amateur naturalist's daughter found "much to interest us in the sea and on land" at Fort Macon. The storm, she recalls, blew away the wind gauge when it reached seventy-five miles per hour. At Charleston, Mrs. Corbusier remembered that "the men were very cordial, but few of their wives called upon us, as they were the last to forget the war was over." They procured the services of an especially good cook at Chattanooga who "liked to surprise us with some very dainty dish." F. Corbusier, "Recollections," 46–52.

9. Established in 1874 near the Spotted Tail [Brulé] Agency in northern Sheridan County, Nebraska, Camp Sheridan was abandoned in 1881. Roberts, *Encyclopedia of Historic Forts*, 487.

10. Born in Philadelphia, Emmet Crawford (1844–86) enlisted in the Seventy-first Pennsylvania Infantry in 1861. Commissioned as an officer three years later, he received two wartime brevets and eventually emerged as a first lieutenant in the regular army. After nearly a year at Camp Verde, Arizona, Crawford fought in the Sioux wars of 1876–77 and was promoted to captain in 1879. Assigned by Crook to command the Indian scouts at San Carlos, Arizona, Crawford led several expeditions into Mexico in pursuit of Geronimo. He was mortally wounded on January 11, 1886, by Mexican irregulars. Altshuler, *Cavalry Yellow and Infantry Blue*, 84–85.

11. Valentine T. McGillycuddy (1849–1939) was born in Michigan and briefly studied medicine before entering government service as a topographer. Crook took McGillycuddy with him during several of his Black Hills expeditions of 1876. After serving as post surgeon at Camp Robinson, Nebraska, McGillycuddy was agent for the Oglala Sioux from 1879-86. John G. Bourke called the energetic McGillycuddy "one of the most competent representatives the Indian Bureau had ever sent beyond the Missouri." He died in Berkeley, California. Thrapp, *Encyclopedia of Frontier Biography*, 2:905; Bourke, *On the Border with Crook*, 424–25.

12. Born in western Nebraska, Red Cloud (1821–1909) became one of the ablest war leaders of the Lakota Sioux, forcing the army to abandon its Bozeman Trail forts in the Treaty of Fort Laramie (1868). Although Red Cloud did not participate in the Great Sioux War (1876–77), he remained an important intermediary between the Lakotas and federal authorities, steadfastly protesting attempts to Americanize his people. Larson, *Red Cloud*.

American Horse (ca. 1840–1908) played an important role in Lakota victories of 1865–67 along the Bozeman Trail. Later, however, his enthusiastic embrace of peaceful relations with the United States and the cultural changes such a position demanded won the enmity of many Lakotas. Garraty and Canes, *American National Biography*, 1:405–06.

Lakota chief Young Man Afraid Of His Horses (ca. 1830–ca. 1900) was a key leader in the successful fights that forced the army to abandon its Bozeman Trail forts. After agreeing to the Treaty of Fort Laramie (1868), Young Man Afraid Of His Horses favored conciliation rather than renewed hostilities but often clashed with Red Cloud over the best means of protecting Lakota interests against white incursions. Thrapp, *Encyclopedia of Frontier Biography*, 3:1614–15.

13. Corbusier is referring to a series of incidents in and around Fort Robinson that culminated in a botched attempt to arrest and remove Crazy Horse, the influential Oglala leader, from the region. Crazy Horse was stabbed in the resulting melee. Buecker, *Fort Robinson and the American West*, 110–18.

14. For brief descriptions of the Sun Dance, which varied from community to community among Plains tribes and was for many years officially prohibited, see Hoxie, *Encyclopedia of North American Indians*, 615–16; and Lamar, *New Encyclopedia of the American West*, 1085–86.

15. In 1849, the War Department purchased the old private trading post long known as Fort Laramie. The army abandoned the post, which was made obsolete by the completion of the Union Pacific and Chicago and Northwestern Railroads, in 1890. Frazer, *Forts of the West*, 181–82.

Established in 1871 to protect the Shoshoni Indians from neighboring tribes, Fort Washakie was located in central Wyoming on the southern edge of the Bighorn River basin. Originally called Camp Brown, it was renamed in 1878 and turned over to the Shoshoni Agency in 1909. Ibid., 186–87.

16. Corbusier's mother had sent the female maid "Louie" to join the family at Camp Sheridan. "Louie was a fine cook and never tired of work," remembered

Mrs. Corbusier, "but about once a month had paroxysms of rage. . . . Her spells always ended with a flood of tears and she would be very repentant and beg to stay with us." After their subsequent move to Fort Washakie, however, Louie "became troublesome," so they sent her back to Elmira, where she reportedly died in an insane asylum. F. Corbusier, "Recollections," 55–56, 70.

17. Mrs. Corbusier implied that the incident had resulted from the intoxication of the driver, who "lay in a half drunken stupor" after the wagon crash. Ibid., 66.

18. New York native Frederick Van Vliet (1841–91) joined the Third Cavalry in 1861, emerging as a brevet lieutenant colonel following the Civil War. Van Vliet served in New Mexico and Arizona before transferring with his regiment to the Department of the Platte in 1871. He returned to the Southwest in 1882 and fought in the Geronimo campaign. Major Van Vliet died from injuries suffered after a fall from a wagon. Altshuler, *Cavalry Yellow and Infantry Blue*, 340; Heitman, *Historical Register and Dictionary*, 1:984.

19. Fort Fetterman was established in 1867 on the Platte River to help protect the Bozeman Trail. The army abandoned it in 1882. Frazer, *Forts of the West*, 180–81.

20. Located in Fremont County, Wyoming, Camp Stambaugh was established in 1870 to protect miners against perceived threats from the Shoshoni Indians. It was abandoned eight years later. Roberts, *Encyclopedia of Historic Forts*, 863.

21. Shoshoni chief Washakie (ca. 1804–1900) long sought alliances with the whites and frequently scouted for the army. Tall and powerfully built, he became an Episcopalian and was buried with military honors. Thrapp, *Encyclopedia of Frontier Biography*, 3:1515–16.

One of the most prominent Arapaho leaders of the period, Black Coal was severely wounded during an army/Shoshoni attack on his village in July 1874. He died in 1893. Trenholm and Carley, *Shoshonis*, 242, 277, 291.

Born in the early 1820s, William Friday was found abandoned on the Santa Fe Trail near the Cimarron River in an emaciated condition by an American frontiersman, Thomas Fitzpatrick, in 1831. Friday lived several years among whites before returning to the Arapahos. He was part of that group's delegation to the Fort Laramie Treaty of 1851 and later successfully pressed for their settlement on the Wind River Reservation of Wyoming. Thrapp, *Encyclopedia of Frontier Biography*, 1:522.

22. Born in Texas, Joseph Franklin Cummings (1851–1912) graduated forty-sixth of forty-eight in his U.S. Military Academy class in 1876. He served in Wyoming, Nebraska, Dakota, and Arizona before entering the School of Application at Fort Leavenworth in 1883. The following year, however, he was court-martialed and dismissed from the army. Cummings died in Washington, D.C. Altshuler, *Cavalry Yellow and Infantry Blue*, 89.

A native of Vermont, Homer Webster Wheeler (1848–1930) went to Kansas in 1868 and accompanied several scouts as a civilian. Commissioned as a second lieutenant in October 1875, he took part in the Sioux and Cheyenne campaigns of 1876–77 and the Bannock War of 1879. He later served in Nebraska, Puerto Rico, the Philippines, Cuba, and Hawaii. Wheeler retired as a colonel in 1911, later writing *The Frontier Trail* (1923) and *Buffalo Days* (1925). Thrapp, *Encyclopedia of Frontier Biography*, 3:1545–46.

23. Canadian-born George Horace Morgan (1855–1948) graduated thirty-second in his West Point class in 1880. He was badly wounded in the Battle of Big Dry Wash (July 17, 1882), for which he would later be awarded a Medal of Honor. Morgan later taught military science at the University of Minnesota and was admitted to that state's bar. Slightly wounded at Santiago, Cuba, he also fought in the Philippines. Colonel Morgan retired from active duty in 1919. Altshuler, *Cavalry Yellow and Infantry Blue*, 236–37.

24. Biochemist, medical administrator, and public health expert, Victor Clarence Vaughan (1851–1929) was a longtime member of the faculty and staff and the University of Michigan Medical School. He and a colleague are credited with establishing the first laboratory course in bacteriology at any American university. William Henry Welch (1850–1934) did much to introduce the work of Robert Koch to American medical schools and helped make the medical facilities and training programs at the Johns Hopkins University some of the finest in the country. Kaufman, Galishoff, and Savitt, *Dictionary of American Medical Biography*, 2:702–03, 788–89.

25. As Mrs. Corbusier notes, this was the first time her husband was not present at her childbirth. F. Corbusier, "Recollections," 78.

26. Until 1892, army surgeons were officially encouraged to care for local civilians in hopes that such practice would familiarize them with local health issues. Gillett, *Army Medical Department*, 56.

27. Fanny recalled that it was Dr. Austin Flint who had recommended a drier climate for Phil's health. For more detailed accounts of their life at Mackinac, see F. Corbusier, "Recollections," 78–87; and H. Corbusier, *A Boy at Fort Mackinac*.

28. Established in 1862 to protect the Tucson-Mesilla road, Fort Bowie was abandoned in 1894 and was transferred to the Interior Department. Frazer, *Forts of the West*, 4.

29. The New Jersey school was recommended by Major Charles L. Davis, who had attended it as a boy and whose uncle served as headmaster. F. Corbusier, "Recollections," 93.

30. Fanny explained that "we never regretted our choice" of Miss Teed, a student at the State Normal School, San Jose. A lover of the outdoors, she "was well equipped for her work and soon adapted herself to the army life." After leaving the Corbusier family, she went to Los Angeles and New York and became an artist. Mr. Cairns "was a clean, decent, well appearing young fellow and hard student, tall, rather loose jointed and with a nose that was somewhat flat at the end, the kind that literary people not infrequently have, but he hadn't the training to impart his knowledge to others as Miss Teed had, so although the boys did well under him, they didn't improve so rapidly as they had done." Ibid., 95, 98–99.

31. Born in Indiana, Anson Mills (1834–1924) attended West Point from 1855–57 and joined the Union army at the outset of the Civil War. Earning three brevets fighting against the Confederates, he remained in the army, serving in campaigns against the Apaches, Sioux, and Northern Cheyennes. He retired as a brigadier general in 1897. His cartridge belt, which he had designed during the 1860s, eventually became standard equipment in the United States and British armies, earning him a fortune. Mills briefly mentions the Corbusiers in his memoirs, *My Story* (233). Altshuler, *Cavalry Yellow and Infantry Blue*, 231–32.

32. Originally known as Fort Fletcher, Fort Hays was established in Ellis County, Kansas, in 1865. Renamed for Brigadier General Alexander Hays, who was killed in the Battle of the Wilderness, the post's garrison protected Kansas Pacific Railroad employees from Indian attack. The army left Fort Hays in November 1889. The reservation now houses part of Fort Hays State University. Roberts, *Encyclopedia of Historic Forts*, 295.

33. "Boot hill" was a western slang term for cemeteries used to bury those who had died by violence. Like many, Corbusier exaggerated the level of frontier gunplay in the Kansas cattle towns. For a sober analysis, see Dykstra, *Cattle Towns*.

34. In 1880, the army established Fort Lewis in southern Colorado in response to recent difficulties with the Ute Indians. The military turned the site over to the Interior Department in 1891, and it later became a branch campus of the state agricultural college. Frazer, *Forts of the West*, 38–39.

35. After enlisting in the army in 1861, Ohio-born Tullius Cicero Tupper (1838–98) rose through the ranks and ended the Civil War as a brevet major. He saw combat against Indians in Indian Territory, Arizona, New Mexico, and South Dakota. In 1890, Tupper was named brevet lieutenant colonel for his actions during the Red River campaign and at Las Animas. He retired in 1893 and died in Cleveland. Altshuler, *Cavalry Yellow and Infantry Blue*, 336–37.

36. Carter N. Berkeley Macauley, born in Minnesota, was appointed assistant surgeon in August 1882. After serving at Fort Columbus, New York, in June 1883 he was named post surgeon at Fort Bennett, Dakota Territory. He died in 1896. *Records of Living Officers*, 62; Heitman, *Historical Register and Dictionary*, 1:652.

37. Born in New York, Henry M. Cronkhite enlisted in the Twenty-sixth New York Infantry in July 1861 but was discharged two years later. Accepting an appointment as assistant surgeon in June 1867, Cronkhite retired as a major in 1895. *Records of Living Officers*, 57; Heitman, *Historical Register and Dictionary*, 1:340.

38. Fort Wayne, Michigan, was originally authorized in 1841 in response to continued animosities between the United States and Britain regarding Canada. Boasting walls seventeen feet thick, it was first officially garrisoned by regular troops in 1861. It was used as a training base and for support functions. The title to the fort was transferred to the city of Detroit in 1949. Roberts, *Encyclopedia of Historic Forts*, 424.

39. During the 1890s, the army commonly detailed its regular army surgeons to National Guard encampments. Gillett, *Army Medical Department*, 55.

40. Columbus Arsenal was built in 1861. Renamed Columbus Barracks in 1875, the post became a major induction center in the twentieth century. Roberts, *Encyclopedia of Historic Forts*, 642.

41. Established in 1868 in Indian Territory near the North Canadian River, Camp Supply served as an important base for army operations in the southern plains. The military abandoned it in 1895. The site was later used as a home for the mentally ill, now called the Western State Psychiatric Center. Frazer, *Forts of the West*, 125.

42. The twelve thousand square miles of north-central Oklahoma known as the "Cherokee strip" were leased by the Cherokee Nation to the Cherokee Livestock Association in 1883, then purchased outright by the federal government in 1891 for $8.5 million. It was opened to the public on September 16, sparking the land "boom" Corbusier describes. *Dictionary of American History*, 2:14.

43. Born in Ohio, Curtis Ethelbert Price was appointed an assistant surgeon in the Twelfth Tennessee Cavalry (Union) in 1864. Promoted to surgeon the following year, he was brevetted to lieutenant colonel for his service at the Battle of Nashville. Mustered out of the army in 1865, Price rejoined the military as an assistant surgeon in June 1875. He was promoted to captain in 1880 and died in 1896. Heitman, *Historical Register and Dictionary*, 1:806; *Records of Living Officers*, 59.

44. Nelson A. Miles (1839–1925) helped raise a company of Massachusetts troops just after the First Battle of Bull Run. Despite having almost no formal military education, he emerged from the Civil War as a major general of volunteers. Miles also gained renown as one of the army's best commanders against the Indians, having played a leading role in the Red River War, the Great Sioux War, the Nez Percé conflict, and the Geronimo campaign. He became commanding general of the U.S. Army in 1895. Wooster, *Nelson A. Miles*.

45. Occupying a commanding position in Virginia guarding the Chesapeake Bay, Fort Monroe, first garrisoned by U.S. troops in 1823, was long the largest and most powerful of the army's coastal defense sites. It has housed several major administrative commands, most recently the U.S. Army Training and Doctrine Command. Roberts, *Encyclopedia of Historic Forts*, 815–16.

46. Located in Detroit, Parke-Davis and Company became one of the most important pharmaceutical firms in the nation during the late nineteenth and early twentieth centuries. The Parke-Davis Research Laboratory was designated a national historic landmark in May 1976. National Park Service, "Parke-Davis and Company Plant and Research Laboratory," website; Michigan Historical Center, "Parke-Davis Research laboratory," website.

47. President Millard Fillmore declared Angel Island, located in San Francisco Bay, a military reserve in 1850. It remained under army control until 1946, serving as a seaboard fortification, immigrant station, quarantine station, and camp for Indian, Japanese, and German war prisoners. The post at Angel Island was officially renamed Fort McDowell in 1900. Roberts, *Encyclopedia of Historic Forts*, 76.

1. Launched in 1874 by the Pacific Mail Steamship Company, the 5,080-ton transport steamer *City of Peking* was chartered for two years by the War Department following George Dewey's dramatic naval victory at Manila. It was scrapped in 1910. Dyal, *Historical Dictionary of the Spanish American War*, 79.

2. Displacing 3,500 tons, the *Peru* was chartered from the Pacific Mail Steamship Company at a daily rate of $1,000 from June 25 to November 2, 1898. It carried fifty officers and one thousand men. McSherry, "The Transport Service," website.

3. Although mix-ups and mistakes occurred, the Medical Department provided better care for the sick and wounded of the Philippines expedition than it did for those who fell ill or were injured in Cuba. In part this resulted from the resources available in San Francisco and the "considerable" administrative abilities of the command's chief surgeon, Lieutenant Colonel Henry Lippincott. Once troops fanned out across the islands, however, shortages of physicians and lack of ready access to supply depots took a grave toll. Gillett, *Army Medical Department*, 133–34.

4. See Introduction, note 12.

5. The Army Nurse Corps was officially established on February 2, 1901. Sarnecky, *A History of the U.S. Army Nurse Corps*, 50–51.

6. Displacing five thousand tons, the *Arizona* was purchased from the Northern Pacific Railway Company in July 1898 for $600,000. It carried elements of the First Colorado, First Nebraska, Tenth Pennsylvania, and the Eighteenth U.S. Infantry regiments. McSherry, "The Transport Service," website.

7. Born in Maine and educated at Colby University, Henry Clay Merriam fought in the battles of Antietam and Fredericksburg before taking command of a regiment of Louisiana black troops in 1863. His gallantry during the assault on Fort Blakely, Alabama, would later be recognized with a Medal of Honor. In 1866, Merriam was appointed a major in the regular army. He saw much service in the Southwest and along the Mexican border. He retired from active duty in 1903 at the rank of major general. Heitman, *Historical Register and Dictionary*, 1:704; *Records of Living Officers*, 238–39.

8. Built in 1889 and displacing 4,375 tons, *Scandia* was purchased from the Hamburg-American Line by the U.S. Navy for $200,000 on July 5, 1898. It transported parts of the First Montana Volunteer Infantry and California Volunteer Heavy Artillery. McSherry, "The Transport Service," website; Swiggum and Kohli, "Hamburg-American Packet Company / Hamburg-American Line," website.

9. Liliuokalani (1838–1917) assumed the throne as queen of Hawaii in 1891. In a power struggle with foreign economic interests led by Sanford B. Dole, however, she was deposed two years later in favor of an independent republic. After a period of house arrest, she worked to preserve Hawaiian traditions and became an accomplished musician. Garraty and Carnes, *American National Biography*, 13:654–55.

10. A native of Indiana, Merritte Weber Ireland was appointed assistant surgeon in 1891. He became a major and surgeon for the Forty-fifth U.S. Volunteer Infantry in 1899. Heitman, *Historical Register and Dictionary*, 1:563.

11. Located just north of Manila, Caloocan was the main railroad terminus in central Luzon. On February 10, 1899, U.S. troops captured the city after heavy fighting. Beede, *War of 1898 and U.S. Interventions*, 305.

12. On January 21, 1899, Malolos, located twenty-five miles north of Manila, was declared the capital of the independent Philippine Republic. After sporadic fighting, General Arthur MacArthur launched a major attack on March 25. Filipino troops evacuated the city six days later. Ibid., 298–300.

13. Chartered for $660 per day from June 7–November 3, 1898, the *Morgan City* displaced 2,300 tons. McSherry, "The Transport Service," website.

14. Pajamas for enlisted men were officially adopted June 1, 1904. Steffen, *Last of the Indian Wars*, 123.

15. To help those soldiers "who had gone to the front in a needy condition," the Daughters of the American Revolution formed a "War Committee." Among the seven members was Mrs. Charles H. Alden, wife of former assistant surgeon general Colonel Charles Henry Alden. Lockwood and Sherwood, *Story of the Records, D.A.R.*, 66; Heitman, *Historical Register and Dictionary*, 1:155.

16. Tagalog, one of eight major Philippine language groups, is spoken in Manila and the island of Luzon. "Tagalog" also refers to the natives of the region. Embree, *Encyclopedia of Asian History*, 4:41.

17. Following the Treaty of Paris, relations between the United States and the Philippine Republic quickly deteriorated as it became evident that American leaders had no intention of granting the islands their independence. On February 4, firing broke out in several Manila suburbs and continued to threaten U.S. interests in the city for nearly a month. Beede, *War of 1898 and U.S. Interventions*, 299, 305.

18. Visayan (or Bisayan) refers to the central Philippines; linguists have identified at least twelve different languages that are commonly dubbed "Visayan." Embree, *Encyclopedia of Asian History*, 3:243–44.

19. The polka redowa is an adoption of the application of waltz rhythms in triple time with traditional polka steps. The versovienne is another polka variation. *International Encyclopedia of Dance*, 5:221–23.

20. Jonah Kuhio Kalanianaole (1871–1922) studied in Hawaii, California, and England and was created a prince by royal proclamation in 1884. Sentenced to a year's imprisonment for his support of the royalist uprising against the Republic of Hawaii in the 1895 revolt, he fought for the British army during the Boer War. Elected as a Republican delegate from the Hawaii Territory, Kalanianaole served from 1903 until his death, having supported Hawaiian statehood, woman suffrage, and homesteading for native Hawaiians. A noted sportsman, he was nicknamed "Prince Cupid" while attending school in Hawaii. Garraty and Carnes, *American National Biography*, 12:943–44.

1. Dr. George Miller Sternberg (1838–1915) entered the army in 1861. An eminent physician and research scientist, he is credited with introducing the breakthroughs of Louis Pasteur and Robert Koch to the United States. Named surgeon general in 1893, Sternberg later established the Typhoid Fever Board (1898) and Walter Reed's Yellow Fever Commission (1900), both of which demonstrated the role of insects in the transmission of certain diseases. A better scientist than bureaucrat, he has been criticized for the Medical Department's lack of preparedness for the conflicts in Cuba and the Philippines. Kaufman, Galishoff, and Savitt, *Dictionary of American Medical Biography*, 2:716–17; Dyal, *Historical Dictionary of the Spanish American War*, 216–17, 310; Spiller, *Dictionary of American Military Biography*, 3:1047–50; Sternberg, *George Miller Sternberg*.

A lawyer and Republican activist, Elihu Root (1845–1937) was appointed secretary of war by President William McKinley in 1899. Selected largely in the hopes that his legal experience would help him establish effective governments in Cuba and the Philippines, Root went on to push through major organizational reforms in the War Department and the army. He later served as secretary of state, U.S. senator, and president of the Carnegie Endowment for International Peace. Spiller, *Dictionary of American Military Biography*, 3:938–42.

2. Governors Island, located about one-half mile from Manhattan, was first occupied by British troops in 1755. A pentagonal work capable of holding one hundred guns, known as Fort Columbus, was completed by the United States in 1808. It was officially renamed Fort Jay in 1904. The army continued to garrison the island until 1966. Roberts, *Encyclopedia of Historic Forts*, 555–56.

3. Established outside Omaha, Nebraska, Fort Crook (named in honor of Major General George Crook) was intended to replace Fort Omaha as a major military depot and post for the central plains. Renamed Offutt in 1924, the site was later developed into an air base and headquarters of the Strategic Command. Frazer, *Forts of the West*, 86.

4. With the outset of the Spanish-American War, the Atlantic Transport Line transferred the passenger ships *Massachusetts, Manitoba,* and *Mobile* to the army, who converted them into the transports *Sheridan, Logan,* and *Sherman* (the latter two mentioned subsequently in the text). Emmons, *American Passenger Ships*.

5. Walter Francis Dillingham (1875–1963) was born in Hawaii into a prominent business family. He developed not only his father's Oahu Railway and Land Company but the powerful Hawaiian Dredging and Construction Company. An opponent of Hawaiian statehood, he was a long-term advisor to Presidents Franklin D. Roosevelt and Dwight D. Eisenhower. *Dictionary of American Biography*, Suppl. 3:184–85.

6. In response to continuing opposition to the United States from the Moros (Philippine Muslims), General Leonard Wood, commanding general of the

Department of Mindanao, established the Moro Province on September 3, 1903. Wood served as first governor of the province, which had its capital at Zamboanga. Beede, *War of 1898 and U.S. Interventions*, 349.

7. In 1905, Major E. C. Carter, commissioner of public health for the Philippines, remarked that "the habit of careless spitting is so general that it is almost impossible to make any impression upon it. It will undoubtedly require years of patient waiting before the results aimed at will begin to show." U.S. Congress, *Annual Reports of the War Department*, 80.

8. Datu Ali was the son of Datu Uttu, a Moro chief who had long resisted Spanish efforts to control Mindanao. In 1903, Ali launched a major uprising against the United States. When traditional defensive tactics against the better-armed Americans proved unsuccessful (the Moros had long built earthen cottas, or forts, to protect their villages), he opted for the hit-and-run methods that would prolong the resistance for three more years. In 1906, Datu Ali was killed by troops led by Captain Frank R. McCoy in Simpetan. Beede, *War of 1898 and U.S. Interventions*, 13.

9. Often referred to as Parang Parang, the post here, which U.S. troops occupied in January 1900, had "barracks for 200 men and good quarters for officers." U.S. Bureau of Insular Affairs, *Pronouncing Gazatteer and Geographical Dictionary*, 475–76.

10. In 1901, the army established Camp Overton on the Bay of Iligan, Moro Province, as a depot for forces seeking to control the northern approaches to Lake Lanao. Beede, *War of 1898 and U.S. Interventions*, 248. In his handwritten diaries, Dr. Corbusier describes the hospital there as being "on a hill 95 feet above the sea level. It is of rough boards and has an asbestos roof. Beds 16." W. H. Corbusier, Diaries, October 12, 1904.

11. Camp Keithley, on the northern edge of Lake Lanao at Marawi, was described by one American serviceman as being "in the heart of the Moro country and the toughest post in the P. I.'s." Willson, "Why I Went to Viet Nam," website.

12. Running *juramentado* and running amok are considered distinct martial practices, but Corbusier seems to conflate the two. Running *juramentado* is a religious rite in which a Muslim warrior seeks to kill Christians, while running amok is a homicidal frenzy with no religious significance. Hurley, "Kris versus Toledo Blade: Juramentados and Amuks," website.

13. Hostilities between U.S. forces and the Moros of the Lake Lanao region of Mindanao continued for years. Fighting was especially heavy in 1902–1903, when Captain John J. Pershing led a series of punitive operations against the Moros following the Battle of Bayang. Although the Americans outgunned their enemies, snipers and guerrilla attacks were always a threat. The religious zealots who killed non-Muslims were sometimes called "amucks." Beede, *War of 1898 and U.S. Interventions*, 248–50, 345–47. A detailed contemporary map of Mindanao entitled "Map of Mindanao, Philippine Islands, Prepared by the War Department, Adju-

tant General's Office, Military Information Division, 1902" can be found at the Geography and Map Division of the Library of Congress.

14. Colonel Frank D. Baldwin established Camp Vicars in May 1902. Over-looking southwestern Lake Lanao, it was named after Lieutenant Thomas A. Vicars, who had been killed in an assault against a Moro fort near the site. Camp Vicars was garrisoned by nearly seven hundred men. After repeated Moro attacks on the camp in August–September 1902, Pershing made it the staging point for several punitive expeditions. Beede, *War of 1898 and U.S. Interventions*, 45, 248–49; Steinbach, *A Long March*, 179–83; Wolfhound History Project, "Camp Vicars Expe-dition," website.

15. Surgeon George Newgarden described the buildings of Malabang, located seventeen miles northwest of Polloc Harbor, as "certainly primitive." His vivid discussion of life there is filled with depictions of battles against rats, bats, snakes, and Moro attacks. See United States Army Surgeon General's Office, "Random Collections of an Army Surgeon;" and U.S. Bureau of Insular Affairs, *Pronouncing Gazatteer and Geographical Dictionar*, 475.

16. In his diary, Corbusier noted that "the Gatling gun in the bow of the boat was uncovered and made ready for use." He went on to explain that Fort Pikit, located on a 138-feet-tall coral hill on the right bank of the Rio Grande, was "square with sort of block houses at the corners," garrisoned by the Forty-eighth Philippine Scout Company and the Twenty-second and Twenty-third Provisional Companies. Forty miles further upriver was the camp at Reina Regente, another small post. W. H. Corbusier, Diaries, October 24–26, 1904; Fort Pikit, October 1906, Returns from U.S. Military Posts, Microfilm M 617, National Archives.

Datu Piang (ca. 1850–1933) was the most powerful leader in southwestern Mindanao. The son of a Chinese trader and a Maguindanaon mother, he proved an expert collaborator with the Spanish and later the American authorities. Some suspect that it was he who provided the intelligence that allowed U.S. troops to surprise and kill his rival, Datu Ali. Dr. Corbusier described Piang as having severely swollen hands "from rheumatism or beri-beri. His hands had some black application and were not clean to shake but he persisted in pushing his hand forward." McKenna, *Muslim Rulers and Rebels*, 91–97; W. H. Corbusier, Diaries, October 24–26, 1904.

17. Corbusier also described preliminary talks in the Fort Pikit-Reina Regente region, noting that over twelve hundred Moros came in for the conference, turn-ing in 137 firearms of various types as a show of their good faith. W. H. Corbusier, Diaries, October 26, 1904.

18. Typically about five hundred men from the Fifteenth U.S. Cavalry gar-risoned Jolo in 1902. Detachments from the base at Jolo frequently patrolled Siasi and Bongao as well (see below). Jolo, Siasi, and Bongao, June 1902, Returns from U.S. Military Posts, Microfilm M 617, National Archives.

Hugh Lenox Scott (1853–1934) was born in Kentucky and graduated from West Point in 1876. After twenty-five years on the frontier, from 1899–1902 Scott served as adjutant general in Cuba. Transferred to the Philippines, he became governor of the Sulu archipelago and commander of Post Jolo. In 1906, Scott was named superintendent of West Point, where he remained for four years. Deeply involved in the army's border skirmishes during the 1910s, he also served as army chief of staff. After retiring from active duty in 1919, Scott served as a member of the Board of Indian Commissioners and chaired the New Jersey State Highway Commission. Beede, *War of 1898 and U.S. Interventions,* 502–04.

19. In September 1899, one company of the Twenty-third Infantry established Camp Gregg at the town of Siasi on the west shore of the island, about forty miles south of Jolo. A company of Filipino scouts garrisoned the little post until its abandonment in September 1913. Siasi, September 1899 and September 14, 1913, Returns from U.S. Military Posts, Microfilm M 617, National Archives.

20. Born in Maine, George Henry Goodwin Gale was appointed to the U.S. Military Academy from Massachusetts. In 1875, he graduated tenth in his class. Securing an appointment to the cavalry, he was promoted to first lieutenant in 1884, captain in 1892, and major in 1901. In 1903, Gale joined the Inspector General's Department. Heitman, *Historical Register and Dictionary,* 1:442.

Paragua was the Spanish name for the island of Palawan. The army established a post at Puerto Princesa, on the east coast of the island, in late May 1901. Puerto Princesa, June 1901–December 1906, Returns from U.S. Military Posts, Microfilm M 617, National Archives.

21. At this time, during a brief trip to Manila (September 4, 1905), Corbusier secured a prescription for eyeglasses. W. H. Corbusier, Diaries, September 2, 1905.

22. Anna Prentice Gate married Sanford Ballard Dole in 1873. Long an advocate of political reform and American interests in Hawaii, her husband was a leader in the 1893 overthrow of Queen Liliuokalani and was named president of the provisional government. Elected president of the Republic of Hawaii in 1894, he was appointed first governor of the Territory of Hawaii in 1900. His cousin, James D. Dole, founded the Hawaiian Pineapple Company. Mrs. Dole died in 1918. Garraty and Carnes, *American National Biography,* 6:705–07.

23. Born in Michigan, John Parke Finley enlisted in the army in 1877. He secured a commission in the Signal Corps seven years later. Transferred to the infantry in 1891, he was promoted to captain in 1898. Heitman, *Historical Register and Dictionary,* 1:420.

24. In his diary, Corbusier is uncharacteristically frank about this short voyage. "A dirty Chinaman does the cooking which is pretty poor and messy. I saw the cook this morning putting articles of food on the plates with his fingers. The ham is rotten, potatoes when fried are still raw, and when boiled soggy and tasteless. Coffee good, bread & rolls sad." W. H. Corbusier, Diaries, December 24, 1905.

25. Originally a Hudson's Bay Company trading post, the site of Vancouver Barracks became a U.S. military post in 1849. Known until 1853 as Columbia Barracks and until 1879 as Fort Vancouver, it was abandoned by the army in 1947 and later made a national historic site. Roberts, *Encyclopedia of Historic Forts,* 838.

1. In 1903, Washington State purchased a 220-acre site south of Tacoma for the use of its National Guard. A more permanent post, called Camp Murray, was established in 1915. The enlarged post became an important National Guard and Army Reserve training site. Roberts, *Encyclopedia of Historic Forts*, 834.

2. Named for Colonel Emerson H. Liscum, who was killed during the Boxer Rebellion, Fort Liscum was established in 1900 near the terminus of the Fairbanks-Valdez Military Road. It was abandoned in 1922. Ibid., 23.

3. Born in Illinois, David H. Kinzie attended the U.S. Military Academy for two years before accepting a lieutenancy in the artillery. During the Civil War, he was brevetted for his outstanding service during the Battles of the Seven Days and Antietam. Kinzie remained in the artillery and by 1901 was a full colonel. Heitman, *Historical Register and Dictionary*, 1:602.

4. The army established a temporary post at Haines, Alaska, in 1898, to serve as a point of entry for five hundred Scandinavian reindeer. Previously referred to as Haines Mission, it was designated a permanent station and renamed Fort William H. Seward, after the secretary of state who had purchased Alaska, in 1904. Renamed Chilkoot Barracks in 1922, it was abandoned in 1943. Roberts, *Encyclopedia of Historic Forts*, 20.

5. Chester Ashley Thomas was born in Los Angeles in 1874. He was educated at Stanford, and after leaving the army, he joined the Yukon Gold Company in 1905 and soon became its "resident manager" in the Yukon. *Canadian Who's Who*, 221; Christy, "First California U.S.V.," website.

6. Fort Egbert was established on the Yukon River at the mining camp of Eagle, Alaska, in 1899. Located six miles west of the Canadian border, the two company post was abandoned in 1911 except for a small detachment left behind to operate the telegraph. Roberts, *Encyclopedia of Historic Forts*, 21.

7. Fort Yukon was garrisoned between September 1897–January 1898 in efforts to provide security during the Klondike gold rush of that period. Fort Yukon, Brief Histories of U.S. Army Commands (Army Posts) and Descriptions of Their Records, Microfilm T 912, National Archives.

Fort Gibbon was established in 1899 near the junction of the Tanana and Yukon Rivers. It was the headquarters for all military posts in the Alaskan interior until its abandonment in 1923. Roberts, *Encyclopedia of Historic Forts*, 21–22.

8. Adolphus W. Greely (1844–1935) volunteered for the army at the outbreak of the Civil War. Commissioned in 1863, he joined the Signal Corps six years later. He was most noted for his controversial leadership of the International Polar Expedition of 1881–84, during which eighteen of the twenty-five members died. Appointed chief Signal Corps officer and brigadier general in 1887, he retired from active duty in 1908 and was awarded the Medal of Honor in 1935. Garraty and Carnes, *American National Biography*, 9:471–72.

New Jersey-born William Sulzer (1863–1941) practiced law in New York City. A Democrat, he served in the state assembly from 1889 to 1894. Entering Congress the following year, Sulzer served nine terms before being elected governor in 1913. He was impeached later that year in a campaign finance scandal. Many, however, attributed his removal to his having challenged powerful Tammany Hall interests. Sulzer was promptly elected to the state assembly as a Progressive. After leaving politics, he devoted himself to his legal practice and his Alaska gold-mining interests. *Dictionary of American Biography*, Suppl. 3:751–52.

Born in Vermont, Thomas Cale (1848–1941) moved to Alaska in 1898. He was engaged in mining and, running as an independent, was elected the territory's delegate to Congress in 1907. He served a single term before returning to South Dakota and later Wisconsin. "Cale, Thomas, 1848–1941," website.

9. The Russians built a stockade at St. Michael in 1833. The U.S. Signal Corps deployed a small detachment there from 1874 to 86, and a regular garrison was dispatched there in 1897. It was abandoned in 1923. Roberts, *Encyclopedia of Historic Forts*, 26–27.

10. Named for Brevet Major General Jefferson Columbus Davis, first U.S. department commander of Alaska, Fort Davis was established at the mouth of the Nome River in 1900. The army abandoned the fort nineteen years later. Ibid., 21.

11. Corbusier initially feared that he had stomach cancer. Along with their father, William Worrall Mayo (1818–1911), brothers Charles Horace Mayo (1865–1939) and William James Mayo (1861–1939) developed their group surgical practice in Rochester, Minnesota, into one of the world's leading health clinics. Woodbury to AG, March 7, 1908, 4565, ACP 1876, Appointments, Commission, and Personal Branch Papers, RG 94, National Archives; Kaufman, Galishoff, and Savitt, *Dictionary of American Medical Biography*, 2:508–09.

12. As a professor of military science at the University of Kentucky, Lieutenant Philip Corbusier was influential in changing the nickname of the school's athletic teams, which originally were known as the Cadets. Following a football game against the University of Illinois in October 1909, Lieutenant Corbusier proclaimed that the team had "fought like wildcats." The label caught on, and the Kentucky Wildcats were born. Day, "From Hoops to Horse Racing," website; "University of Kentucky Traditions and Songs," website.

13. Originally displacing 8,850 tons, *Lake Manitoba* began service for the Canadian Pacific Line in 1903. It was taken over by the Beaver Line in 1918 and rebuilt to 9,674 tons. Gutted by fire later that year, it was sold to the Bishop Navigation Company and renamed the *Iver Heath*. Swiggum and Kohli, "Canadian Pacific Line," website.

14. The *Lapland* sailed for the White and Red Star Lines from 1908 until 1933, when it was sold in Japan for scrap. Swiggum and Kohli, "White Star Line," website; Swiggum and Kohli, "Red Star Line," website.

15. Opened in 1917, Camp Merritt was the port of embarkation for nearly 600,000 U.S. servicemen headed for Europe during World War I. It was dis-

continued as a military post three years later. Roberts, *Encyclopedia of Historic Forts*, 512.

Built in 1899, the ten thousand-ton *Rhein* was interned in Baltimore in August 1914. It was taken over by the U.S. Navy three years later and finally broken up in 1929. Emmons, *American Passenger Ships*, 32.

The First Antiaircraft Battalion was attached to the First Army Corps for most of World War I, serving in the Château-Thierry and Aisne-Marne operations. *Order of Battle*, 193–95.

16. The *Cedric* sailed from 1902 to 1932 for the famous White Star Line. It was scrapped at Inverkeithing. Swiggum and Kohli, "White Star Line," website.

Corbusier also included the following in his original text:

Headquarters Port of Embarkation, Hoboken, New Jersey, August 18, 1919. Colonel William H. Corbusier, U.S. Army, Retired, Hoboken, N.J., My dear Colonel Corbusier[,] In accordance with orders from the War Department, you have been relieved from duty at this port as a member of the General Court-Martial on duty here. Our records show that you have been continuously on duty since July 26, 1918. During the whole of this time you have had a very important duty as member of the Court-Martial and indeed it has been performed in a most efficient and satisfactory way. I desire to thank you for the cheerful spirit with [which] you placed your services at the disposal of the Government, and to say that I greatly appreciate the services you have rendered. A copy of this letter is being forwarded to the War Department with the request that it be placed on file with your record in the Office of the Adjutant General. Very truly yours, signed, David D. Shanks, Major General, U.S.A.

17. To help finance the war, the Wilson administration orchestrated one "victory loan" and four "liberty loan" campaigns, which raised over $21 billion. The fourth comprised just under $7 billion. To drum up popular support, the government organized liberty loan committees, featuring public speakers, the clergy, and mass meetings. *Dictionary of American History*, 4:143.

18. The Canadian Pacific Line acquired the *Melita*, which displaced nearly fourteen thousand tons, in 1918. It was eventually sold to the Italia Line and renamed the troopship *Liguria*. Swiggum and Kohli, "Canadian Pacific Line," website.

19. Opened in 1876 and originally known as the San Antonio Quartermaster Depot, the post was officially designated Fort Sam Houston in 1890. Expanded on several occasions, it was the center for airborne infantry maneuvers during World War II. It was later the headquarters of the U.S. Army Medical Command and has been designated a national historic landmark. Roberts, *Encyclopedia of Historic Forts*, 775–76.

20. Phyllis and William ("Billy"), Phil and Ida Corbusier's children, were ages seventeen and eleven, respectively, at the time of the flood. Ancestry.com, *Kentucky 1910 Miracode Index*, website.

21. Established in 1917 at San Antonio, Camp Travis served as an important basic training center during World War I. It was merged into Fort Sam Houston in 1922. Ibid., 779.

22. Born in New York, Raymond Franklin Metcalfe (1877–1959) secured his medical degree in 1900 and was commissioned in the Army Medical Corps the following year. He served two tours in the Philippines as well as in World War I. He retired as a brigadier general in May 1941 but was recalled to active duty during World War II. Ancell, *Biographical Dictionary of World War II*, 222.

23. Captain Richard Henry Pratt established the Carlisle Indian Industrial School in 1879. Hoping to assimilate Indians into white society, Pratt insisted that his students divorce themselves completely from all tribal traditions. Prucha, *Great Father*, 234–37.

24. In 1917, Thomas Edward Campbell was turned out of the governor's office by a contested recount but was reelected for two full terms in 1919 and 1921. Sobel and Raimo, *Biographical Directory of the Governors*, 50–51.

25. The site of fourteenth-century Hohokam ruins, the Casa Grande Ruins Reservation was designated for federal protection in 1892. The first archaeological ruin preserved by the federal government, it was later reclassified as a national monument. Phillips and Axelrod, *Encyclopedia of the American West*, 1:253.

26. Letterman General Hospital served military patients from the Philippines, Hawaii, and the western half of the United States. Gillett, *Army Medical Department*, 337–38.

27. Born in Georgia in 1886, Winn received his medical degree in 1910. He was commissioned in the Army Medical Corps in 1917 and advanced to the rank of brigadier general. *Who Was Who in America*, 7:620.

28. Gilman was one of the founders of the Pacific Coast Surgical Association. Regents of the University of California, "Physicians at Mount Zion," website.

29. Having written several books on the region, Frank Hayward Severance (1856–1931) was recognized as the leading authority on the Buffalo / Niagara area during the early twentieth century. *Who Was Who in America*, 1:663.

Ophthalmologist Lucien Howe's (1848–1928) work in neonatal preventive medicine helped eradicate much infant blindness. He served on the University of Buffalo faculty and at the Buffalo General Hospital before directing the Howe Laboratory of Ophthalmology at Harvard University. Kaufman, Galishoff, and Savitt, *Dictionary of American Medical Biography*, 1:368.

30. These "old battle fields" were sites of key battles between the United States and Britain during the War of 1812.

31. George Henderson Kelly (1854–1929) was born in Missouri but moved to Arizona in 1887, where he became a newspaper editor and publisher and a Democratic Party activist. He was appointed state historian in 1923. *Who Was Who in America*, 1:663.

32. Displacing 10,508 tons and capable of twenty knots, the ship originally known as *City of New York* was launched as a civilian liner in 1888. With the out-

break of the Spanish-American War, the U.S. Navy, valuing the ship's speed and size, took it over, renamed it *Harvard*, and converted it into an armed liner. It was refitted after the war and resumed its service as a passenger liner until World War I, when the U.S. Navy once again took it over as a transport. It was scrapped at Genoa. Dyal, *Historical Dictionary of the Spanish American* War, 151–52.

33. Chronically undersupplied and undergarrisoned, Camp Stotsenburg was located in the central Luzon Valley about sicty-five miles from Manila. Its garrison could theoretically respond to invasion forces from either the Lingayen Gulf or the Bataan Peninsula. It was also the site of the Air Corps base at Clark Field. Linn, *Guardians of Empire*, 70.

34. Army officer and lawyer Garrick Mallery (1831–94) joined the Bureau of American Ethnology in 1879, from whose offices he conducted several pioneering studies that remain a foundation for American Indian research. Garraty and Carnes, *American National Biography*, 14:372.

BIBLIOGRAPHY

Manuscript Collections

Burns, Mike. Typescript. Ed. Robert D. Sullivan. Nancy Corbusier Knox Collection, Santa Fe, N. Mex.

Corbusier Family. Letters. Nancy Corbusier Knox Collection, Santa Fe, N. Mex.

Corbusier, Fanny Dunbar. "Recollections of Her Life in the Army." Center for American History. University of Texas at Austin.

Corbusier, William H. "Ancestry of William Henry Corbusier, Lieutenant Colonel, United States Army, Retired, and Fanny Dunbar Corbusier, His Wife." New York Public Library, New York.

———. Diaries. Nancy Corbusier Knox Collection, Santa Fe, N. Mex.

Knox, Nancy. "The Longer View: George Towers Dunbar, 1812–1848." In possession of editor.

Lauderdale, John V. Letterbooks. Beinecke Rare Book and Manuscript Library. Yale University.

United States Army Surgeon General's Office. "Random Collections of an Army Surgeon" by George Newgarden. MS C 444: 98–129. National Library of Medicine, Bethesda, Md.

———. "Record of William Henry Corbusier, Colonel, U.S. Army, Retired." Autobiographical Sketches of U.S. Army Medical Officers Collection. Box 1. MS C 44. National Library of Medicine, Bethesda, Md.

———. "The System of Personal Identification by Finger Prints Recently Adopted for the U.S. Army." Correspondence. MS C 5. National Library of Medicine, Bethesda, Md.

National Archives and Records Administration (NARA)

Appointments, Commission, and Personal Branch Papers. Adjutant General's Office. Box 409. RG 94.

Brief Histories of U.S. Army Commands (Army Posts) and Descriptions of Their Records. Microfilm T 912.

Descriptive Commentaries from the Medical Histories of Posts. Roll 3. Microfilm M 903.

Enlistment Papers, U.S. Army Indian Scouts. File 1176, Box 8 (Mike Burns); Files 209, 216, 247, Box 10 (Captain Charley); Files 229, 234, 248, 261, Box 27 (Kelho); Files 210, 240, Box 48 (Snook). RG 94.

Index to Compiled Service Records of Confederate Soldiers Who Served in Organizations from the State of Louisiana. Roll 50. Microfilm M 320.

Index to Compiled Service Records of Volunteer Soldiers Who Served during the War of 1812. Roll 151. Microfilm M 602.

Index to Compiled Service Records of Volunteer Union Soldiers Who Served in Organizations from the State of Illinois. Rolls 22, 97. Microfilm M 1539.

Letters Received by the Office of Indian Affairs, 1824–1880. Roll 13. Microfilm M 234.

Personal Papers of Medical Officers and Physicians. Box 129. RG 94.

Returns from U.S. Military Posts, 1800–1916. Roll 1492 (Amite, Louisiana); Roll 925 (Fort Pikit); Roll 1170 (Jolo, Siasi, and Bongao); Roll 979 (Puerto Princesa). Microfilm M 617.

Station Cards, Acting Assistant Surgeons, 1862–68, 1898–1901. Box 2. RG 94.

U.S. Manuscript Census. 1840, 1850, 1860, 1870, 1880.

Books

Adams, George Washington Adams. *Doctors in Blue: The Medical History of the Union Army in the Civil War.* New York: Henry Schuman, 1952.

Adjutant General's Office. *Chronological List of Actions, etc., with Indians from January 15, 1837 to January, 1891.* 1891. Reprint, Fort Collins, Colo.: Old Army Press, 1979.

Alberts, Don E. *The Battle of Glorieta: Union Victory in the West.* College Station: Texas A&M University Press, 1998.

Altshuler, Constance Wynn. *Cavalry Yellow and Infantry Blue: Army Officers in Arizona between 1851 and 1886.* Tucson: Arizona Historical Society, 1991.

Ancell, R. Manning. *The Biographical Dictionary of World War II: Generals and Flag Officers; the U.S. Armed Forces.* Westport, Conn.: Greenwood Press, 1996.

Ashburn, P. M. *History of the Medical Department of the United States Army.* Boston: Houghton Mifflin, 1929.

Bancroft, Hubert Howe. *History of California.* Vol. 23, *The Works of Hubert Howe Bancroft.* San Francisco: The History Company, 1888.

Beede, Benjamin R., ed. *The War of 1898 and U.S. Interventions, 1898–1934: An Encyclopedia.* New York: Garland Publishing, 1994.

Bergeron, Arthur W., Jr. *Guide to Louisiana Confederate Military Units, 1861–1865.* Baton Rouge: Louisiana State University Press, 1989.

Boatner, Mark M., III. *The Civil War Dictionary.* Rev. ed. New York: David McKay, 1959.

Bourke, John G. *On the Border with Crook.* 1891. Reprint, Lincoln: University of Nebraska Press, 1971.

Buecker, Thomas R. *Fort Robinson and the American West, 1874–1899.* Lincoln: Nebraska State Historical Society, 1999.

Burrows, Edwin G., and Mike Wallace. *Gotham: A History of New York City to 1898.*
New York: Oxford University Press, 1999.

Byrne, Bernard J. *A Frontier Army Surgeon.* New York: Exposition Press, 1962.

The Canadian Who's Who. Toronto: Musson Book Co., 1910.

Carroll, Bret E. *Spiritualism in Antebellum America.* Bloomington: Indiana University Press, 1997.

Cassidy, Frederic G., ed. *Dictionary of American Regional English.* 3 vols. Cambridge: Belknap Press of Harvard University Press, 1985.

Conrad, Glenn R., ed. *A Dictionary of Louisiana Biography.* New Orleans: Louisiana Historical Association, 1988.

Corbusier, Harold Dunbar. *A Boy at Fort Mackinac: The Diary of Harold Dunbar Corbusier, 1883–84, 1892.* Ed. Phil Porter. Mackinac Island, Mich.: Corbusier Archives and Mackinac State Historic Park, 1984.

Corbusier, William T. *Verde to San Carlos: Recollections of a Famous Army Surgeon and His Observant Family on the Western Frontier, 1869–1886.* Tucson: Dale Stuart King, 1969.

Crooke, George. *General George Crook: His Autobiography.* Ed. Martin F. Schmitt. 1946. Reprint, Norman: University of Oklahoma Press, 1960.

Current, Richard N., ed. *Encyclopedia of the Confederacy.* New York: Simon and Schuster, 1993.

Dabbs, Jack Autrey. *The French Army in Mexico, 1861–1867: A Study in Military Government.* The Hague: Mouton, 1963.

Dictionary of American Biography. 22 vols., 10 suppls. New York: Charles Scribner's Sons, 1928–95.

Dictionary of American History. 8 vols. Rev. ed. New York: Scribner, 1976–78.

Donald, David Herbert. *Lincoln.* New York: Simon and Schuster, 1995.

Dyal, Donald H., ed. *Historical Dictionary of the Spanish American War.* Westport, Conn.: Greenwood Press, 1996.

Dykstra, Robert. *The Cattle Towns.* New York: Alfred A. Knopf, 1968.

Embree, Ainslie T. *The Encyclopedia of Asian History.* 4 vols. New York: Charles Scribner's Sons, 1988.

Emmons, Frederick E. *American Passenger Ships: The Ocean Lines and Liners, 1873–1983.* Newark: University of Delaware Press, 1985.

Essin, Emmett M. *Shavetails and Bell Sharps: The History of the U.S. Army Mule.* Lincoln: University of Nebraska Press, 1997.

Ewen, David, ed. *American Popular Songs from the Revolutionary War to the Present.* New York: Random House, 1966.

Fitzgerald, Emily. *An Army Doctor's Wife on the Frontier: Letters From Alaska and the Far West, 1874–1878.* Ed. Abe Laufe. 1962. Reprint, Lincoln: University of Nebraska Press, 1986.

Foner, Eric, and John A. Garraty, eds. *Reader's Companion to American History.* Boston: Houghton-Mifflin, 1991.

Frazer, Robert W. *Forts of the West: Military Forts and Presidios and Posts Commonly Called Forts West of the Mississippi River to 1898*. Norman: University of Oklahoma Press, 1965.

Garraty, John A., and Mark C. Carnes, eds. *American National Biography*. 24 vols. New York: Oxford University Press, 1999.

Garrison, Fielding H. *John Shaw Billings: A Memoir*. New York: G. P. Putnam's Sons, 1915.

Gifford, E. W. *Northeastern and Western Yavapai*. Vol. 34, no. 4, *University of California Publications in American Archaeology and Ethnology*. Berkeley and Los Angeles: University of California Press, 1935.

Gillett, Mary C. *The Army Medical Department, 1865–1917*. Army Historical Series. Washington: Center of Military History, United States Army, 1995.

Gudde, Erwin G. *California Gold Camps: A Geographical and Historical Dictionary of Camps, Towns, and Localities Where Gold Was Found and Mined; Wayside Stations and Trading Centers*. Berkeley and Los Angeles: University of California Press, 1975.

Hartnoll, Phyllis. *The Oxford Companion to the Theatre*. New York: Oxford University Press, 1985.

Haskins, Charles W. *The Argonauts of California, Being the Reminiscences of Scenes and Incidents That Occurred in California in Early Mining Days. . . .* New York: Fords, Howard, and Hulbert, 1890.

Heiser, Victor G. *An American Doctor's Odyssey: Adventures in Forty-five Countries*. New York: W. W. Norton, 1936.

Heitman, Francis B. *Historical Register and Dictionary of the United States Army, from Its Organization, September 29, 1789, to March 2, 1903*. 2 vols. Washington: Government Printing Office, 1903.

Heizer, Robert F. *California*. Vol. 8, *Handbook of North American Indians*. Washington: Smithsonian Institution, 1978.

History of the Ninth Regiment Illinois Cavalry Volunteers. Chicago: Donohue and Henneberry, 1888.

Hitchcock, H. Wiley, and Stanley Sadie, eds. *The New Grove Dictionary of American Music*. 4 vols. New York: Macmillan, 1986.

Hogan, Robert, ed. *Dictionary of Irish Literature*. Westport, Conn.: Greenwood Press, 1979.

Hoxie, Frederick E., ed. *Encyclopedia of North American Indians*. Boston: Houghton Mifflin, 1996.

Hurst, Jack. *Nathan Bedford Forrest: A Biography*. New York: Alfred A. Knopf, 1993.

International Encyclopedia of Dance. 6 vols. New York: Oxford University Press, 1998.

Kaufman, Martin, Stuart Galishoff, and Todd L. Savitt, eds. *Dictionary of American Medical Biography*. 2 vols. Westport, Conn.: Greenwood Press, 1984.

Khera, Sigrid, and Patricia S. Mariela. "Yavapai." In *Handbook of North American Indians*. Vol. 10. Washington: Smithsonian Institution, 1983.

Kimball, Maria B. *A Soldier Doctor of Our Army*. Boston: Houghton Mifflin, 1917.

Kober, George M. *Reminiscences of George Martin Kober, M.D., LL.D.* Washington: Kober Foundation of Georgetown University, 1930.

Lamar, Howard, ed. *The New Encyclopedia of the American West*. New Haven: Yale University Press, 1998.

Lankevich, George J. *American Metropolis: A History of New York City*. New York: New York University Press, 1998.

Larson, Robert W. *Red Cloud: Warrior-Statesman of the Lakota Sioux*. Norman: University of Oklahoma Press, 1997.

Leckie, William H., and Shirley A. Leckie. *Unlikely Warriors: General Benjamin H. Grierson and His Family*. Norman: University of Oklahoma Press, 1984.

Linderman, Gerald F. *Embattled Courage: The Experience of Combat in the American Civil War*. New York: Free Press, 1987.

Linn, Brian McAllister. *Guardians of Empire: The U.S. Army and the Pacific, 1902–1940*. Chapel Hill: University of North Carolina Press, 1997.

Lockwood, Mary S., and Emily Lee Sherwood. *Story of the Records, D.A.R.* Washington: George E. Howard, 1906.

McChristian, Douglas C. *The U.S. Army in the West, 1870–1880: Uniforms, Weapons, and Equipment*. Norman: University of Oklahoma Press, 1995.

McDonough, James Lee, and Thomas L. Connelly. *Five Tragic Hours: The Battle of Franklin*. Knoxville: University of Tennessee Press, 1983.

McGrew, Roderick E. *Encyclopedia of Medical History*. New York: McGraw Hill, 1985.

McHenry, Robert, ed. *Webster's American Military Biographies*. New York: Dover Publications, 1978.

McKenna, Thomas M. *Muslim Rulers and Rebels: Everyday Politics and Armed Separation in the Southern Philippines*. Berkeley and Los Angeles: University of California Press, 1998.

McPherson, James M. *Ordeal by Fire: The Civil War and Reconstruction*. New York: Alfred A. Knopf, 1982.

Magill, Frank N., ed. *Dictionary of World Biography*. 10 vols. Pasadena: Salem Press, 1999.

Magnusson, Magnus, ed. *Cambridge Biographical Dictionary*. Cambridge: Cambridge University Press, 1990.

Mahon, John K. *History of the Militia and the National Guard*. New York: Macmillan, 1983.

Malinowski, Sharon, and Anna Sheets, eds. *The Gale Encyclopedia of Native American Tribes*. Vol. 2. Detroit: Gale Publishing, 1998.

Mills, Anson. *My Story*. Washington: The author, 1918.

Office of the Chief of Naval Operations. *Dictionary of American Naval Fighting Ships*. Vol. 2. 1963. Reprint, Washington: Navy Department, 1977.

Order of Battle of the United States Land Forces in the World War. Vol. 1, *American Expeditionary Forces: General Headquarters, Armies, Army Corps, Services of Supply,*

Separate Forces. 1937. Reprint, Washington: Center of Military History, United States Army, 1988.

Phillips, Charles, and Alan Axelrod, eds. *Encyclopedia of the American West.* 4 vols. New York: Simon and Schuster Macmillan, 1996.

Prucha, Francis Paul. *The Great Father: The United States Government and the American Indians.* Abr. ed. Lincoln: University of Nebraska Press, 1986.

Records of Living Officers of the United States Army. Philadelphia: L. R. Hamersly and Co., 1884.

Roberts, Robert B. *Encyclopedia of Historic Forts: The Military, Pioneer, and Trading Posts of the United States.* New York: Macmillan, 1988.

Russell, Don. *Campaigning with King: Charles King, Chronicler of the Old Army.* Ed. Paul L. Hedren. Lincoln: University of Nebraska Press, 1991.

Sarnecky, Mary T. *A History of the U.S. Army Nurse Corps.* Philadelphia: University of Pennsylvania Press, 1999.

Sherman, William Tecumseh. *Memoirs of General W. T. Sherman.* 1885. Reprint, New York: Library of America, 1990.

Shumsky, Neil Larry, ed. *Encyclopedia of Urban America: The Cities and Suburbs.* 2 vols. Santa Barbara: ABC-Clio, 1998.

Sobel, Robert, and John Raimo, eds. *Biographical Directory of the Governors of the United States, 1789–1978.* 1978. Reprint, Westport, Conn.: Meckler Group, 1988.

Spann, Edward K. *New Metropolis: New York City, 1840–1857.* New York: Columbia University Press, 1981.

Spiller, Roger J., ed. *Dictionary of American Military Biography.* 3 vols. Westport, Conn.: Greenwood Press, 1984.

Steffen, Randy. *The Last of the Indian Wars, the Spanish-American War, the Brink of the Great War, 1881–1916.* Vol. 3, *The Horse Soldier, 1776–1943.* Norman: University of Oklahoma Press, 1978.

Steinbach, Robert H. *A Long March: The Lives of Frank and Alice Baldwin.* Austin: University of Texas Press, 1989.

Sternberg, Martha L. *George Miller Sternberg: A Biography.* Chicago: American Medical Association, 1920.

Summerhayes, Martha. *Vanished Arizona: Recollections of the Army Life of a New England Woman.* 1911. Reprint, Lincoln: University of Nebraska Press, 1979.

Thrapp, Dan L. *Al Sieber: Chief of Scouts.* Norman: University of Oklahoma Press, 1964.

———. *Encyclopedia of Frontier Biography.* 3 vols. Glendale, Calif.: Arthur H. Clark, 1988.

Trenholm, Virginia Cole, and Maurine Carley. *The Shoshonis: Sentinels of the Rockies.* Norman: University of Oklahoma Press, 1964.

U.S. Bureau of Insular Affairs. *A Pronouncing Gazatteer and Geographical Dictionary of the Philippine Islands. . . .* Washington: Government Printing Office, 1902.

U.S. Congress. House. *Annual Reports of the War Department.* Vol. 11, pt. 2. 59th Cong., 1st sess., 1905. H. Doc. 2

Utley, Robert M. *The Indian Frontier of the American West, 1846–1890.* Albuquerque: University of New Mexico Press, 1984.

Waldman, Carl. *Who Was Who in Native American History: Indians and Non-Indians from Early Contacts through 1900.* New York: Facts on File, 1990.

Waterstrait, Elaine. *Hoomothya's Long Journey, 1865–1897: The True Story of a Yavapai Indian.* Fountain Hills, Ariz.: Mount McDowell Press, 1998.

Whitman, Walt. *The Complete Poetry and Prose of Walt Whitman, as Prepared by Him for the Deathbed Edition.* 2 vols. New York: Pellegrini and Cudahy, 1948.

Who Was Who in America. 7 vols. Chicago: Marquis Who's Who, 1963.

Wilmeth, Don B., and Tice L. Miller, eds. *Cambridge Guide to American Theatre.* Cambridge: Cambridge University Press, 1993.

Wilson, Charles Reagan, and William Ferris, eds. *Encyclopedia of Southern Culture.* Chapel Hill: University of North Carolina Press, 1989.

Wooster, Robert. *The Civil War 100: A Ranking of the Most Influential People in the War between the States.* New York: Citadel Press, 1998.

————. *Nelson A. Miles and the Twilight of the Frontier Army.* Lincoln: University of Nebraska Press, 1993.

Articles and Unpublished Papers

Abbott, A. C. "Acting Assistant Surgeons in the Philippines." *Boston Medical and Surgical Journal* 142 (1900): 178.

Anderson, L. G. "Notes of an Army Surgeon in the Recent War," *American Medicine* 3 (1902): 475–78.

Banister, John M. "Medical and Surgical Observations During a Three-Year Tour of Duty in the Philippines." *Journal of the Association of Military Surgeons of the United States* 18 (1906): 149–69, 259–77, 318–34.

Buecker, Thomas R. "A Surgeon at the Little Big Horn: The Letters of Dr. Holmes O. Paulding." *Montana: The Magazine of Western History* 32 (autumn 1982): 34–49.

Corbusier, William H. "The Apache-Yumas and Apache-Mojaves." *The American Antiquarian* 8 (September 1886): 276–84; (November 1886): 325–39.

Eaton, George. "Stopping an Apache Battle." Ed. Don Russell. *Journal of the U.S. Cavalry Association* 42 (July–August 1933).

Hume, Edgar Erskine. "Admission to the Medical Department of the Army Half a Century Ago: The Experience of Brigadier General William Hemple Arthur." *Military Surgeon* 79 (1936): 197–202.

Hyde, Samuel C., Jr. "Bushwhacking and Barn Burning: Civil War Operations and the Florida Parishes' Tradition of Violence." *Louisiana History* 36 (spring 1995): 171–86.

Linn, Brian. "The Long Twilight of the Frontier Army." Paper presented at the Yale Conference on the Military and the History of the American West, New Haven, Conn., 1991.

Luce, Edward S., ed. "The Diary and Letters of Dr. James M. DeWolf." *North Dakota History* 25 (April–July 1958): 33–81.

Mallery, Garrick. "Sign Language among North American Indians Compared with That among Other Peoples and Deaf-Mutes." *First Annual Report of the Bureau of Ethnology to the Secretary of the Smithsonian Institution* (1879–80): 263–552.

Mattison, Ray H., ed. "The Diary of Surgeon Washington Matthews, Fort Rice, D.T." *North Dakota History* 2 (1954): 5–74.

Olch, Peter D. "Medicine in the Indian-Fighting Army, 1866–1890." *Journal of the West* 21 (July 1982): 32–41.

Seamen, Gilbert E. "Some Observations of a Medical Officer in the Philippines." *Milwaukee Medical Journal* 10 (1902): 181–89.

Turnbull, Wilfrid. "Reminiscences of an Army Surgeon in Cuba and the Philippines." *American Historical Collection* 2 (1974): 31–49.

Newspapers

New York Herald, April 3, 1867.
New York Times, July 5, 1854; February 9, 1930.
Washington Post, June 1, 1998.

Internet Sources

Ancestry.com. *Civil War Pension Index.* N.d. <www.ancestry.com/search/rectype/military/cwpi/main.htm>. (August 28, 2002).

———. *Civil War Research Database.* N.d. <www.ancestry.com/search/rectype/military/cwrd/main.htm>. (August 21, 2002).

———. *Kentucky 1910 Miracode Index.* N.d. <http://www.ancestry.com/search/rectype/inddbs/5185a.htm>. (November 7, 2002).

"Cale, Thomas, 1848–1941." Biographical Directory of the United States Congress. N.d. <http://bioguide.Congress.gov/scripts/biodisplay. pl?index=C000042>. (September 19, 2002).

Christy, Julie. "First California U.S.V." *San Francisco History.* N.d. <www.zpub.com/sf50/sf/hgcal.htm>. (September 19, 2002).

Day, Teresa. "From Hoops to Horse Racing." *Lexington, Kentucky, Convention and Visitors Bureau.* May 2002. <www.visitlex.com/quick/sports.html>. (September 19, 2002).

Hurley, Vic. "Kris versus Toledo Blade: Juramentados and Amuks." *Swish of the Kris: The Story of the Moros.* September 1997. <http://www.bakbakan.com/swishk/swk2-14.html>. (November 6, 2002).

Illinois USGenWeb Project. "Roster of Field and Staff, 9th Illinois Cavalry." *Illinois in the Civil War.* N.d. <www.rootsweb.com/~ilcivilw/f&s/cavo09-fs.htm>. (August 21, 2002).

————. "Roster of Field and Staff, 6th Illinois Cavalry." *Illinois in the Civil War*. N.d. <www.rootsweb.com/~ilcivilw/f&s/cavoo6-fs.htm>. (August 21, 2002).

Lawson, Steve. *"Newbern." California Wreck Divers*. N.d. <www.cawreckdivers.org/Wrecks/Newbern.htm>. (August 28, 2002).

Library of Congress. "Epilogue." *1492: An Ongoing Voyage*. October 12, 2001. <http://www.loc.gov/exhibits/1492/epilogue.html>. (August 15, 2002).

McSherry, Patrick. "The Transport Service." *The Spanish American War Centennial Website*. N.d. <www.spanamwar.com/transports.htm>. (September 13, 2002).

Michigan Historical Center. "Parke-Davis Research Laboratory." *National Historic Landmarks in Michigan*. January 9, 2002. <www.sos.state.mi.us/history/preserve/phissite/parkedav.html>. (September 11, 2002).

National Park Service. "Parke-Davis and Company Plant and Research Laboratory." *Detroit: A National Register of Historic Places Travel Itinerary*. April 25, 2000. <www.cr.nps.gov/nr/travel/detroit/d8.htm>. (September 11, 2002).

Regents of the University of California. "Physicians at Mount Zion." *UCSF Medical Center at Mount Zion*. January 26, 2001. <http://mountzion.ucsfmedical-center.org/pastandpresent/docpic.html>. (September 20, 2002).

"Steamers." *Iowa in the Civil War*. N.d. <www.iowa-counties.com/civilwar/27th_inf/steamers.htm>. (August 21, 2002).

Swiggum, S., and M. Kohli. "Canadian Pacific Line." *The Ships List*. February 12, 2002. <www.theshipslist.com/ships/lines/cp.html>. (September 19, 2002).

————. "Hamburg-American Packet Company / Hamburg-American Line." *The Ships List*. May 24, 2002. <www.theshipslist.com/ships/lines/hamburg.html>. (September 13, 2002).

————. "Panama Route Ships." *The Ships List*. June 9, 2002. <www.theshipslist.com/ships/descriptions/panamafleet.html>. (August 15, 2002).

————. "Red Star Line." *The Ships List*. February 27, 2002. <www.theshipslist.com/ships/lines/redstar.html>. (September 19, 2002).

————. "White Star Line." *The Ships List*. February 28, 2002. <www.theshipslist.com/ships/lines/whitestar.html.> (September 19, 2002).

"University of Kentucky Traditions and Songs." *University of Kentucky*. August 6, 2002. <www.uky.edu/Home/GeneralInfo/traditions.html>. (September 19, 2002).

Watson, Kathie. "Music of the War between the States." *Poetry and Music of the War between the States*. July 2, 2002. <http://users.erols.com/kfraser/music/index.html>. (August 21, 2002).

Willson, David A. "Why I Went to Viet Nam." *The Sixties Project*. N.d. <http://lists.village.virginia.edu/sixties/HTML_docs/Texts/Narrative/Willson_Why_I_Went.html>. (September 17, 2002).

Wolfhound History Project. "Camp Vicars Expedition." *The United States 27th Infantry Regiment "Wolfhounds" Online*. December 31, 2000. <http://www.kolchak.org/History/Hunt1931/chapter%202/Ch2PI7.htm>. (September 17, 2002).

INDEX